PRACTICE – ASSESS – DIAGNOSE

180 Days of MATH for Kindergarten

Developed by
Jodene Smith

Shell Education

Publishing Credits

Dona Herweck Rice, *Editor-in-Chief*; Lee Aucoin, *Creative Director*; Don Tran, *Print Production Manager;* Timothy J. Bradley, *Illustration Manager*; Chris McIntyre, M.A.Ed., *Editorial Director*; Sara Johnson, M.S.Ed., *Senior Editor*; Aubrie Nielsen, M.S.Ed., *Associate Education Editor*; Juan Chavolla, *Cover/Interior Layout Designer;* Meg Clark, *Production Artist;* Corinne Burton, M.A.Ed., *Publisher*

Shell Education
5482 Argosy Avenue
Huntington Beach, CA 92649-1030
www.tcmpub.com/shell-education

ISBN 978-1-4258-0803-7

Printed by: 51497
Printed in: China

TABLE OF CONTENTS

INTRODUCTION AND RESEARCH

The Need for Practice

In order to be successful in today's mathematics classroom, students must deeply understand both concepts and procedures so that they can discuss and demonstrate their understanding. Demonstrating understanding is a process that must be continually practiced in order for students to be successful. According to Marzano (2010, 83), "practice has always been, and will always be, a necessary ingredient to learning procedural knowledge at a level at which students execute it independently." Practice is especially important to help students apply their concrete, conceptual understanding to a particular procedural skill.

Understanding Assessment

In addition to providing opportunities for frequent practice, teachers must be able to assess students' understanding of mathematical procedures, terms, concepts, and reasoning (Kilpatrick, Swafford, and Findell 2001). This is important so that teachers can adequately address students' misconceptions, build on their current understanding, and challenge them appropriately.

Assessment is a long-term process that often involves careful analysis of student responses from a lesson discussion, project, practice sheet, or test. When analyzing the data, it is important for teachers to reflect on how their teaching practices may have influenced students' responses and to identify those areas where additional instruction may be required. In short, the data gathered from assessments should be used to inform instruction: slow down, speed up, or reteach. This type of assessment is called *formative assessment* and is used to provide a seamless connection between instruction and assessment (McIntosh 1997).

HOW TO USE THIS BOOK

180 Days of Math for Kindergarten offers teachers and parents a full page of daily mathematics practice activities for each day of the school year.

Easy to Use and Standards-Based

These activities reinforce grade-level skills across a variety of mathematical concepts. The questions are provided as a full practice page, making them easy to prepare and implement as part of a classroom morning routine, at the beginning of each mathematics lesson, or as homework.

Every kindergarten practice page provides 6 questions, each tied to a specific mathematical concept. Students are given the opportunity for regular practice in each mathematical concept, allowing them to build confidence through these quick standards-based activities.

Kindergarten students may need additional support in order to complete the practice pages. Depending on students' reading skills and readiness levels, teachers, classroom volunteers, or parents may need to read the questions aloud to students. Have students write the answers on their own, or if needed, have them say their answers aloud and assist them with recording the answers.

Question	Mathematics Concept	NCTM Standards
1	**1-to-1 Correspondence, Number Identification, or Comparing Numbers**	Understands numbers, ways of representing numbers, relationships among numbers, and number systems; Counts with understanding and recognizes "how many" in sets of objects; Develops a sense of whole numbers and represents and uses them in flexible ways
2	**Addition or Subtraction**	Understands meanings of operations and how they relate to one another; Computes fluently and makes reasonable estimates; Understands various meanings of addition and subtraction of whole numbers
3	**Patterns**	Understands patterns, relations, and functions; Recognizes, describes, and extends patterns
4	**Measurement**	Understands measurable attributes of objects and the units, systems, and processes of measurement; Recognizes the attributes of length, volume, weight, area, and time
5	**Geometry**	Analyzes characteristics and properties of two-dimensional and three-dimensional geometric shapes and develops mathematical arguments about geometric relationships; Recognizes, names, builds, draws, compares, and sorts two- and three-dimensional shapes
6	**Story Problem or Mathematical Reasoning**	Builds new mathematical knowledge through problem solving; Solves problems that arise in mathematics and in other contexts

Standards are listed with the permission of the National Council of Teachers of Mathematics (NCTM). NCTM does not endorse the content or validity of these alignments.

HOW TO USE THIS BOOK *(cont.)*

Using the Practice Pages

As outlined on page 4, every question is aligned to a mathematics concept and standard.

Practice pages provide instruction and assessment opportunities for each day of the school year.

Each question ties student practice to a specific mathematics concept.

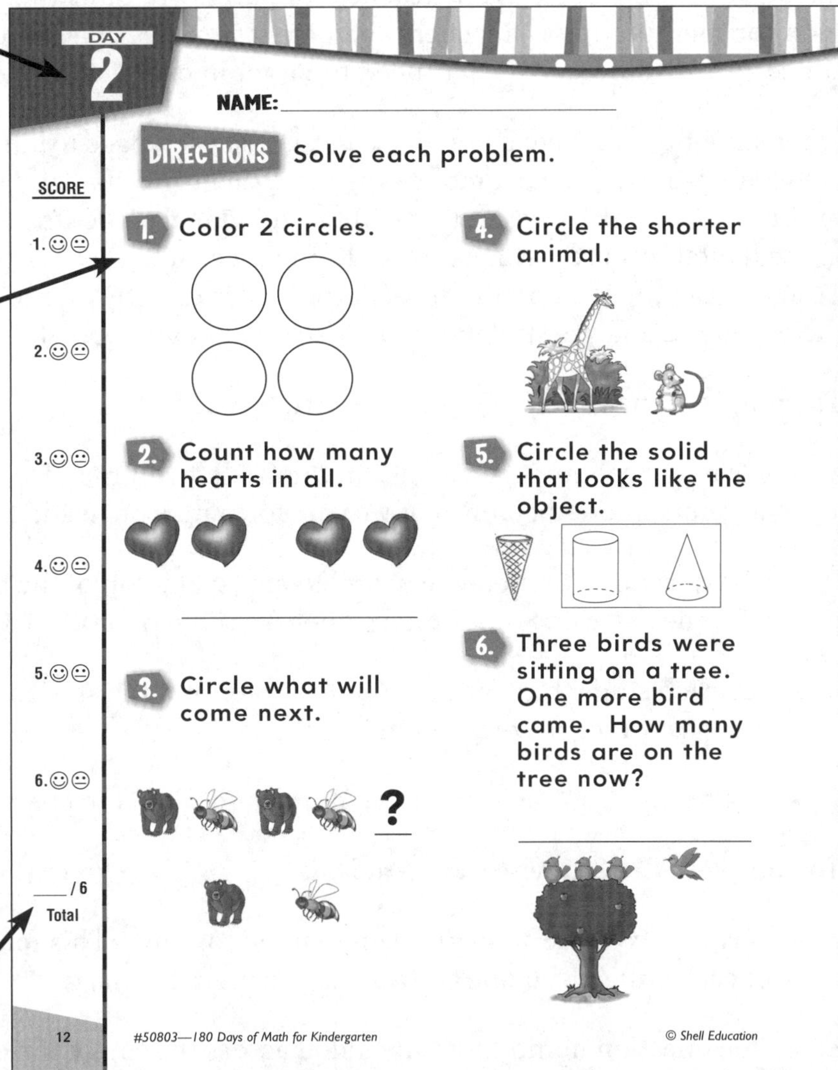
DAY 2

NAME:

SCORE

1. ☺😐
2. ☺😐
3. ☺😐
4. ☺😐
5. ☺😐
6. ☺😐

___ / 6 Total

DIRECTIONS Solve each problem.

1. Color 2 circles.
2. Count how many hearts in all.
3. Circle what will come next.
4. Circle the shorter animal.
5. Circle the solid that looks like the object.
6. Three birds were sitting on a tree. One more bird came. How many birds are on the tree now?

12 #50803—180 Days of Math for Kindergarten © Shell Education

Using the Scoring Guide

Use the scoring guide along the side of each practice page to check answers and see at a glance which skills may need more reinforcement.

Fill in the appropriate circle for each problem to indicate correct (☺) or incorrect (😐) responses. You might wish to indicate only incorrect responses to focus on those skills. (For example, if students consistently miss numbers 2 and 6, they may need additional help with those concepts as outlined in the table on page 4.) Use the answer key at the back of the book to score the problems, or you may call out answers to have students self-score or peer-score their work.

HOW TO USE THIS BOOK *(cont.)*

Diagnostic Assessment

Teachers can use the practice pages as diagnostic assessments. The data analysis tools included with the book enable teachers or parents to quickly score students' work and monitor their progress. Teachers and parents can see at a glance which mathematics concepts or skills students may need to target in order to develop proficiency.

After students complete a practice page, grade each page using the answer key (pages 191–201). Then, complete the *Practice Page Item Analysis* (page 7) for the whole class, or the *Student Item Analysis* (page 8) for individual students. These charts are also provided in the digital resources (filenames: GK_practicepage_analysis.pdf, GK_studentanalysis.pdf). Teachers can input data into the electronic files directly on the computer, or they can print the pages and analyze students' work using paper and pencil.

To complete the Practice Page Item Analysis:

- Write or type students' names in the far-left column. Depending on the number of students, more than one copy of the form may be needed or you may need to add rows.
- The question numbers are included across the top of the chart. Each item correlates with the matching question number from the practice page.
- For each student, record an *X* in the column if the student has the item incorrect. If the item is correct, leave the item blank.
- Count the *X*s in each row and column and fill in the correct boxes.

To complete the Student Item Analysis:

- Write or type the student's name on the top row. This form tracks the ongoing progress of each student, so one copy per student is necessary.
- The question numbers are included across the top of the chart. Each item correlates with the matching question number from the practice page.
- For each day, record an *X* in the column if the student has the item incorrect. If the item is correct, leave the item blank.
- Count the *X*s in each row and column and fill in the correct boxes.

Practice Page Item Analysis

Directions: Record an *X* in cells to indicate where students have missed questions. Add up the totals. You can view: (1) which questions/concepts were missed per student; (2) the total correct score for each student; and (3) the total number of students who missed each question.

Day: ______	Question #	1	2	3	4	5	6	# Correct
Student Name								
Sample Student			X			X	X	3/6
# of Students Missing Each Question								

HOW TO USE THIS BOOK *(cont.)*

Student Item Analysis

Directions: Record an *X* in cells to indicate where the student has missed questions. Add up the totals. You can view: (1) which questions/concepts the student missed; (2) the total correct score per day; and (3) the total number of times each question/concept was missed.

Student Name: Sample Student							
Question	1	2	3	4	5	6	# Correct
Day							
1		X			X	X	3/6

HOW TO USE THIS BOOK *(cont.)*

Using the Results to Differentiate Instruction

Once results are gathered and analyzed, teachers can use the results to inform the way they differentiate instruction. The data can help determine which concepts are the most difficult for students and which need additional instructional support and continued practice. Depending on how often the practice pages are scored, results can be considered for instructional support on a daily or weekly basis.

Whole-Class Support

The results of the diagnostic analysis may show that the entire class is struggling with a particular concept or group of concepts. If these concepts have been taught in the past, this indicates that further instruction or reteaching is necessary. If these concepts have not been taught in the past, this data is a great pre-assessment and demonstrates that students do not have a working knowledge of the concepts. Thus, careful planning for the length of the unit(s) or lesson(s) must be considered, and extra frontloading may be required.

Small-Group or Individual Support

The results of the diagnostic analysis may show that an individual or small group of students is struggling with a particular concept or group of concepts. If these concepts have been taught in the past, this indicates that further instruction or reteaching is necessary. Consider pulling aside these students while others are working independently to instruct further on the concept(s). Teachers can also use the results to help identify individuals or groups of proficient students who are ready for enrichment or above-grade level instruction. These students may benefit from independent learning contracts or more challenging activities. Students may also benefit from extra practice using games or computer-based resources.

Digital Resources

Reference page 203 for information about accessing the digital resources and an overview of the contents.

HOW TO USE THIS BOOK *(cont.)*

NCTM Standards

The lessons in this book are aligned to the National Council of Teachers of Mathematics (NCTM) standards. The standards listed on page 4 support the concepts and skills that are consistently presented on each of the practice pages.

Standards Correlations

Shell Education is committed to producing educational materials that are research and standards based. In this effort, we have correlated all of our products to the academic standards of all 50 states, the District of Columbia, and the Department of Defense Dependent Schools, as well as to the college and career readiness standards.

How to Find Standards Correlations

To print a customized correlation report of this product for your state, visit our website at **www.tcmpub.com/shell-education** and follow the on-screen directions. If you require assistance in printing correlation reports, please contact Customer Service at 1-877-777-3450.

Purpose and Intent of Standards

The No Child Left Behind legislation mandates that all states adopt academic standards that identify the skills students will learn in kindergarten through grade twelve. While many states had already adopted academic standards prior to NCLB, the legislation set requirements to ensure the standards were detailed and comprehensive.

Standards are designed to focus instruction and guide adoption of curricula. Standards are statements that describe the criteria necessary for students to meet specific academic goals. They define the knowledge, skills, and content students should acquire at each level. Standards are also used to develop standardized tests to evaluate students' academic progress.

Teachers are required to demonstrate how their lessons meet state standards. State standards are used in development of all of our products, so educators can be assured they meet the academic requirements of each state.

DAY 1

NAME: ______________________

DIRECTIONS Solve each problem.

1. Color 3 blocks.

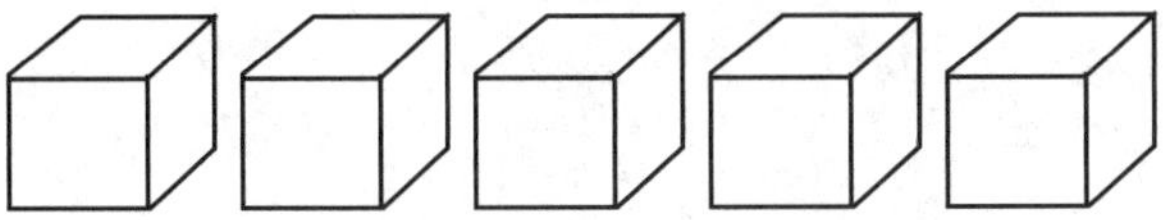

2. Count how many stars in all.

____

3. Circle what will come next.

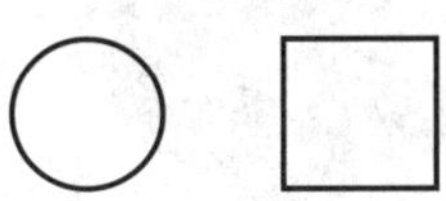

4. What time is it?

_______ o'clock

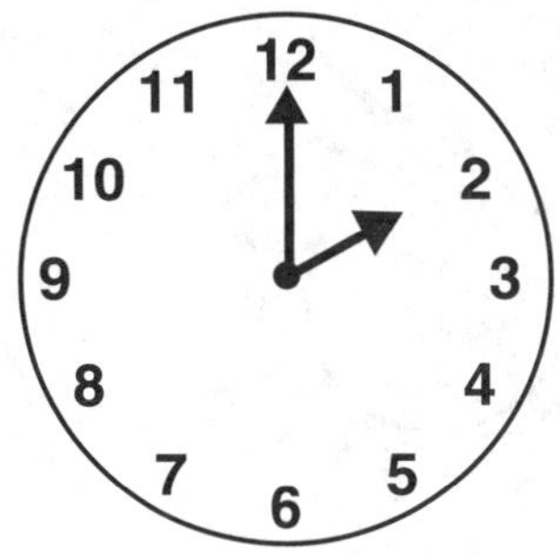

5. Color the circles.

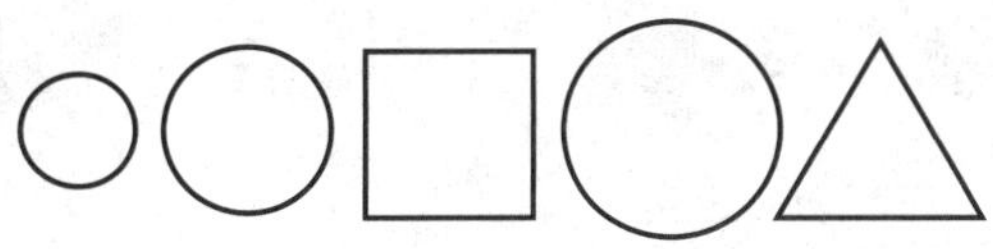

6. How many legs are on these 2 chairs?

____

SCORE

1. ☺ 😐

2. ☺ 😐

3. ☺ 😐

4. ☺ 😐

5. ☺ 😐

6. ☺ 😐

____ / 6
Total

DAY 2

NAME: ______________________________

DIRECTIONS Solve each problem.

SCORE

1. ☺ 😐
2. ☺ 😐
3. ☺ 😐
4. ☺ 😐
5. ☺ 😐
6. ☺ 😐

____ / 6 Total

1. Color 2 circles.

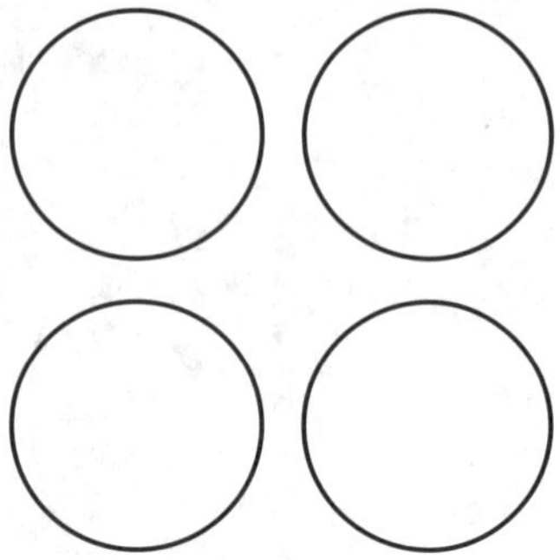

2. Count how many hearts in all.

____

3. Circle what will come next.

?

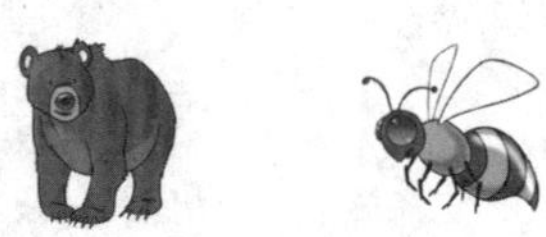

4. Circle the shorter animal.

5. Circle the solid that looks like the object.

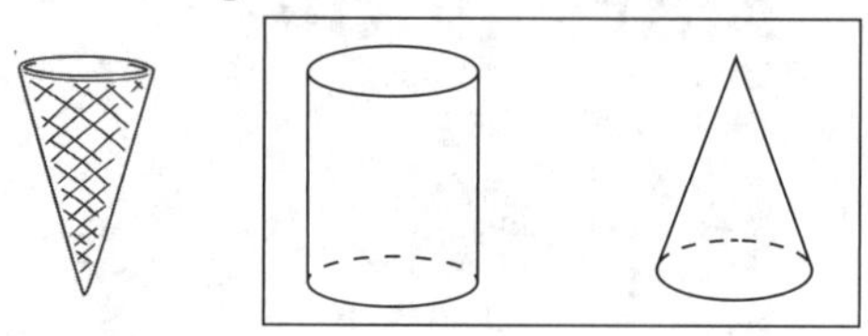

6. Three birds were sitting on a tree. One more bird came. How many birds are on the tree now?

____

DAY 3

NAME: ____________________

DIRECTIONS Solve each problem.

1. Draw more circles to make a set of 5.

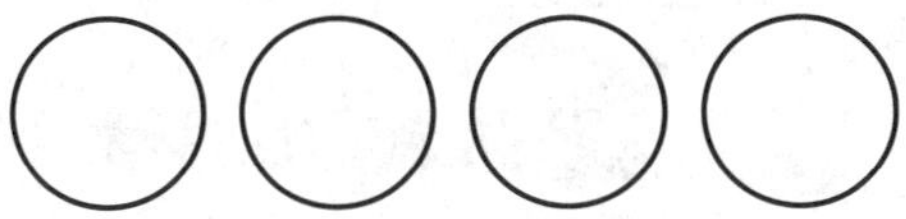

2. Count how many balloons in all.

____

3. Color the beads. What color will come next?

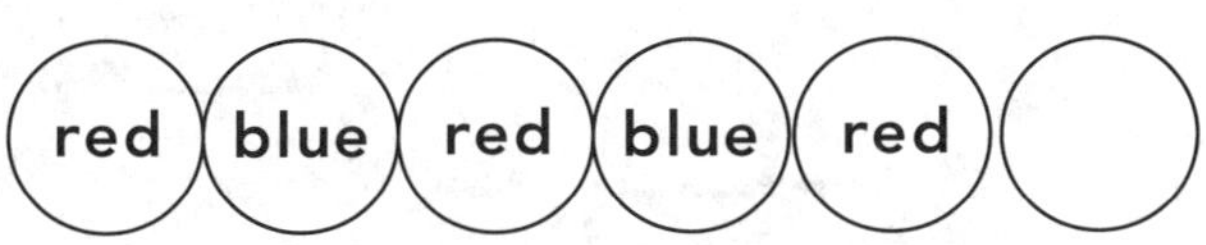

4. Circle about how many children are in your classroom.

3 30

5. Draw 1 fishbowl for the fish.

6. I am the number that comes after 2. What number am I?

____

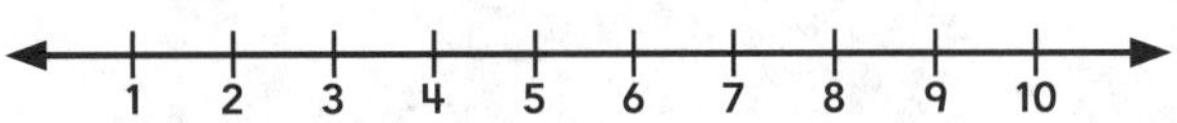

SCORE

1. ☺ 😐

2. ☺ 😐

3. ☺ 😐

4. ☺ 😐

5. ☺ 😐

6. ☺ 😐

____ / 6 Total

DAY
4

NAME: ______________________________

DIRECTIONS Solve each problem.

SCORE

1. ☺ 😐

2. ☺ 😐

3. ☺ 😐

4. ☺ 😐

5. ☺ 😐

6. ☺ 😐

____ / 6
Total

1. Circle the bowl that has more fish.

2. Count how many animals in all.

____

3. Circle who will come next.

4. How long is the stick?

______ cubes

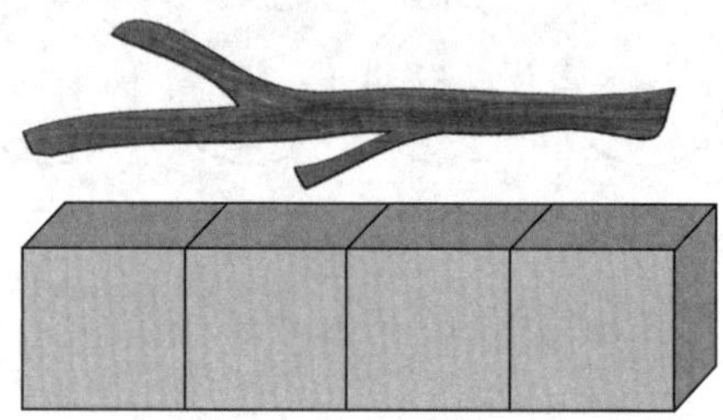

5. Draw a triangle.

6. Circle all the large paperclips.

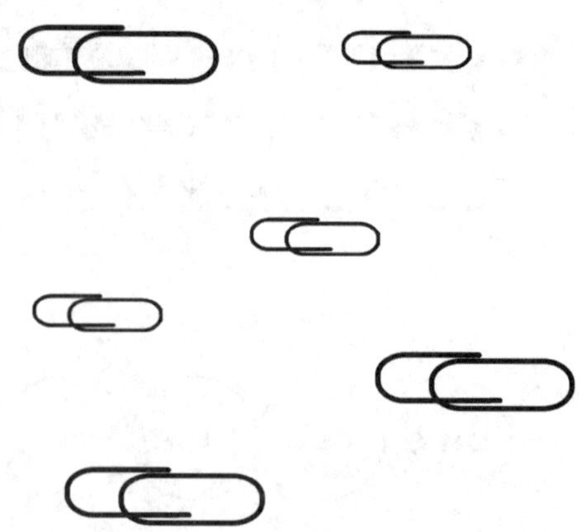

NAME: ____________________

DIRECTIONS Solve each problem.

1. Circle the number of moons.

6 7 8

2. Count how many apples in all.

____

3. Circle what will come next.

?

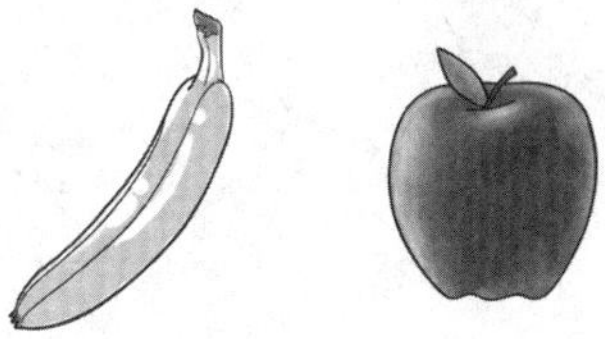

4. Circle the best time for breakfast.

7:00 in the morning

3:00 in the afternoon

5. How many sides does a triangle have?

____

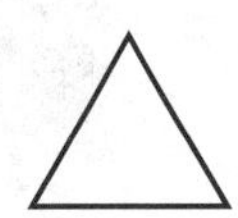

6. Draw 5 petals on the flower.

SCORE

1. ☺ 😐

2. ☺ 😐

3. ☺ 😐

4. ☺ 😐

5. ☺ 😐

6. ☺ 😐

___ / 6
Total

NAME: ______________________

DIRECTIONS Solve each problem.

SCORE

1.

2.

3.

4.

5.

6.

___ /6 Total

1. Will every bunny get a carrot?

Circle the answer.

yes no

2. Count how many flowers in all.

____

3. Circle what will come next.

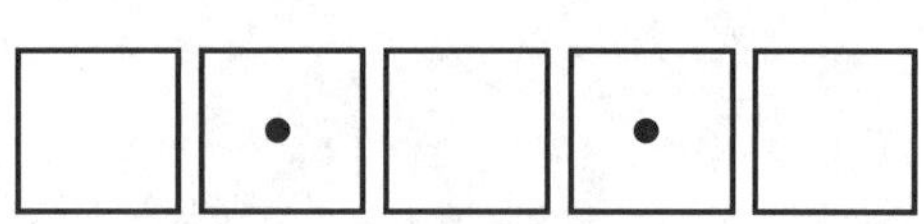

?

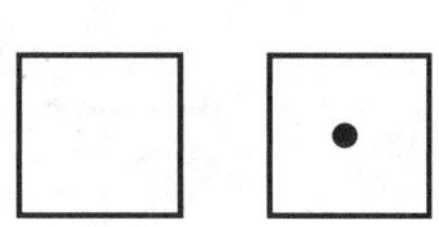

4. Circle the tool you can use to measure time.

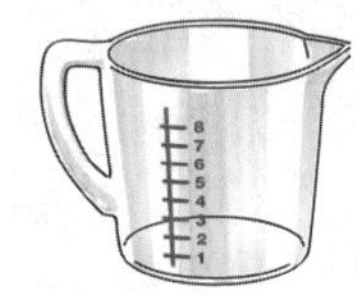

5. Circle what shelf the ball is on.

top middle bottom

6. Draw more bananas so there are 4.

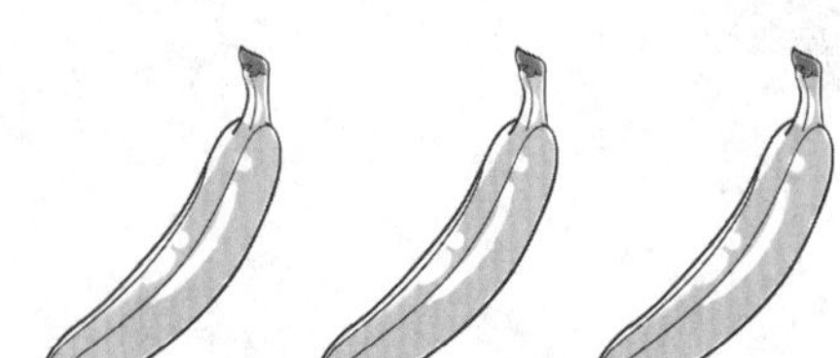

DAY
7

NAME: ______________________________

DIRECTIONS Solve each problem.

1. Count the apples. Draw an equal set of circles.

2. Count how many turtles in all.

____

3. Circle what will come next.

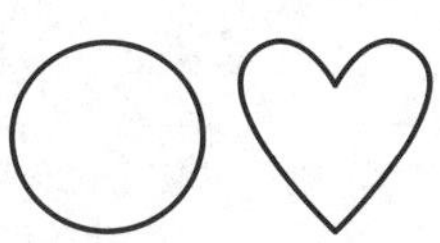

4. Circle the object that weighs more.

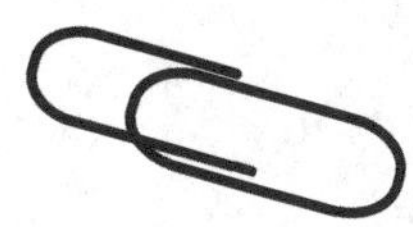

5. Is this figure open or closed? Circle the answer.

open closed

6. Three snails are on the sidewalk. One snail crawls away. How many snails are left?

____

SCORE

1.

2.

3.

4.

5.

6.

___ / 6 Total

DAY

8

NAME: ______________________________

DIRECTIONS Solve each problem.

SCORE

1. ☺ 😐

2. ☺ 😐

3. ☺ 😐

4. ☺ 😐

5. ☺ 😐

6. ☺ 😐

____ / 6
Total

1. Draw 4 legs on the cat.

2. Count how many suns in all.

____

3. Circle what will come next.

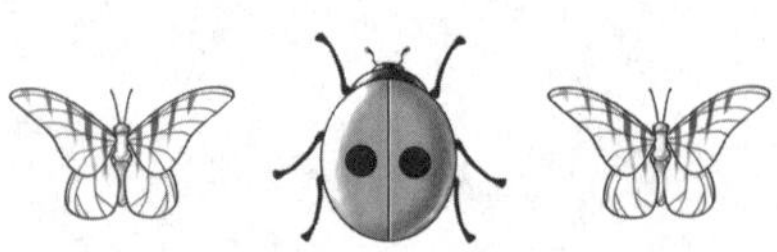

? ___

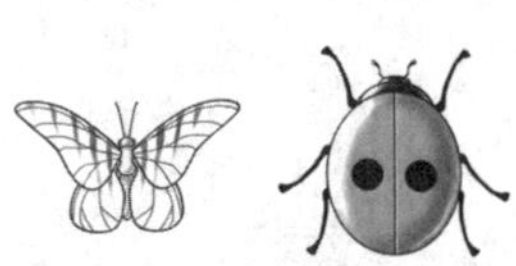

4. Circle what day comes after Monday.

Friday Tuesday

5. Will the object roll? Circle the answer.

yes no

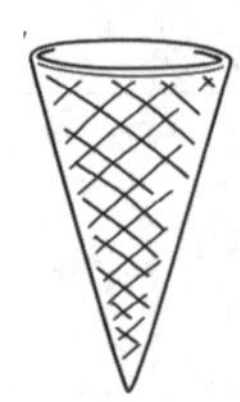

6. Circle the object that is a fruit.

DAY
9

NAME: ____________________________

DIRECTIONS Solve each problem.

1. Circle the hive with 3 bees.

2. Count how many crayons in all.

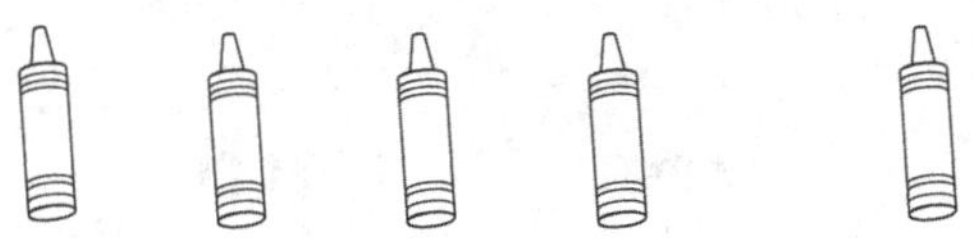

____

3. Color the squares. What color will come next?

red	green	red	green	red	

4. Circle how long it takes to comb your hair.

1 minute 1 hour

5. Circle where the food is.

on the plate

under the plate

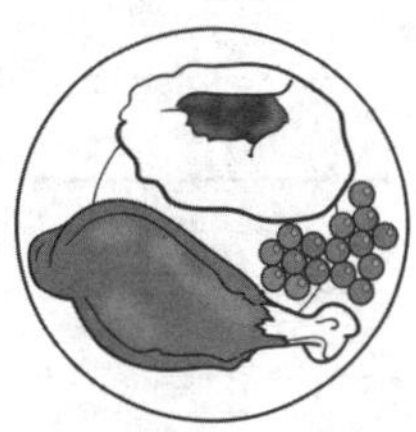

6. Max ate 2 eggs. The next day he ate 2 eggs. Draw how many eggs he ate in all.

SCORE

1. ☺ 😐
2. ☺ 😐
3. ☺ 😐
4. ☺ 😐
5. ☺ 😐
6. ☺ 😐

____ / 6
Total

NAME: ______________________

DIRECTIONS Solve each problem.

SCORE

1. ☺ 😐
2. ☺ 😐
3. ☺ 😐
4. ☺ 😐
5. ☺ 😐
6. ☺ 😐

____ / 6
Total

1. Color 4 apples.

2. Count how many umbrellas in all.

____

3. Circle what will come next.

4. Circle the container that holds more.

5. Does the shape have symmetry? Circle the answer.

yes no

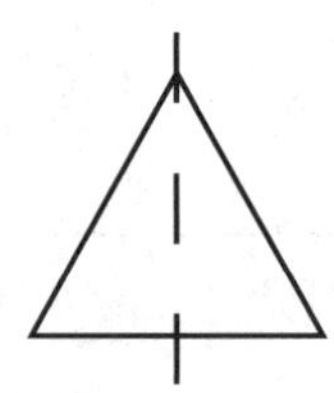

6. Show 5 dots. Add or cross out dots.

NAME: ____________________

DIRECTIONS Solve each problem.

1. Circle 2 seals.

2. Count how many cookies in all.

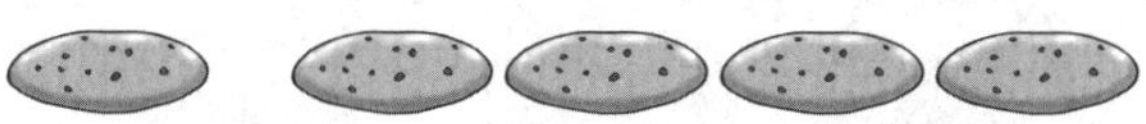

____

3. Circle what will come next.

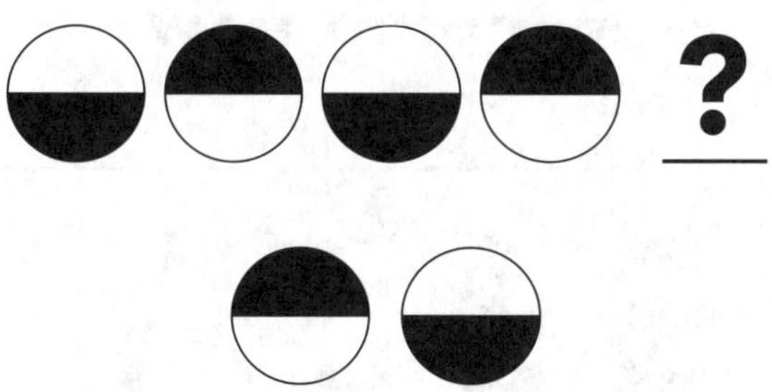

4. What time is it?

______ o'clock

5. Color the squares.

6. How many legs are on 2 dogs?

____

SCORE

1. ☺ 😐
2. ☺ 😐
3. ☺ 😐
4. ☺ 😐
5. ☺ 😐
6. ☺ 😐

____ / 6
Total

NAME: ______________________

DIRECTIONS Solve each problem.

SCORE

1. ☺ 😐
2. ☺ 😐
3. ☺ 😐
4. ☺ 😐
5. ☺ 😐
6. ☺ 😐

____ / 6 Total

1. Circle the number that is one more than 4.

3 4 5

2. Count how many leaves in all.

____

3. Circle what will come next.

4. Circle the shorter person.

5. Circle the solid that looks like the object.

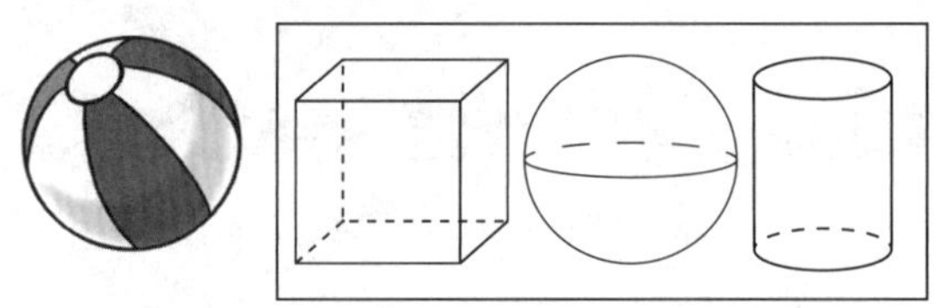

6. Two children are on the swings. One more child comes to swing. How many children are swinging now?

____

DAY 13

NAME: ______________________

DIRECTIONS Solve each problem.

1. Draw more to make a set of 10.

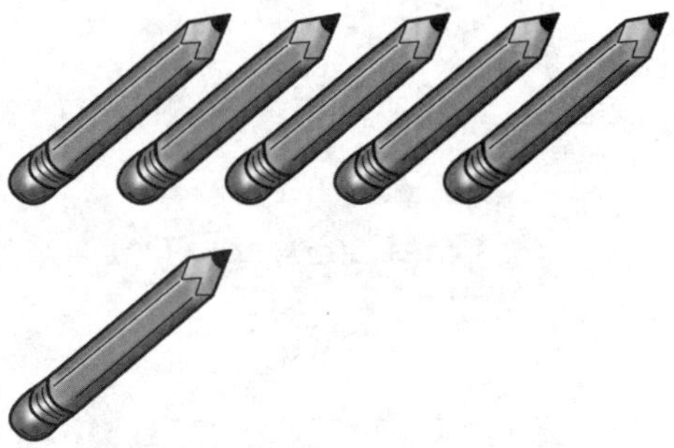

2. Count how many bugs in all.

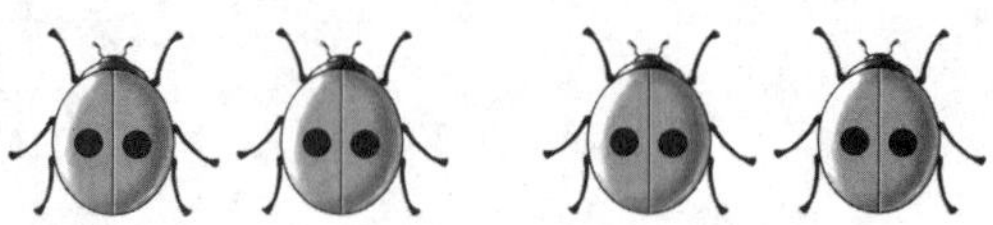

____

3. Circle what will come next.

 **?** ____

4. Circle how many pennies you can grab with one hand.

10 100

5. Draw a road under the car.

6. Which numbers are made with only straight lines?

_____ _____ _____

0 1 2 3 4

5 6 7 8 9

SCORE

1. ☺ 😐

2. ☺ 😐

3. ☺ 😐

4. ☺ 😐

5. ☺ 😐

6. ☺ 😐

___ / 6 Total

NAME: ______________________________

DIRECTIONS Solve each problem.

SCORE

1. ☺ 😐

2. ☺ 😐

3. ☺ 😐

4. ☺ 😐

5. ☺ 😐

6. ☺ 😐

____ / 6

Total

1. Circle the machine that has less gum.

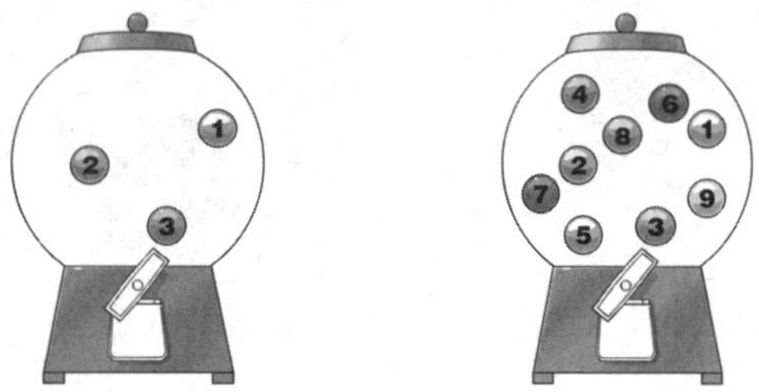

2. Count how many books in all.

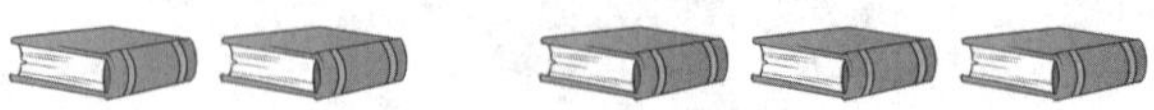

____

3. Circle who will come next.

4. How long is the plane?

_____ cubes

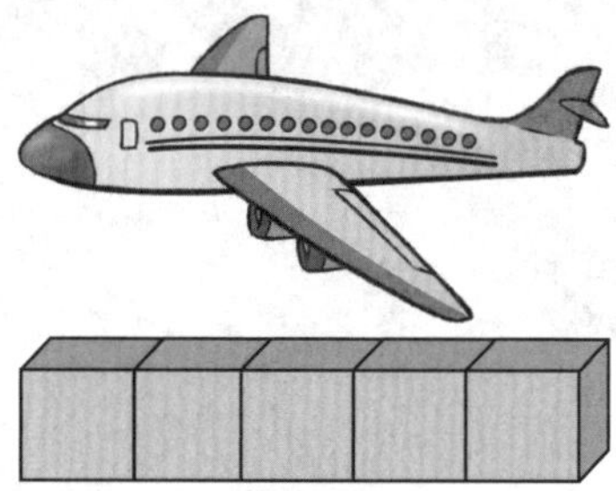

5. Draw a circle.

6. Cross out the shape that does not belong.

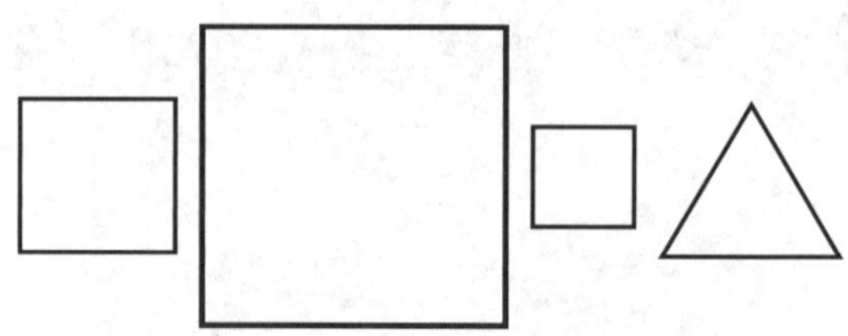

NAME: ______________________________

DIRECTIONS Solve each problem.

1. Circle how many mittens there are.

6 7 8

2. Count how many fish in all.

____

3. Color the triangles. What color will come next?

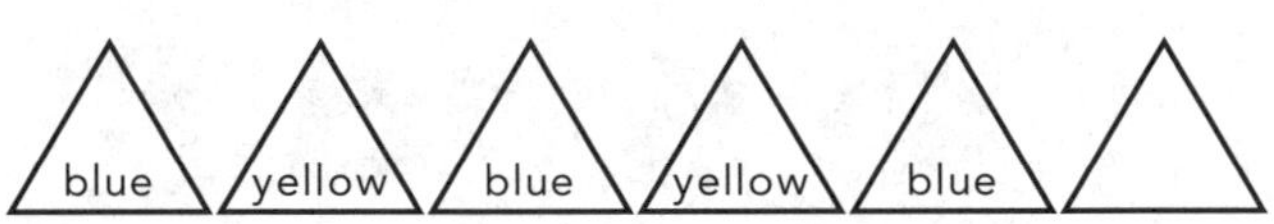

4. Circle when school ends.

in the morning

in the afternoon

5. Does this solid have any flat surfaces? Circle the answer.

yes no

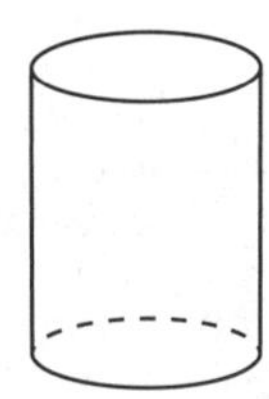

6. Write the number of hearts.

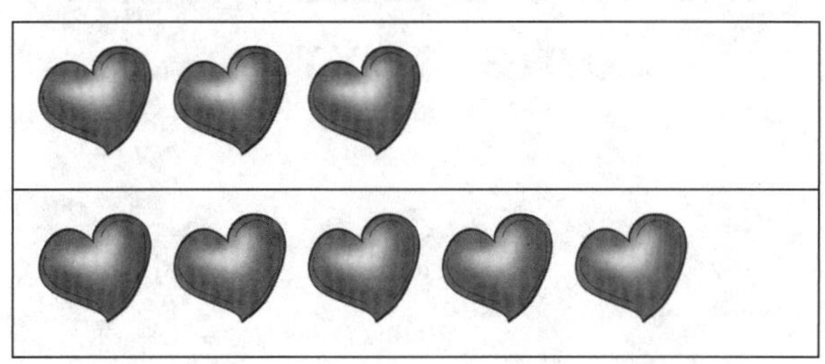

____

SCORE

1. ☺ 😐

2. ☺ 😐

3. ☺ 😐

4. ☺ 😐

5. ☺ 😐

6. ☺ 😐

____ / 6

Total

DAY
16

NAME: ______________________

DIRECTIONS Solve each problem.

SCORE

1. ☺ 😐
2. ☺ 😐
3. ☺ 😐
4. ☺ 😐
5. ☺ 😐
6. ☺ 😐

___ / 6
Total

1. Will every boy get a cap? Circle the answer.

yes no

2. Add. How many in all?

____

3. Circle what will come next.

 **?** ___

4. Circle the tool to measure weight.

5. Circle where the spoon is.

left right

6. Which animal is right before the mouse?

____

NAME: ____________________

DIRECTIONS Solve each problem.

1. Count the worms. Draw an equal set of circles.

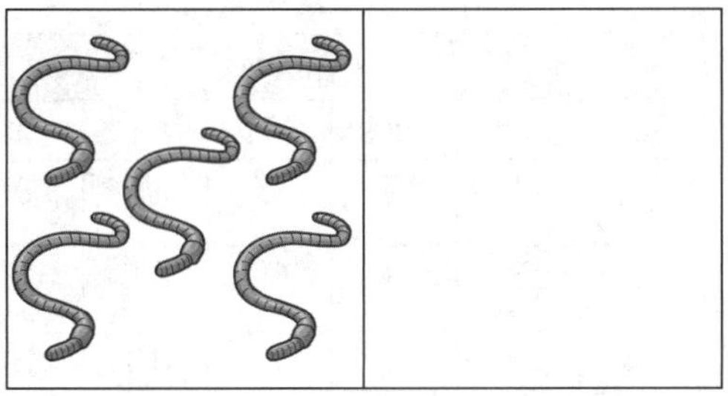

2. Add. How many in all?

____

3. Circle what will come next.

4. Circle the object that weighs less.

5. Is this figure open or closed? Circle the answer.

open closed

W

6. Jose sees 2 lizards on the wall. One runs away. How many lizards are left?

____

SCORE

1. ☺ 😐

2. ☺ 😐

3. ☺ 😐

4. ☺ 😐

5. ☺ 😐

6. ☺ 😐

____ / 6

Total

DAY 18

NAME: ______________________________

DIRECTIONS Solve each problem.

SCORE

1. ☺ 😐
2. ☺ 😐
3. ☺ 😐
4. ☺ 😐
5. ☺ 😐
6. ☺ 😐

___ / 6 Total

1. Draw 2 legs on the person.

2. Add. How many in all?

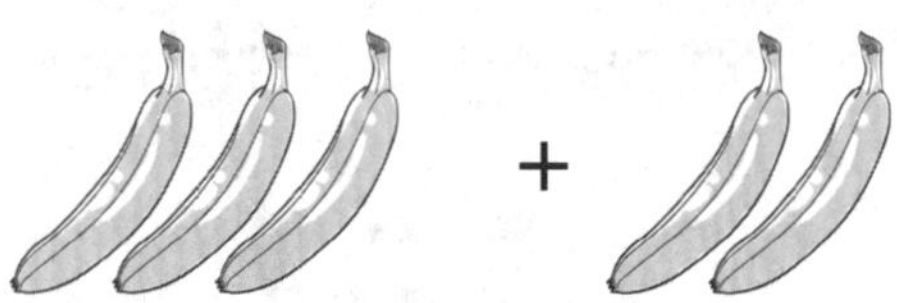

____

3. Circle what will come next.

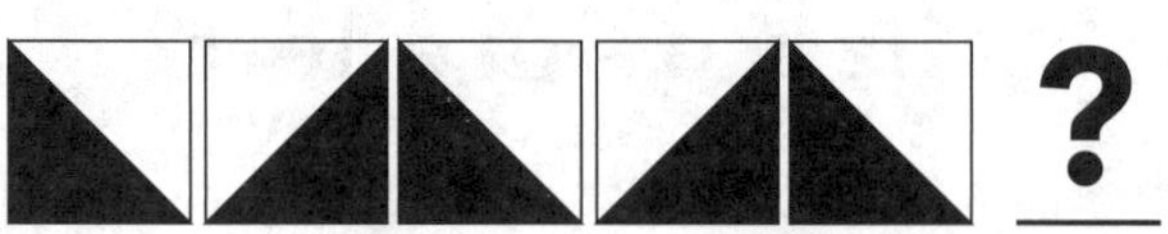

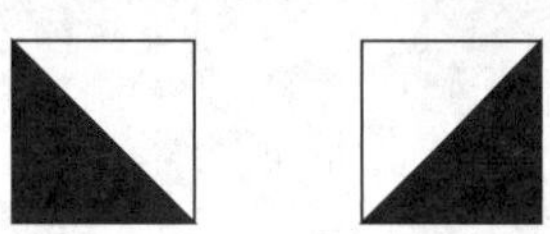

4. What is the name of the month?

____

May						
Sun	Mon	Tues	Wed	Thurs	Fri	Sat
	1	2	3	4	5	6
7	8	9	10	11	12	13
14	15	16	17	18	19	20
21	22	23	24	25	26	27
28	29	30	31			

5. Will the solid stack? Circle the answer.

yes no

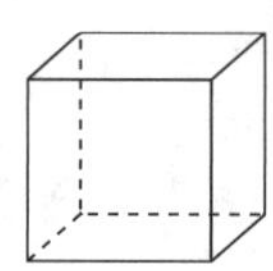

6. Circle the largest triangle.

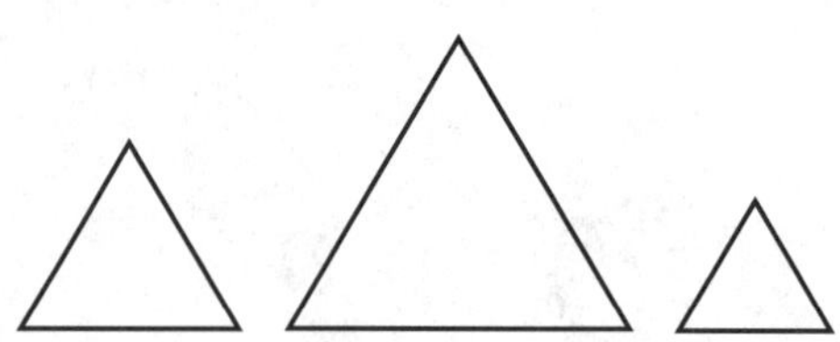

NAME: ____________________

DIRECTIONS Solve each problem.

1. Circle the log with 5 frogs.

2. Add. How many in all?

____

3. Circle what will come next.

 ?

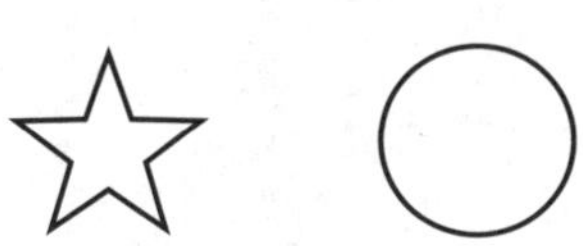

4. Circle about how long it takes to run across the playground.

1 minute   1 hour

5. Circle the picture that shows a dog in the doghouse.

6. Sandy started counting like this:

1 2 3 4 5

How is Sandy counting? Circle the answer.

forward   backward

SCORE

1. ☺ 😐

2. ☺ 😐

3. ☺ 😐

4. ☺ 😐

5. ☺ 😐

6. ☺ 😐

____ / 6 Total

DAY 20

NAME: ____________________

DIRECTIONS Solve each problem.

SCORE

1. ☺ 😐
2. ☺ 😐
3. ☺ 😐
4. ☺ 😐
5. ☺ 😐
6. ☺ 😐

____ / 6

Total

1. Color 5 pumpkins.

2. Add. How many in all?

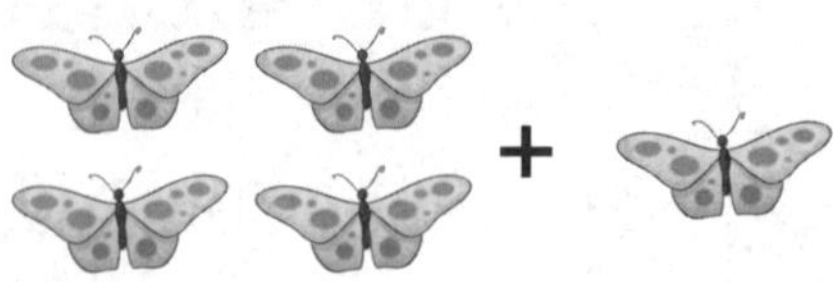

____

3. Circle what will come next.

4. Circle the container that holds less.

5. Does the shape have symmetry? Circle the answer.

yes no

6. Draw 1 sun.

Draw 3 clouds.

NAME: ______________________________

DIRECTIONS Solve each problem.

1. Color 4 cars.

2. Add. How many in all?

____

3. Color the squares. What color will come next?

green	blue	green	blue	green	

4. What time is it?

____ : ____

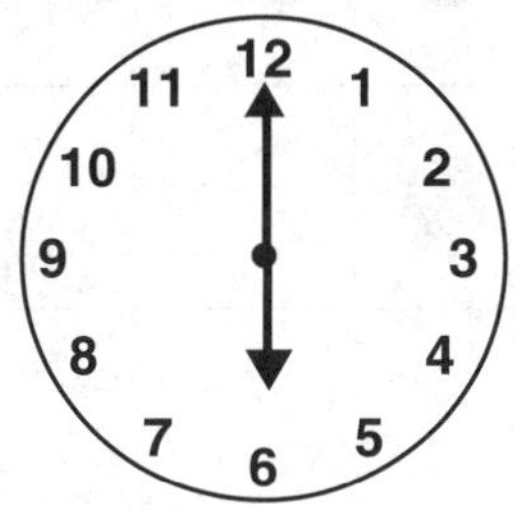

5. Color the triangles.

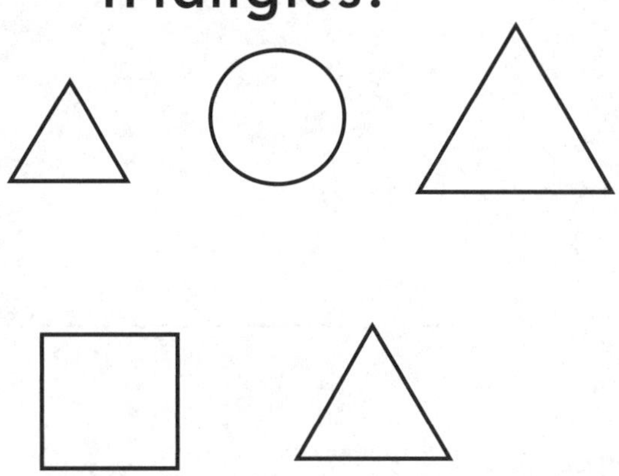

6. How many legs are on 3 birds?

____

SCORE

1. ☺ 😐

2. ☺ 😐

3. ☺ 😐

4. ☺ 😐

5. ☺ 😐

6. ☺ 😐

___ / 6
Total

DAY 22

NAME: ______________________________

DIRECTIONS Solve each problem.

SCORE

1. ☺ 😐
2. ☺ 😐
3. ☺ 😐
4. ☺ 😐
5. ☺ 😐
6. ☺ 😐

____ / 6 Total

1. Add dots to make 10.

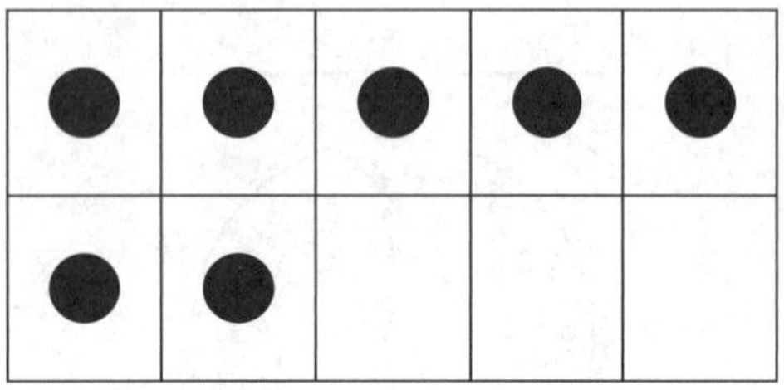

2. Add. How many in all?

____

3. Circle who will come next.

4. Draw an object that is taller than a door.

5. Circle the solid that looks like the object.

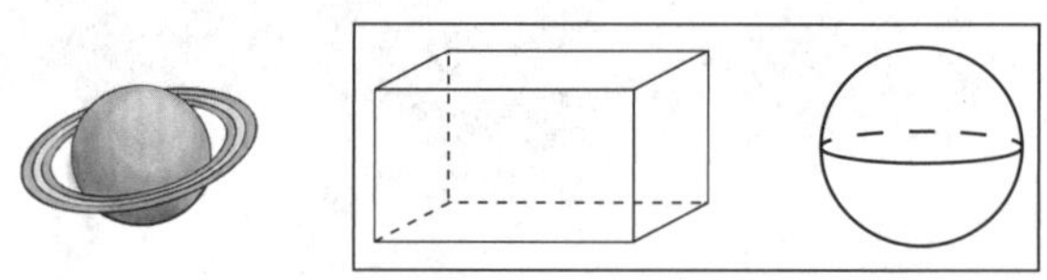

6. Mindy had 1 dog. Her dog had 4 puppies. How many dogs are there now?

____

NAME: ____________________

DIRECTIONS Solve each problem.

1. Add dots to make 10.

●	●	●	●	●

2. Add. How many in all?

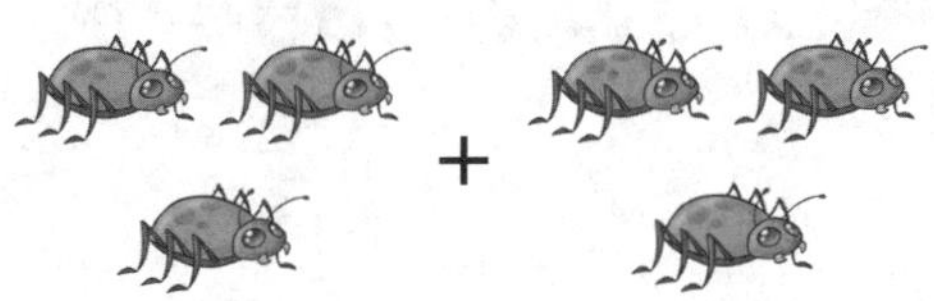

____

3. Circle who will come next.

? ____

4. Circle about how many apples fit in a cup.

1 10

5. Draw an apple in the bowl.

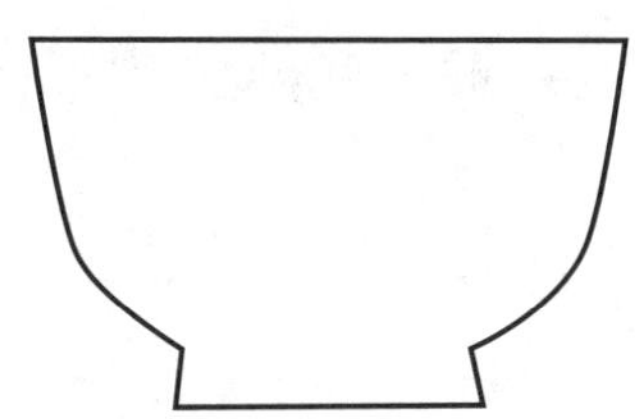

6. I am the number that comes after 5. What number am I?

____

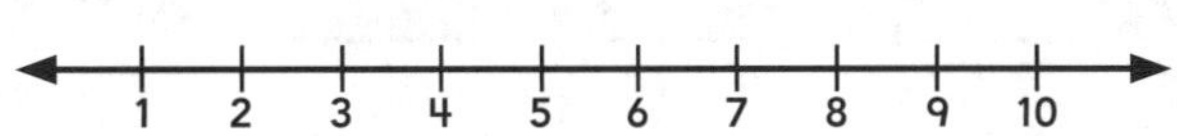

SCORE

1. ☺ 😐

2. ☺ 😐

3. ☺ 😐

4. ☺ 😐

5. ☺ 😐

6. ☺ 😐

____ / 6 Total

DAY 24

NAME: ____________________

DIRECTIONS Solve each problem.

1. Circle the cup that has more pencils.

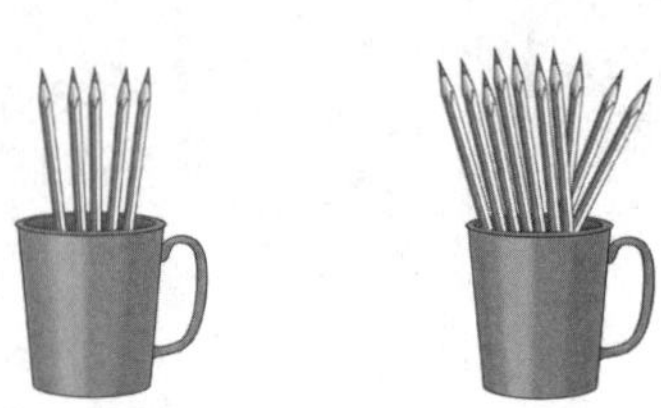

2. Add. How many in all?

____

3. Circle what will come next.

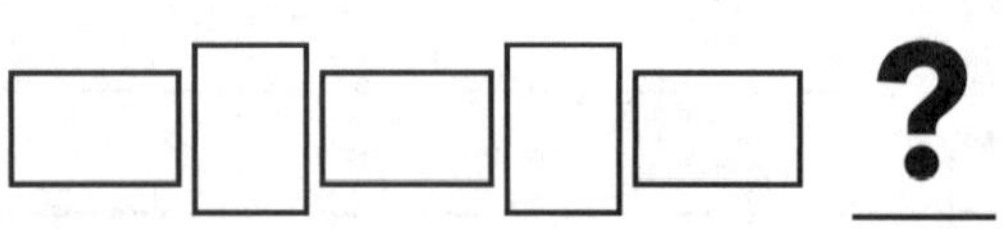

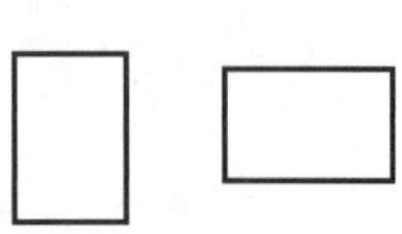

4. How long is the pencil?

_____ paperclips

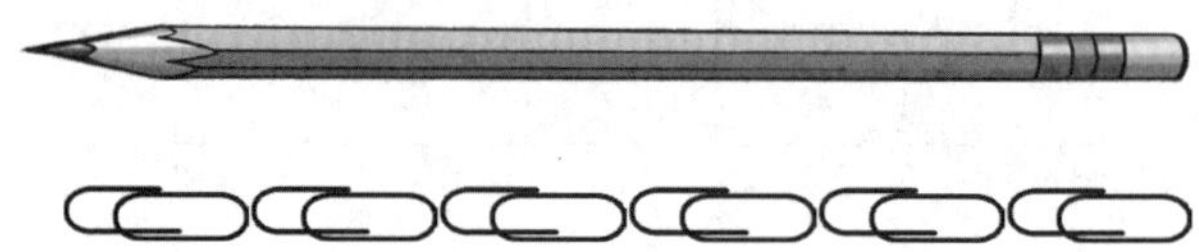

5. Draw a square.

6. Circle the small buttons.

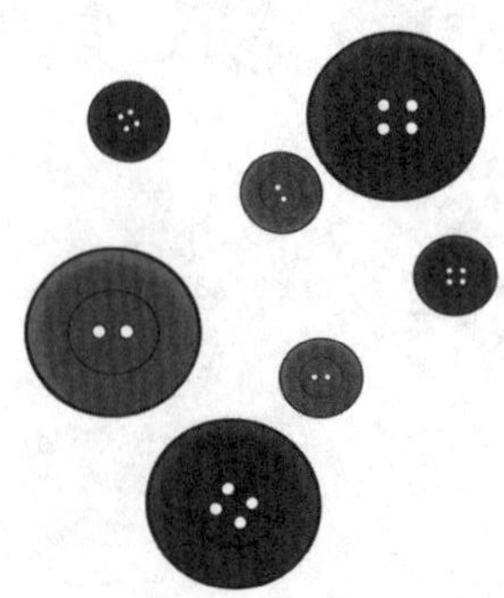

SCORE

1. ☺ 😐

2. ☺ 😐

3. ☺ 😐

4. ☺ 😐

5. ☺ 😐

6. ☺ 😐

_____ / 6 Total

NAME: ____________________

DIRECTIONS Solve each problem.

1. Circle how many bats there are.

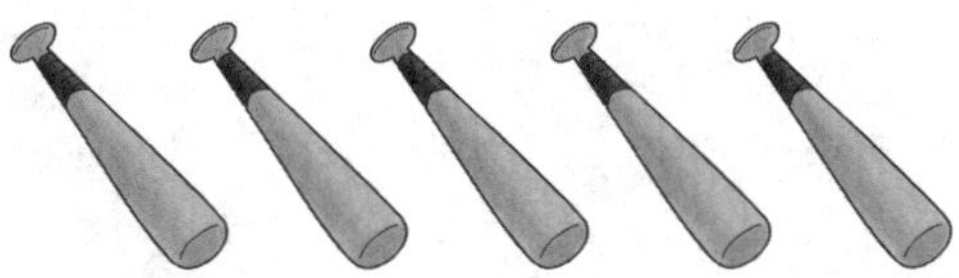

5 6 7

2. Add. How many in all?

____

3. Circle what will come next.

4. Circle the best time for lunch.

12:00 in the afternoon

7:00 in the evening

5. How many sides does a square have?

____

6. Look at the shape below. Draw a shape with more sides.

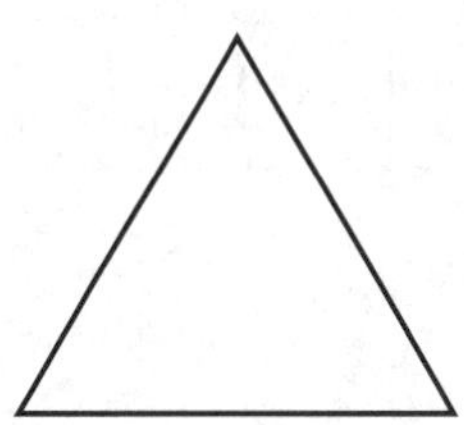

SCORE

1.

2.

3.

4.

5.

6.

____ / 6 Total

NAME: ____________________

DIRECTIONS Solve each problem.

SCORE

1.

2.

3.

4.

5.

6.

___/6 Total

1. Circle the group that has more fish.

2. Add.

3 + 2 = __________

3. Color the squares. What color will come next?

red	yellow	red	yellow	red	

4. Circle the tool to measure length.

5. Circle where the dog is.

above the desk

under the desk

6. Draw more apples so there are 7.

NAME: ______________________

DIRECTIONS Solve each problem.

1. Count the crayons. Draw an equal set of circles.

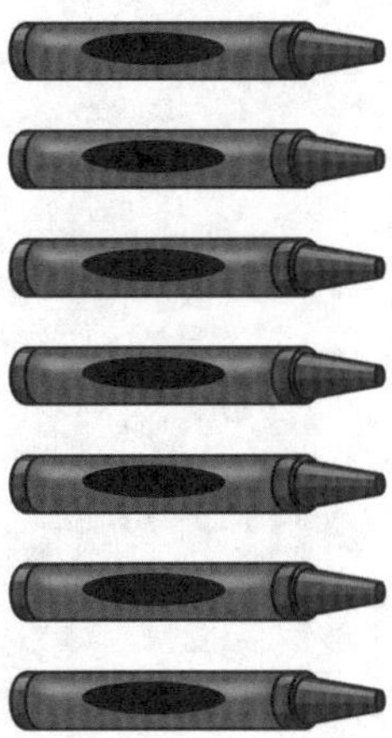

2. Add.

1 + 3 = __________

3. Write what number will come next.

1 2 1 2 1 ☐

4. Circle the object that weighs more.

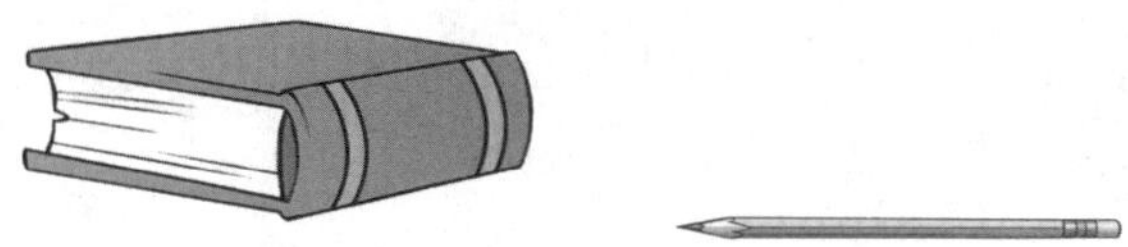

5. Is this figure open or closed? Circle the answer.

open closed

D

6. Pat saw 4 butterflies flying in the garden. Then they all flew away. How many butterflies are left?

____

SCORE

1. ☺ 😐

2. ☺ 😐

3. ☺ 😐

4. ☺ 😐

5. ☺ 😐

6. ☺ 😐

___ / 6 Total

DAY
28

NAME: ____________________

DIRECTIONS Solve each problem.

SCORE

1. ☺ 😐
2. ☺ 😐
3. ☺ 😐
4. ☺ 😐
5. ☺ 😐
6. ☺ 😐

____ / 6
Total

1. Draw 6 legs on the bug.

2. Add.

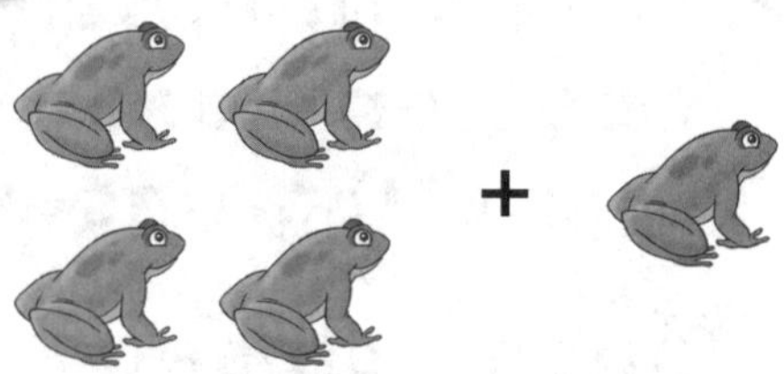

4 + 1 = ____________

3. Circle who will come next.

 ?

4. Circle what day comes after Saturday.

Monday Sunday

5. Will the solid roll? Circle the answer.

yes no

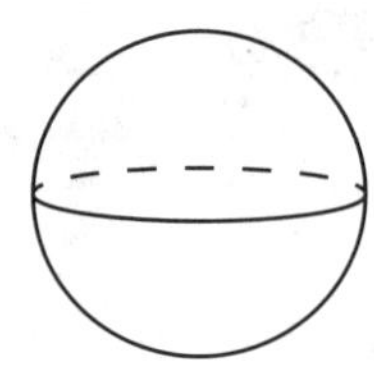

6. Circle the object you use at school.

NAME: ____________________

DIRECTIONS Solve each problem.

1. Circle the animal with 4 legs.

2. Add.

2 + 1 = __________

3. Write what letter will come next.

A B A B A ☐

4. Circle the time it takes to do 10 jumping jacks.

1 minute 1 hour

5. Circle where the spider is.

on the web

next to the web

6. Paul has two bowls with two fish in each bowl. How many fish does Paul have?

____

SCORE

1. ☺ 😐

2. ☺ 😐

3. ☺ 😐

4. ☺ 😐

5. ☺ 😐

6. ☺ 😐

___ / 6

Total

DAY 30

NAME: ____________________

DIRECTIONS Solve each problem.

SCORE

1.

2.

3.

4.

5.

6.

____ / 6

Total

1. Circle 3 suns.

2. Add.

2 + 2 = ________

3. Circle what will come next.

4. Circle the container that holds less.

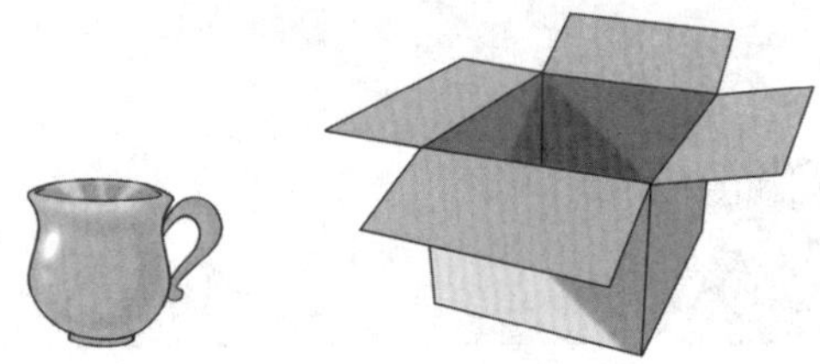

5. Does the picture have symmetry? Circle the answer.

yes no

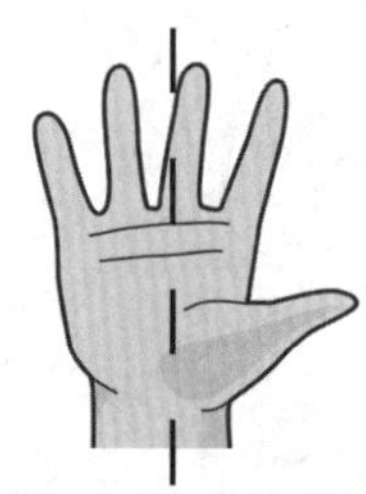

6. Show 7 squares. Add or cross out squares.

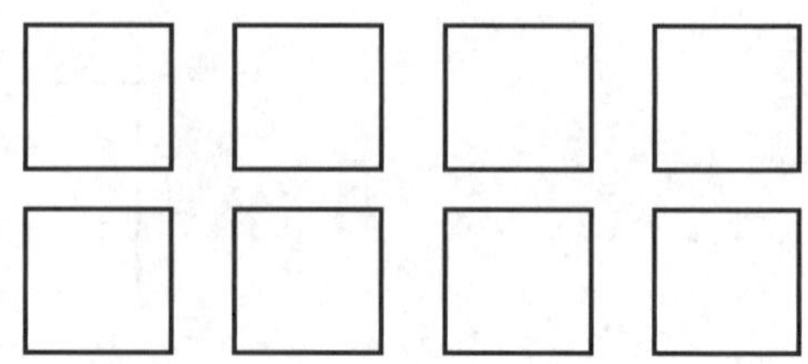

DAY 31

NAME: ____________________

DIRECTIONS Solve each problem.

1. Color 7 bells.

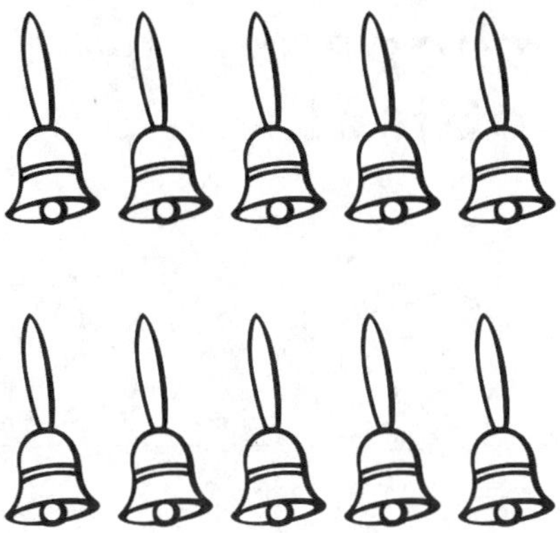

2. Add.

2 + 3 = ________

3. Circle what will come next.

4. What time is it?

______ o'clock

5. Color the rectangles.

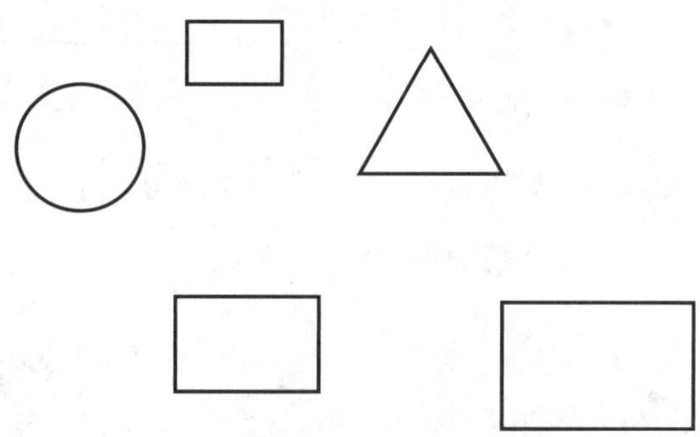

6. How many fingers are on 2 hands?

____

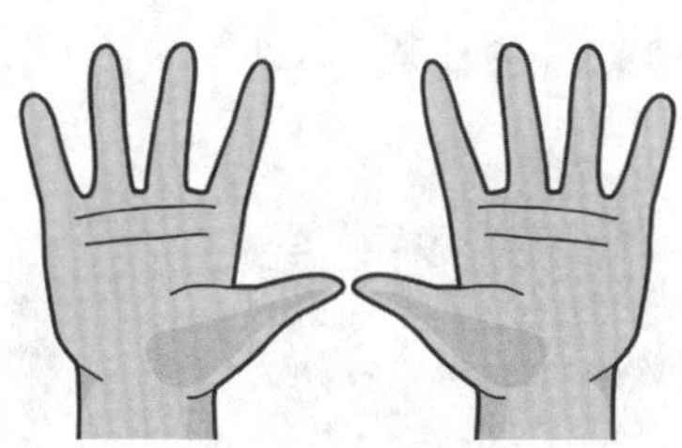

SCORE

1. ☺ 😐

2. ☺ 😐

3. ☺ 😐

4. ☺ 😐

5. ☺ 😐

6. ☺ 😐

___ / 6 Total

DAY

32

NAME: ______________________________

DIRECTIONS Solve each problem.

SCORE

1. ☺ 😐

2. ☺ 😐

3. ☺ 😐

4. ☺ 😐

5. ☺ 😐

6. ☺ 😐

____ / 6

Total

1. Circle the number that comes after 6.

3 5 7

2. Add.

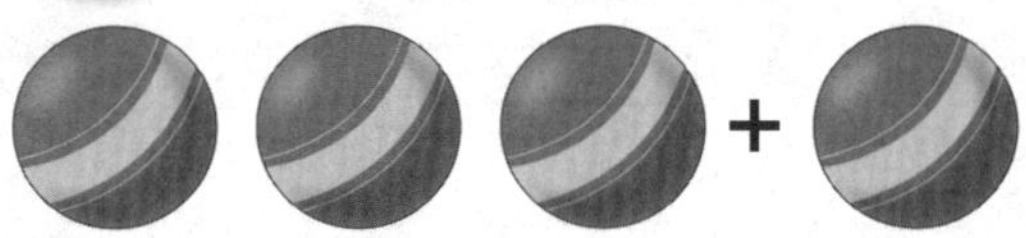

3 + 1 = __________

3. Circle what will come next.

?

4. Circle the shorter object.

5. Circle the solid that is the same shape as the object.

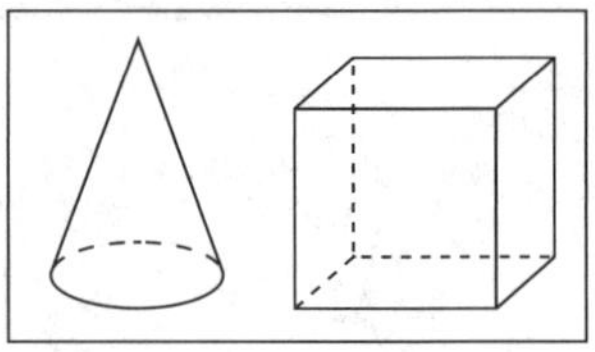

6. Three caterpillars were sitting on a leaf. One more caterpillar comes along. How many caterpillars are on the leaf now?

____

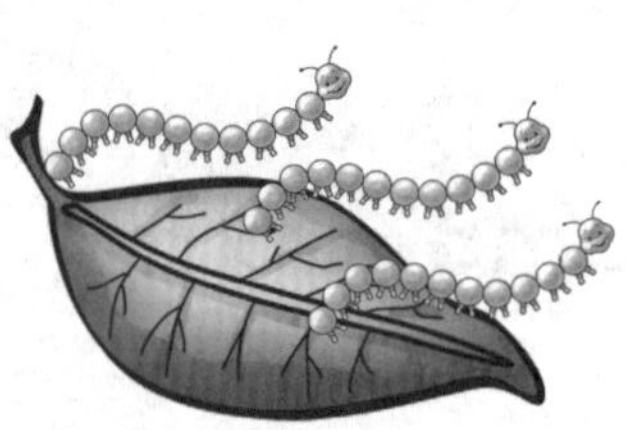

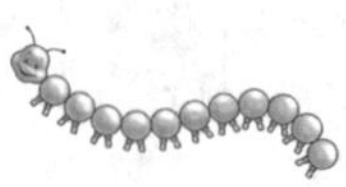

NAME: ______________________

DIRECTIONS Solve each problem.

1. Draw more to make a set of 10.

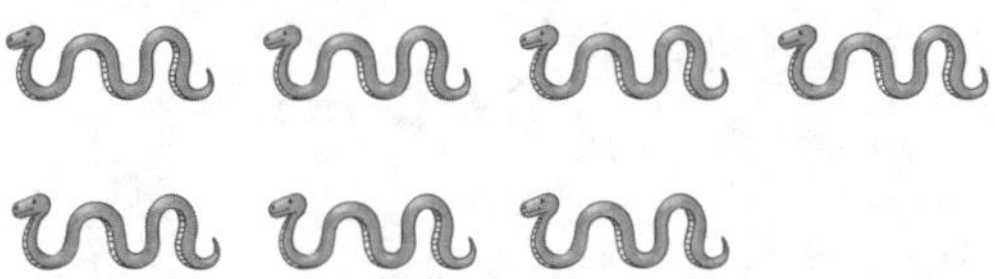

2. Add.

+

3 + 3 = __________

3. Color the circles. What color will come next?

(red) (green) (red) (green) (red) ( )

4. About how many cans of soup fit in a grocery bag? Circle the answer.

2   20

5. Draw a bee outside of the hive.

6. Draw 4 circles. Color one circle red and the rest blue. How many circles are blue?

____

SCORE

1. ☺ 😐
2. ☺ 😐
3. ☺ 😐
4. ☺ 😐
5. ☺ 😐
6. ☺ 😐

____ / 6 Total

DAY 34

NAME: ____________________

DIRECTIONS Solve each problem.

SCORE

1. ☺ 😐
2. ☺ 😐
3. ☺ 😐
4. ☺ 😐
5. ☺ 😐
6. ☺ 😐

____ / 6 Total

1. Circle the box with fewer flowers.

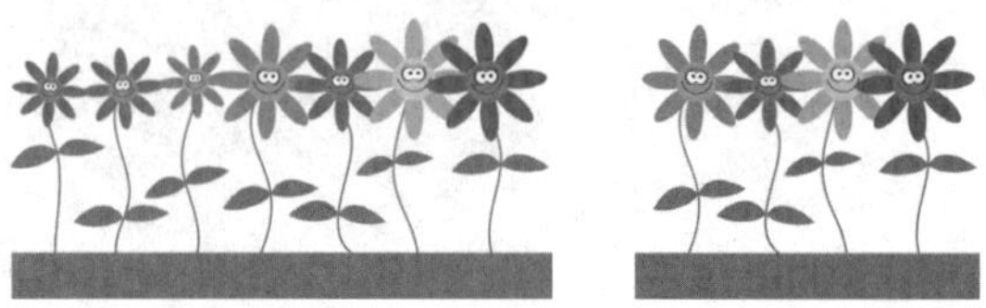

2. Add.

1 + 2 = ________

3. Circle who will come next.

4. How tall is the mouse?

_____ cubes

5. Draw a rectangle.

6.

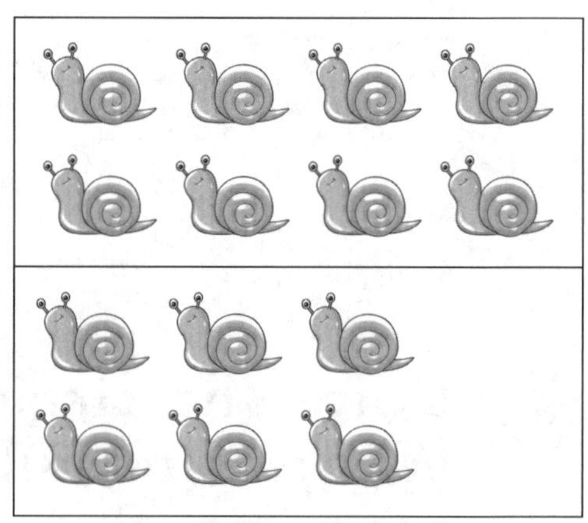

Write the missing numbers.

_____ is more

than _____

NAME: ____________________

DIRECTIONS Solve each problem.

1. How many bones are there?

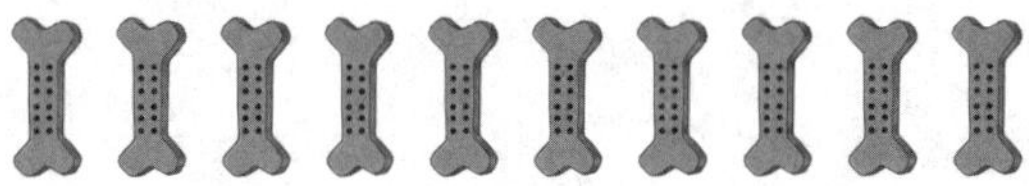

8 9 10

2. Add.

3 + 2 = ________

3. What will come next?

4. Circle the best estimate for bedtime.

11:00 in the morning

8:00 in the evening

5. Does the solid have any curved surfaces? Circle the answer.

yes no

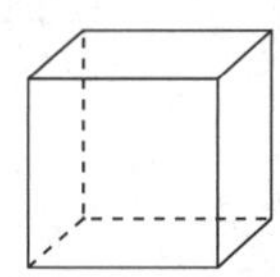

6. How many cats are there?

____

SCORE

1. ☺ 😐

2. ☺ 😐

3. ☺ 😐

4. ☺ 😐

5. ☺ 😐

6. ☺ 😐

____ / 6 Total

NAME: ____________________

DIRECTIONS Solve each problem.

SCORE

1. ☺ 😐
2. ☺ 😐
3. ☺ 😐
4. ☺ 😐
5. ☺ 😐
6. ☺ 😐

___ / 6 Total

1. Will every dog get a bone? Circle the answer.

yes no

2. Add.

1 + 3 = ________

3. Circle what will come next.

4. Circle the tool you use to measure days.

5. Circle where the bird is.

in the nest

under the nest

6. Cross out the shape that does not belong.

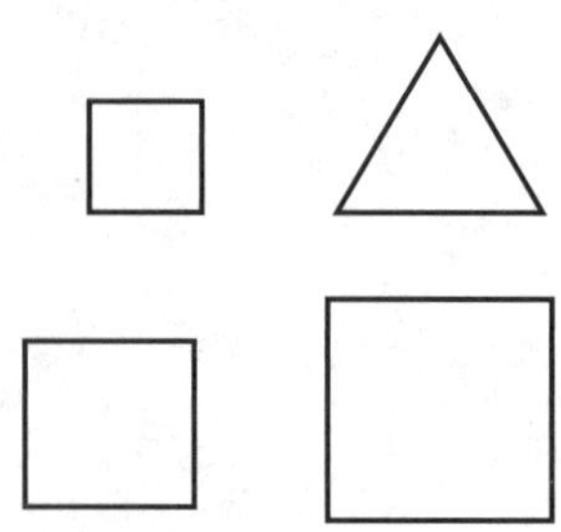

NAME: ______________________________

DIRECTIONS Solve each problem.

1. Count the teacups. Draw an equal set of circles.

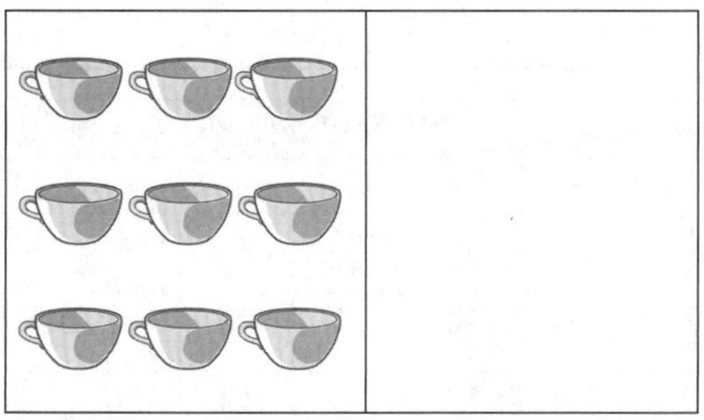

2. Add. Write the number sentence.

_____ + _____ = _____

3. Circle what will come next.

 ?
___

4. Circle the object that weighs less.

5. Is this figure open or closed? Circle the answer.

open closed

H

6. Jahir saw a grasshopper in his backyard. Then the grasshopper hopped away. How many grasshoppers are left?

____

SCORE

1. ☺ 😐

2. ☺ 😐

3. ☺ 😐

4. ☺ 😐

5. ☺ 😐

6. ☺ 😐

____ / 6
Total

DAY 38

NAME: ____________________

DIRECTIONS Solve each problem.

SCORE

1. ☺ 😐
2. ☺ 😐
3. ☺ 😐
4. ☺ 😐
5. ☺ 😐
6. ☺ 😐

____ / 6
Total

1. Draw 3 circles.

2. Add. Write the number sentence.

____ + ____ = ____

3. Write what letter will come next.

O P O P O ☐

4. How many days are in the month of November?

____

November						
Sun	Mon	Tues	Wed	Thurs	Fri	Sat
1	2	3	4	5	6	7
8	9	10	11	12	13	14
15	16	17	18	19	20	21
22	23	24	25	26	27	28
29	30					

5. Will the object roll? Circle the answer.

yes　　no

6. How are these sorted? Circle the answer.

size　　color

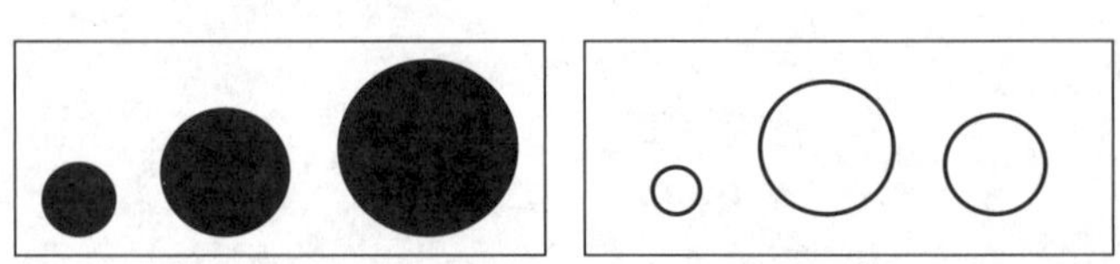

NAME: ____________________

DIRECTIONS Solve each problem.

1. Circle the box with 5 paint colors.

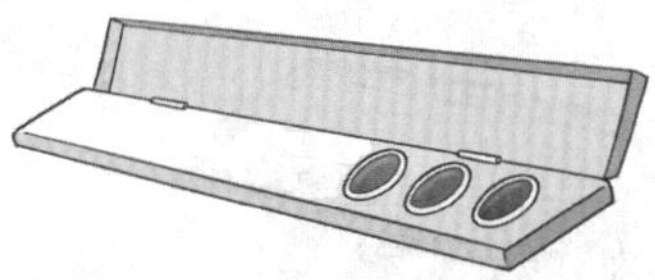

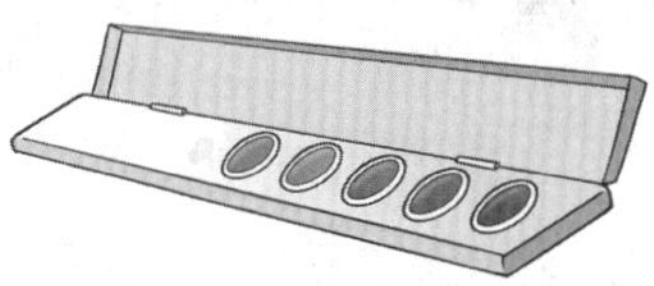

2. Add.

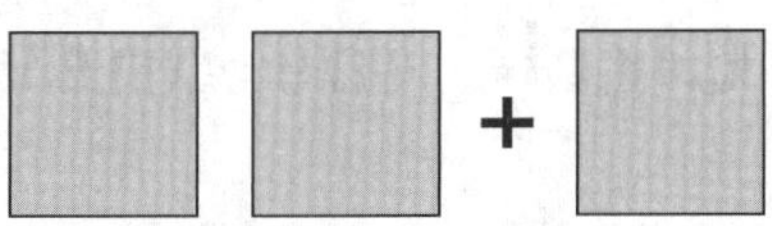

2 + 1 = ________

3. Color the triangles. What color will come next?

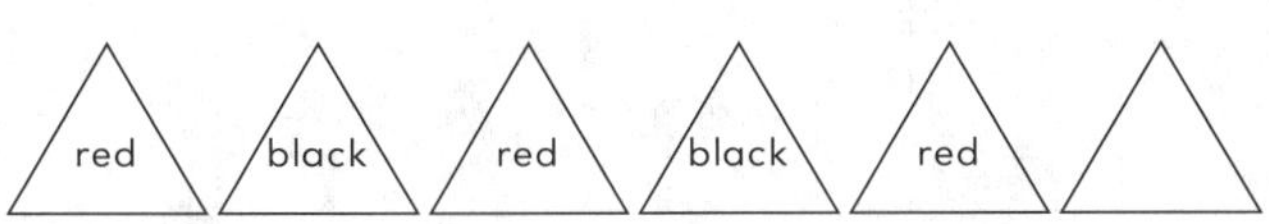

4. Circle about how long it takes to watch a TV show.

1 minute 1 hour

5. Circle the picture that shows the robot in the box.

6. Draw 2 plates. Draw a cracker on each plate.

Are there the same number of plates and crackers?

____

SCORE

1. ☺ 😐

2. ☺ 😐

3. ☺ 😐

4. ☺ 😐

5. ☺ 😐

6. ☺ 😐

____ / 6

Total

NAME: ____________________________

DIRECTIONS Solve each problem.

SCORE

1. ☺ 😐
2. ☺ 😐
3. ☺ 😐
4. ☺ 😐
5. ☺ 😐
6. ☺ 😐

____ / 6
Total

1. Color 5 crayons.

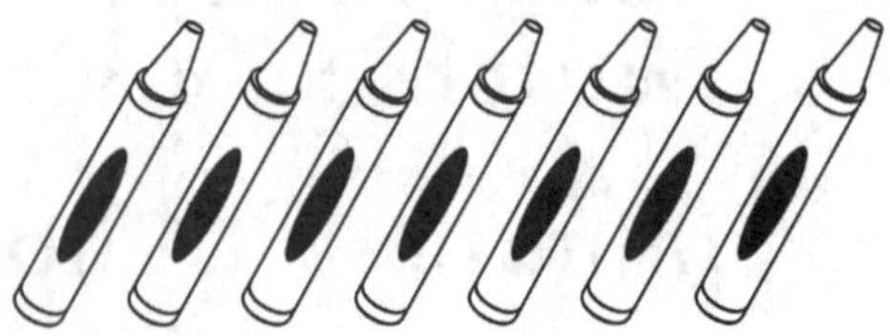

2. Write the number sentence.

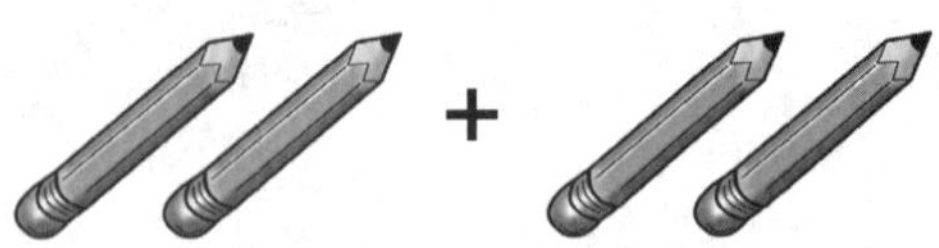

______ + ______ = ______

3. Circle what will come next.

?
____

4. Circle the container that holds more.

5. Does the object have symmetry? Circle the answer.

yes no

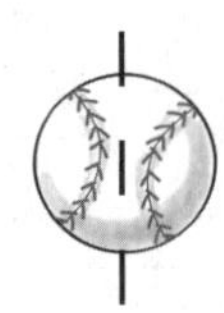

6. Circle who is to the left of Pat.

Tim Pat Meg Rex

DAY 41

NAME: ____________________

DIRECTIONS Solve each problem.

1. Color 9 pretzels.

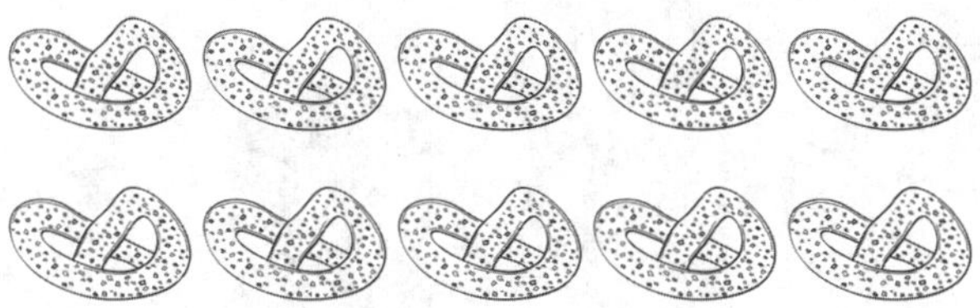

2. How many fish are left?

____

3. Circle what will come next.

? ___

4. What time is it?

_____ o'clock

5. Circle the shapes with 3 sides.

6. How many legs are on 3 stools?

____

SCORE

1. ☺ 😐

2. ☺ 😐

3. ☺ 😐

4. ☺ 😐

5. ☺ 😐

6. ☺ 😐

___ / 6 Total

NAME: ______________________

DIRECTIONS Solve each problem.

SCORE

1. ☺ 😐
2. ☺ 😐
3. ☺ 😐
4. ☺ 😐
5. ☺ 😐
6. ☺ 😐

____ / 6
Total

1. Write the number that comes next.

7 8 9 ____

2. How many crayons are left?

____

3. Draw what will come next.

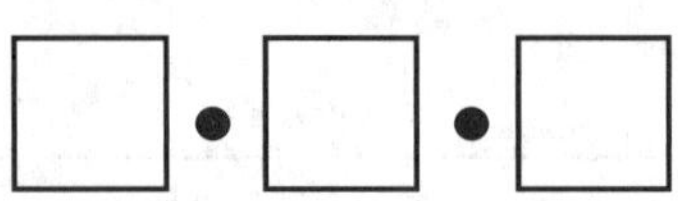 ____

4. Circle the taller object.

5. Circle the solid that looks like the object.

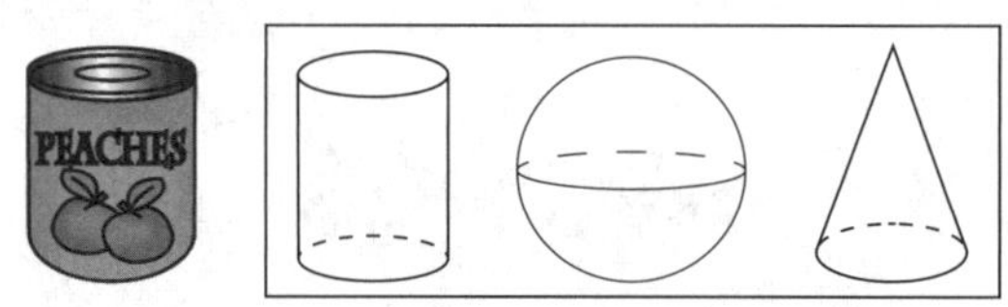

6. Two cars are in the parking lot. Two more cars come. How many cars are there now?

____

NAME: ____________________

DIRECTIONS Solve each problem.

1. Draw more to make a set of 10.

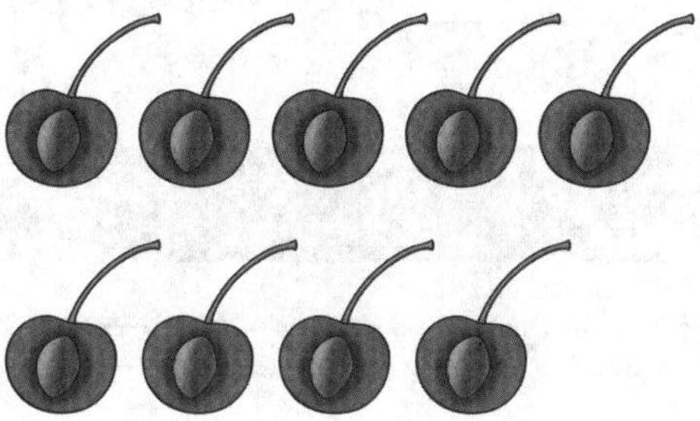

2. Add.

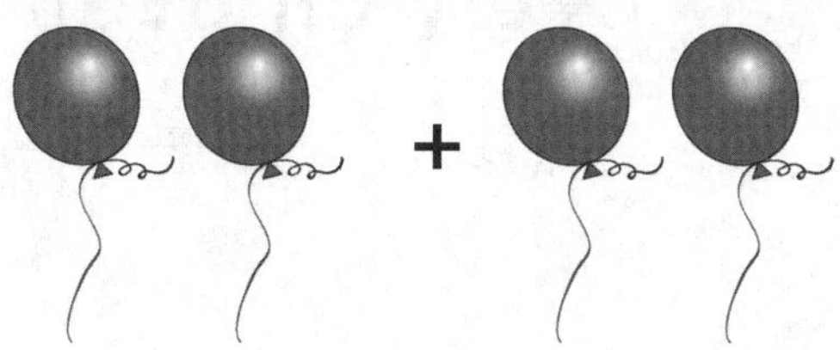

___ + ___ = ____

3. Circle what will come next.

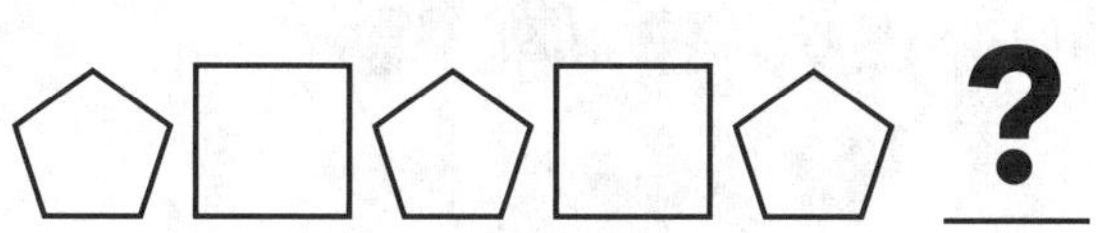

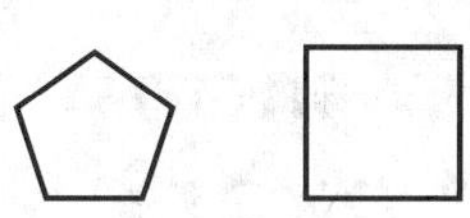

4. About how many pencils can you hold in 1 hand? Circle the answer.

10 100

5. Draw a butterfly below the net.

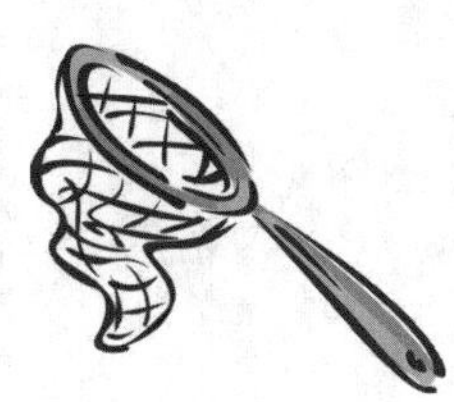

6. I am the number that comes after 8. What number am I?

____

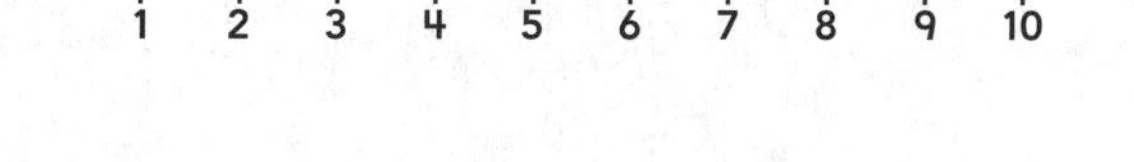

SCORE

1. ☺ 😐

2. ☺ 😐

3. ☺ 😐

4. ☺ 😐

5. ☺ 😐

6. ☺ 😐

___ / 6 Total

DAY 44

NAME: ______________________________

DIRECTIONS Solve each problem.

SCORE

1. ☺ 😐
2. ☺ 😐
3. ☺ 😐
4. ☺ 😐
5. ☺ 😐
6. ☺ 😐

____ / 6 Total

1. Put an X on the group that has more.

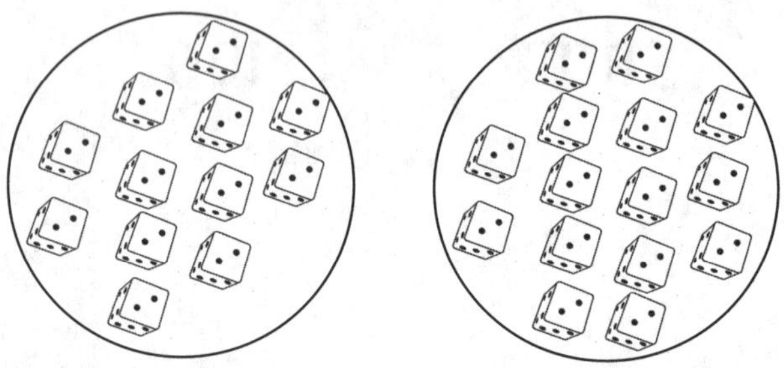

2. How many bugs are left?

____

3. Write what letter will come next in the pattern.

A E A E A ☐

4. How long is the crayon?

______ paperclips

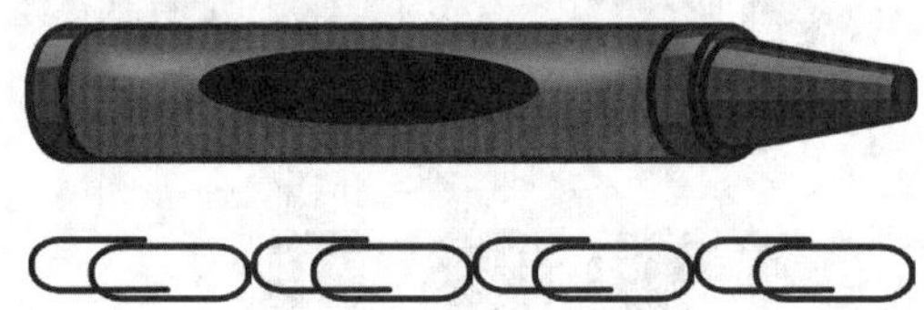

5. Draw an oval.

6. Circle 10.

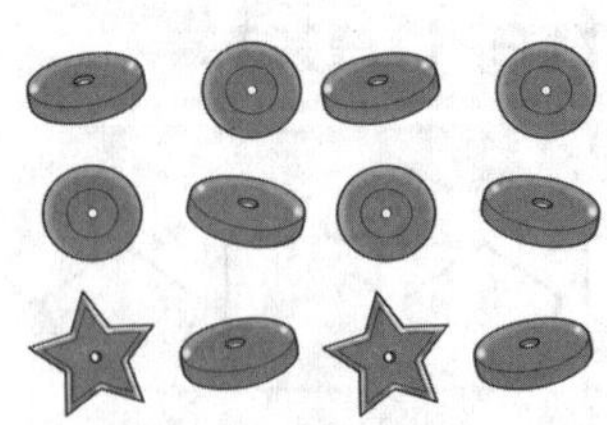

How many are left over?

____

NAME: ____________________

DIRECTIONS Solve each problem.

1. Circle the number of rings.

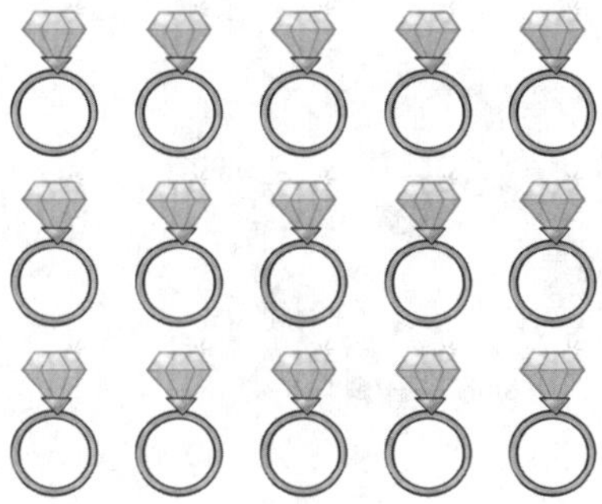

14 15 16

2. Write the number sentence.

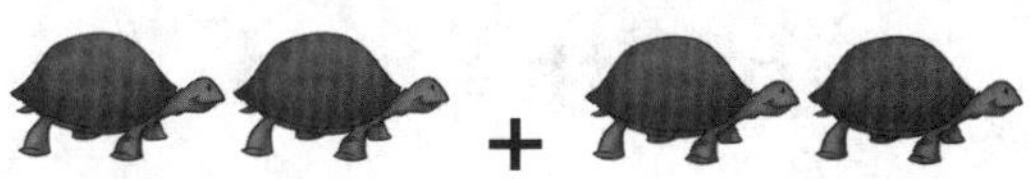

____ + ____ = ____

3. Color the diamonds. What color comes next?

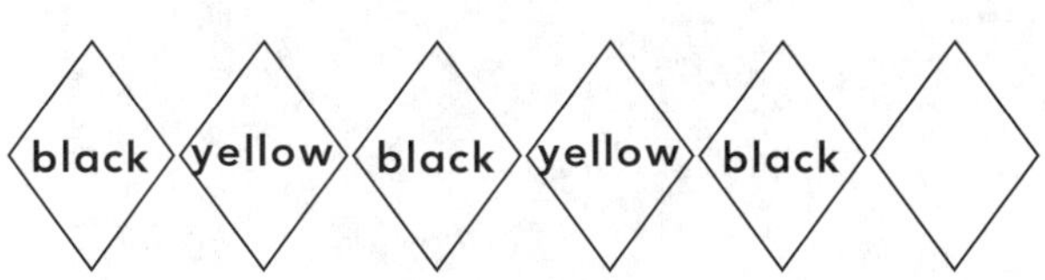

4. Circle when you go to recess.

in the morning

in the evening

5. How many sides does a triangle have?

____

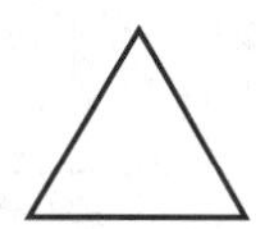

6. Circle the large leaves.

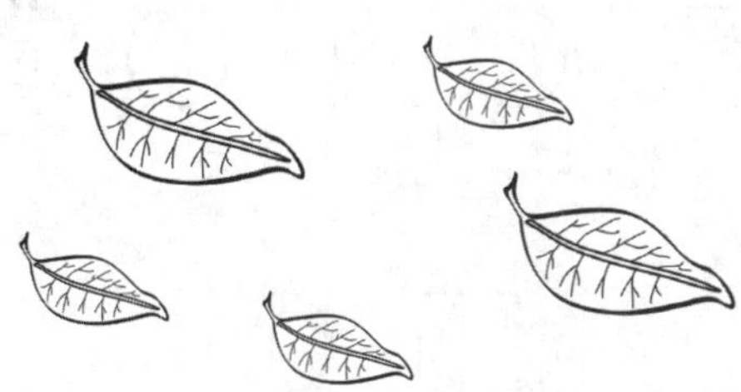

SCORE

1. ☺ 😐
2. ☺ 😐
3. ☺ 😐
4. ☺ 😐
5. ☺ 😐
6. ☺ 😐

____ / 6 Total

NAME: ____________________

DIRECTIONS Solve each problem.

SCORE

1. 😊 😐

2. 😊 😐

3. 😊 😐

4. 😊 😐

5. 😊 😐

6. 😊 😐

____ / 6 Total

1. Will every boy get a jacket? Circle the answer.

yes no

2. How many boats are left?

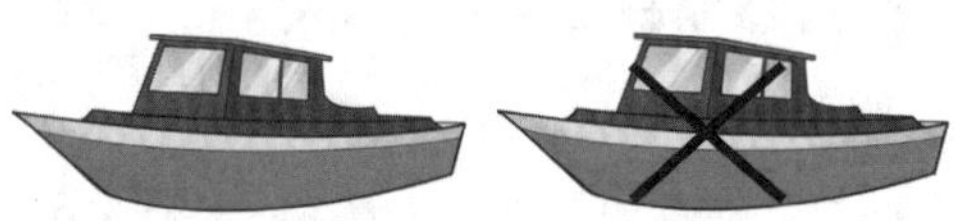

____

3. Circle what will come next.

 ?

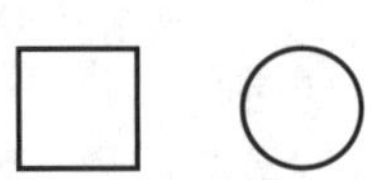

4. Circle the tool to measure water.

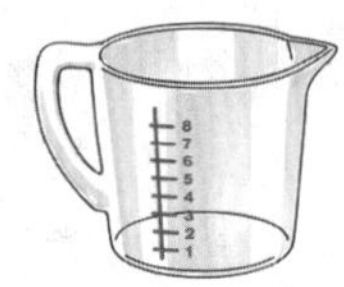

5. Where is the teddy bear? Circle the answer.

on the bed

off the bed

6. Draw more clouds so there are 9.

DAY 47

NAME: ______________________________

DIRECTIONS Solve each problem.

1. Count the bones. Draw an equal set of circles.

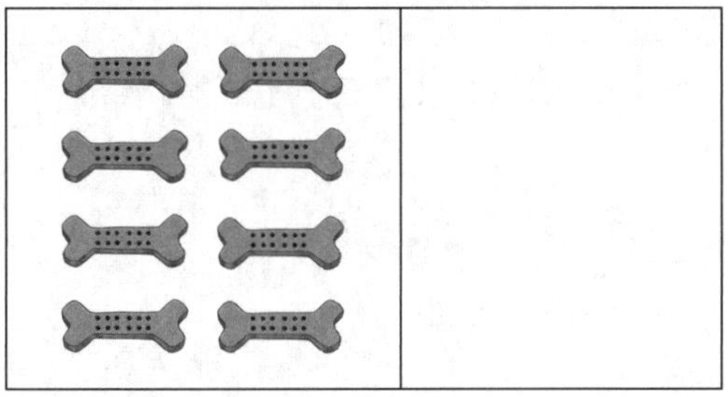

2. Add.

_____ + _____ = _____

3. Write what letter will come next in the pattern.

A A B A A B ☐

4. Circle the person who weighs more.

5. Is this figure open or closed? Circle the answer.

open closed

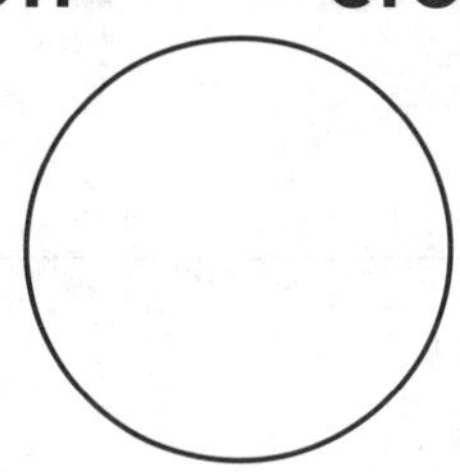

6. There were 4 fish. Three swam away. How many fish were left?

____

SCORE

1. ☺ 😐

2. ☺ 😐

3. ☺ 😐

4. ☺ 😐

5. ☺ 😐

6. ☺ 😐

___ / 6
Total

DAY 48

NAME: ______________________

DIRECTIONS Solve each problem.

1. Draw 1 string on the kite.

4. Circle the day that comes after Thursday.

Wednesday

Friday

2. How many apples are left?

____

5. Will the solid stack? Circle the answer.

yes no

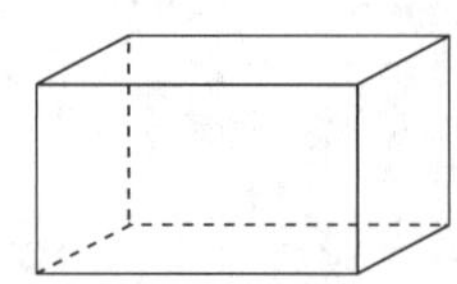

3. Color the beads. What color will come next?

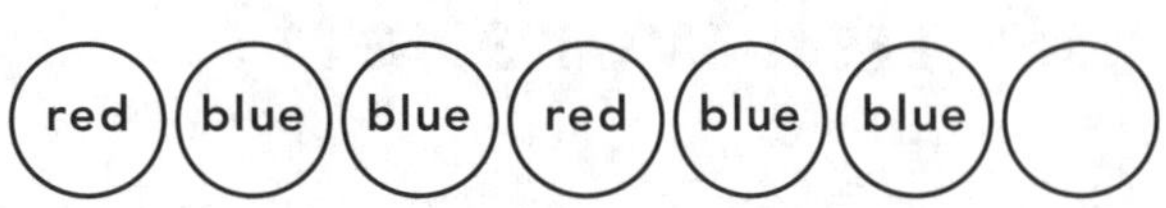

6. Circle the child in the middle.

SCORE

1.

2.

3.

4.

5.

6.

____ / 6
Total

NAME: ______________________________

DIRECTIONS Solve each problem.

1. Circle the ladybug with 10 spots.

2. Write the number sentence.

_____ + _____ = _____

3. Circle who will come next.

? ___

4. Circle how long it takes to write your name.

1 minute   1 hour

5. Circle where the corn is.

in the pot

by the pot

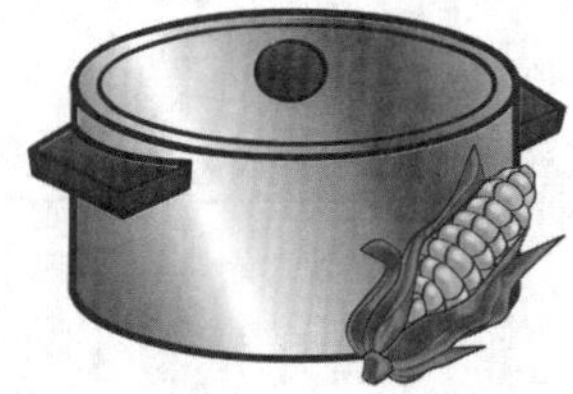

6. Circle the object you would put in a group with shapes.

 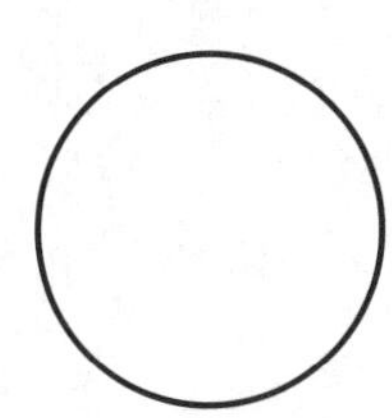

SCORE

1. ☺ 😐

2. ☺ 😐

3. ☺ 😐

4. ☺ 😐

5. ☺ 😐

6. ☺ 😐

___ / 6 Total

DAY 50

NAME: ______________________

DIRECTIONS Solve each problem.

SCORE

1. ☺ 😐
2. ☺ 😐
3. ☺ 😐
4. ☺ 😐
5. ☺ 😐
6. ☺ 😐

____ / 6 Total

1. Circle the number of pumpkins.

9   10   11

2. Write the number sentence.

____ + ____ = ____

3. Circle what will come next.

 ?

4. Circle the container that holds more.

5. Does the picture have symmetry? Circle the answer.

yes   no

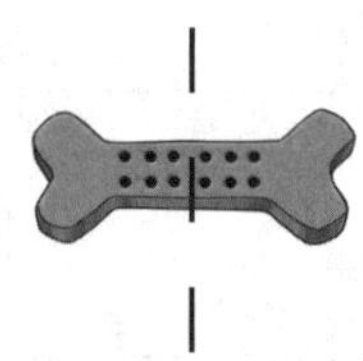

6. Show 8 triangles. Add or cross out triangles.

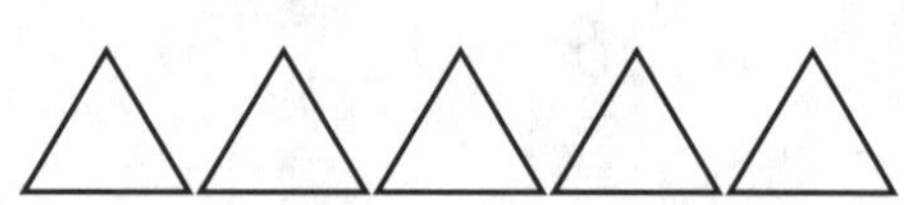

NAME: ____________________

DIRECTIONS Solve each problem.

1. Color 10 stars.

2. Subtract.

3 – 1 = ________

3. Circle what will come next.

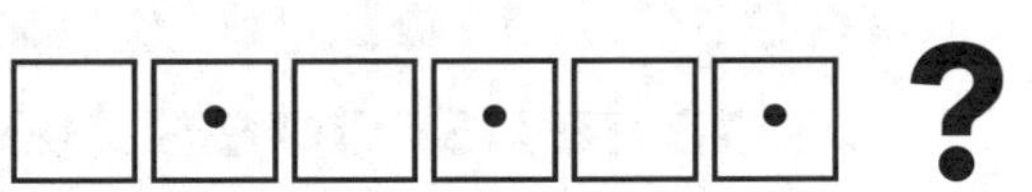

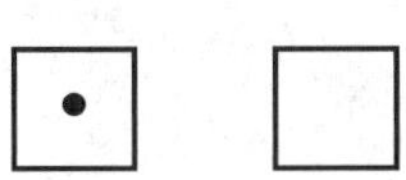

4. What time is it?

______ o'clock

5. Color the shapes with 4 sides.

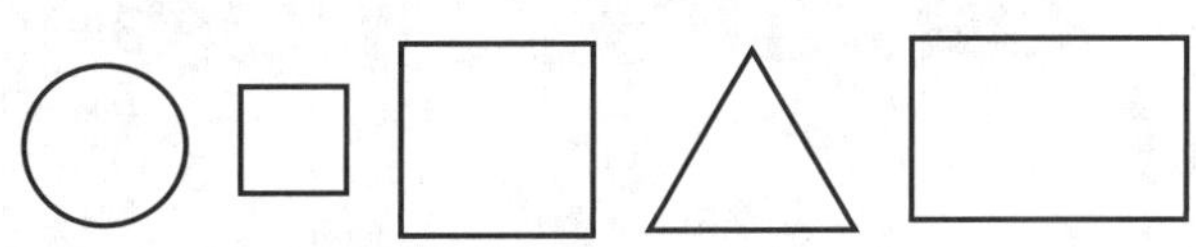

6. How many eyes are on 3 children?

____

SCORE

1. ☺ 😐

2. ☺ 😐

3. ☺ 😐

4. ☺ 😐

5. ☺ 😐

6. ☺ 😐

____ / 6

Total

DAY
52

NAME: ______________________________

DIRECTIONS Solve each problem.

SCORE

1. ☺ 😐
2. ☺ 😐
3. ☺ 😐
4. ☺ 😐
5. ☺ 😐
6. ☺ 😐

____ / 6 Total

1. Write what number comes next.

9 10 11 ______

2. Write the number sentence.

______ + ______ = ______

3. Circle what will come next.

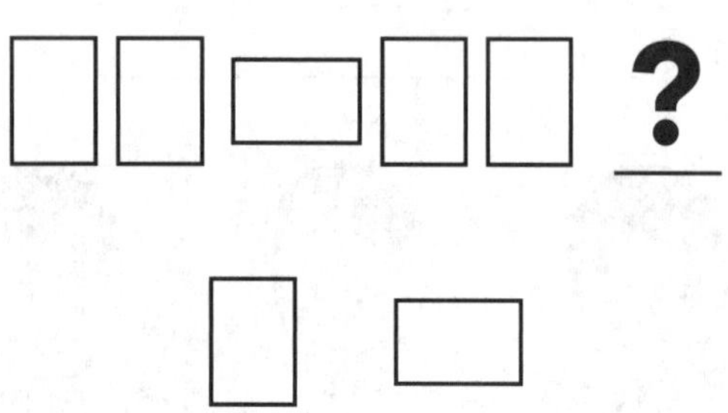

4. Draw an object that is shorter than a woman.

5. Circle the solid that looks like the object.

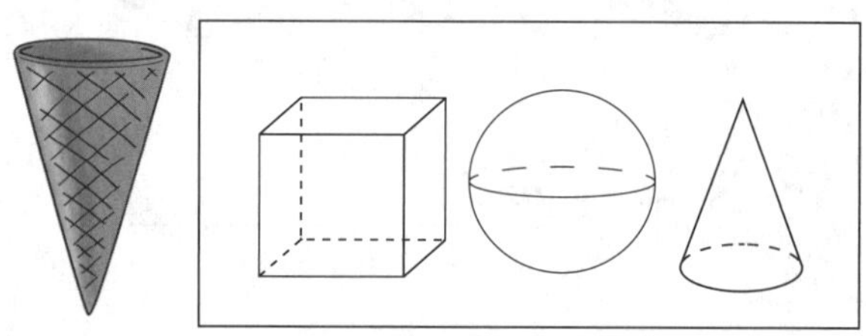

6. John finds 4 seashells. Then he finds one more. How many seashells does he have now?

______

NAME: ____________________

DIRECTIONS Solve each problem.

1. Draw more to make a set of 10.

2. Subtract.

$3 - 2 = \square$

3. Circle what will come next.

? ___

4. Circle how many raisins can fit on a spoon.

8 80

5. Draw a bird in the tree.

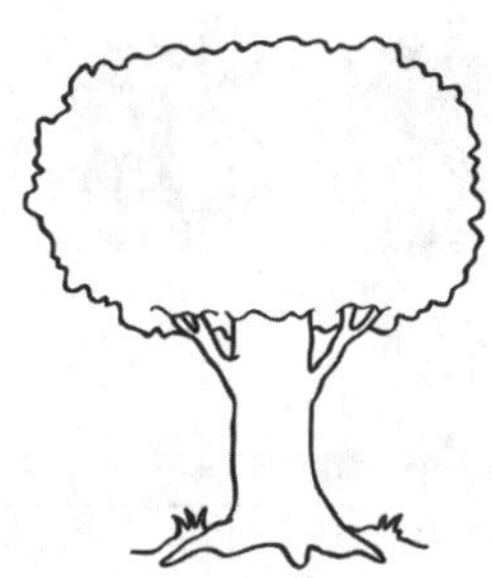

6. How many cats are there?

____

Dogs	Birds	Cats
4	2	3

SCORE

1.

2.

3.

4.

5.

6.

___ / 6
Total

DAY
54

NAME: ______________________________

DIRECTIONS Solve each problem.

SCORE

1. ☺ 😐
2. ☺ 😐
3. ☺ 😐
4. ☺ 😐
5. ☺ 😐
6. ☺ 😐

___/6
Total

1. Circle the group with more worms.

4 worms 5 worms

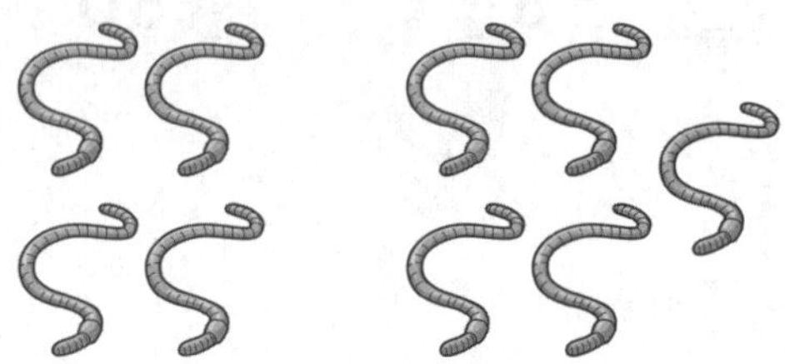

2. Subtract.

4 – 4 = _____

3. Color the squares. What color will come next?

red	green	green	red	green	green	

4. How tall is the toy?

_____ cubes

5. Draw a heart.

6. Jack started counting like this:

10 9 8 7 6

How is Jack counting? Circle the answer.

forward backward

NAME: ____________________

DIRECTIONS Solve each problem.

1. Circle the number of shells.

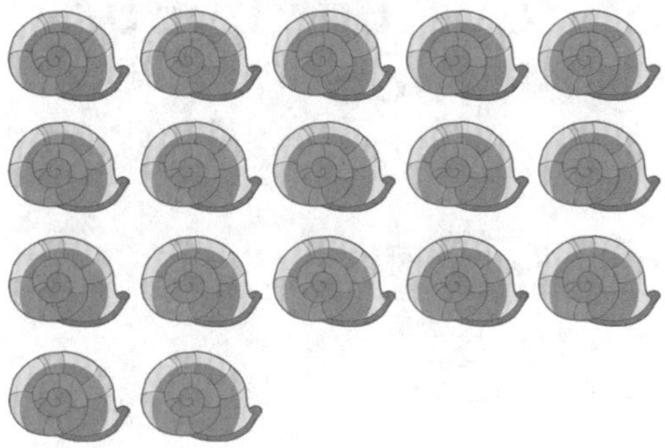

17 18 19

2. Write the number sentence.

 + 

_____ + _____ = _____

3. Circle what will come next.

 ?

4. Circle the best time for dinner.

9:00 in the morning

5:00 in the evening

5. Does the solid have any flat surfaces? Circle the answer.

yes no

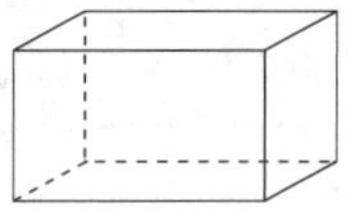

6. Circle groups of 2. How many groups of 2 can you make?

____

SCORE

1. ☺ 😐

2. ☺ 😐

3. ☺ 😐

4. ☺ 😐

5. ☺ 😐

6. ☺ 😐

____ / 6

Total

DAY
56

NAME: ______________________

DIRECTIONS Solve each problem.

SCORE

1. ☺ 😐
2. ☺ 😐
3. ☺ 😐
4. ☺ 😐
5. ☺ 😐
6. ☺ 😐

____ / 6

Total

1. Will every bird get a worm? Circle the answer.

yes no

2. Write the number sentence.

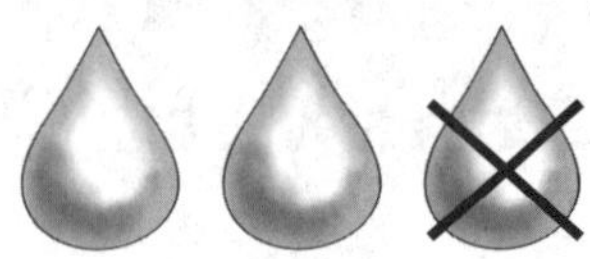

____ – ____ = ____

3. Circle what will come next.

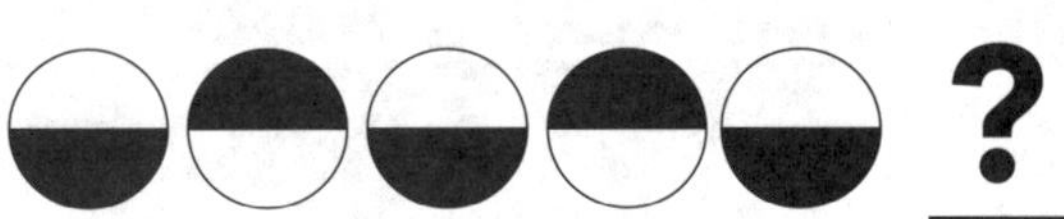

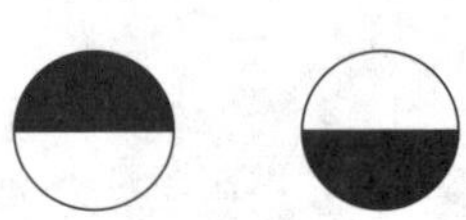

4. Circle the tool you use to measure days until your birthday.

5. The cat is ____ the television.

on under in

6. Cross out the shape that does not belong.

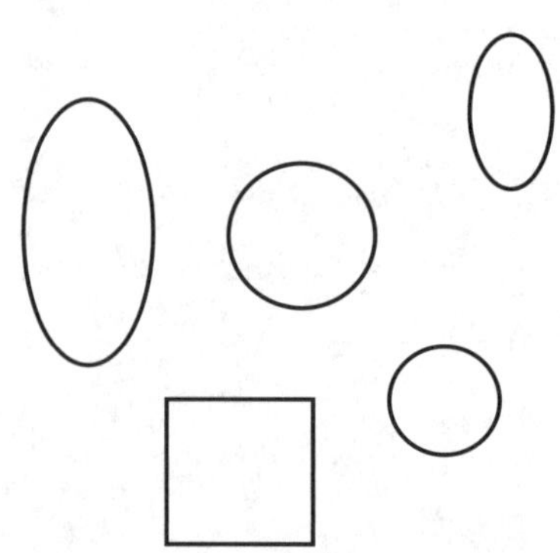

NAME: ______________________________

DIRECTIONS Solve each problem.

1. Count the donuts. Draw an equal set of circles.

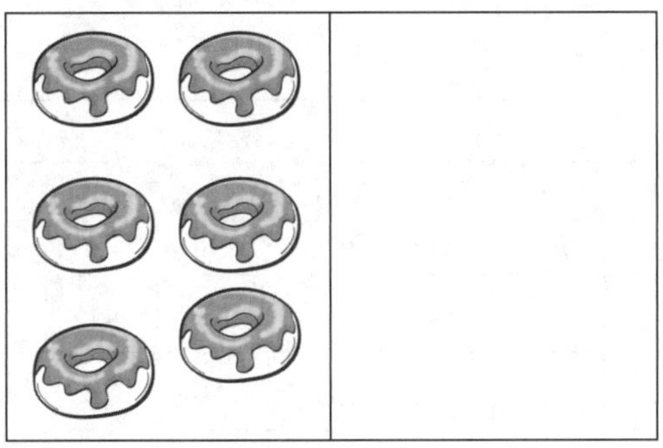

2. Add.

3 + 3 = ________

3. Circle the part that repeats.

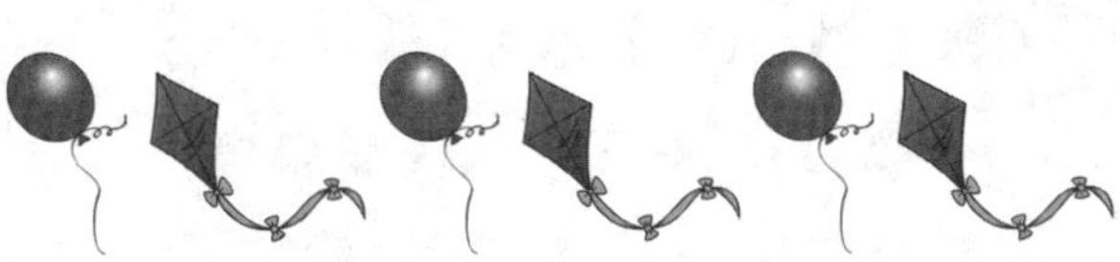

4. Circle the object that weighs less.

5. Is this figure open or closed? Circle the answer.

open   closed

6. Two cats are on a wall. One of the cats runs away. How many cats are still on the wall?

____

SCORE

1. ☺ 😐

2. ☺ 😐

3. ☺ 😐

4. ☺ 😐

5. ☺ 😐

6. ☺ 😐

____ / 6
Total

DAY **58**

NAME: ______________________________

DIRECTIONS Solve each problem.

SCORE

1. ☺ 😐
2. ☺ 😐
3. ☺ 😐
4. ☺ 😐
5. ☺ 😐
6. ☺ 😐

____ / 6 Total

1. Draw 2 legs on the bird.

2. Write the number sentence.

_____ + _____ = _____

3. Circle what will come next.

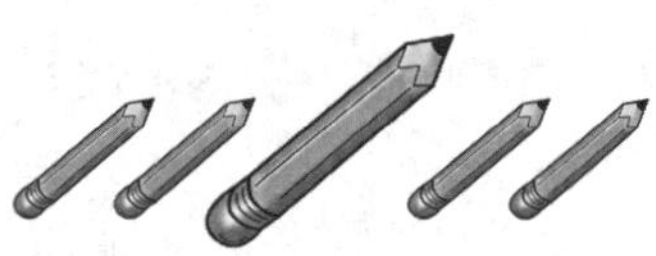

? ____

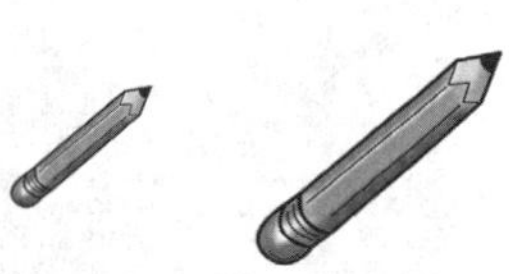

4. What day of the week is December 1st?

____

December						
Sun	Mon	Tues	Wed	Thurs	Fri	Sat
			1	2	3	4
5	6	7	8	9	10	11
12	13	14	15	16	17	18
19	20	21	22	23	24	25
26	27	28	29	30	31	

5. Will the solid slide? Circle the answer.

yes   no

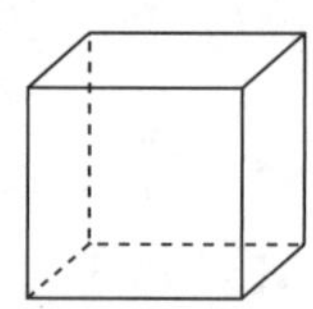

6. John has 10 apples. Susan has 12 apples. Circle who has fewer apples.

John   Susan

DAY 59

NAME: ____________________

DIRECTIONS Solve each problem.

1. Circle the machine with 11 pieces of gum.

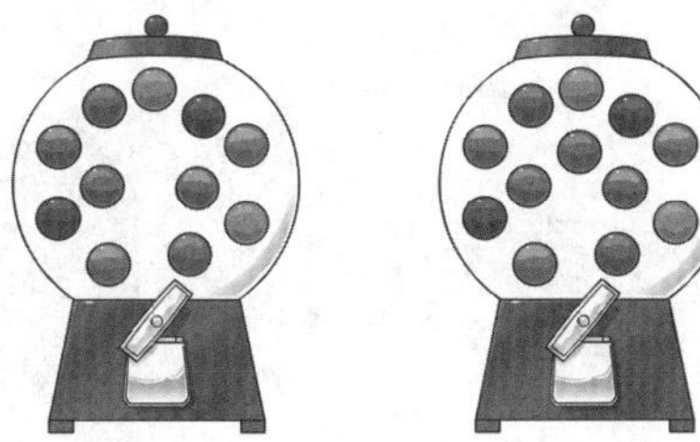

2. Subtract.

3 – 0 = ______

3. Circle who will come next.

? ____

4. Circle the time it takes to brush your teeth.

1 minute   1 hour

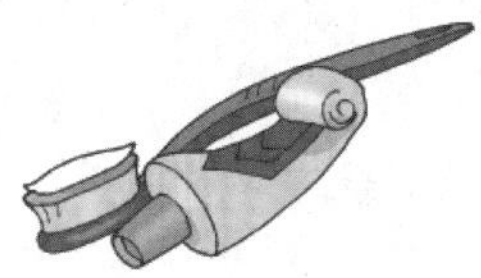

5. Circle the picture that shows glasses to the right of the book.

6. Draw 3 apples. Draw 3 bananas.

Are there the same number of bananas and apples?

____

SCORE

1.

2.

3.

4.

5.

6.

____ / 6 Total

DAY
60

NAME: ______________________

DIRECTIONS Solve each problem.

SCORE

1. ☺ 😐
2. ☺ 😐
3. ☺ 😐
4. ☺ 😐
5. ☺ 😐
6. ☺ 😐

____ / 6
Total

1. Circle the number of snakes.

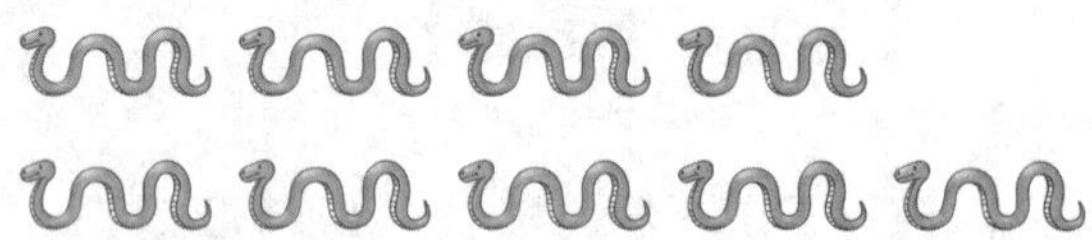

8 9 10

2. Write the number sentence.

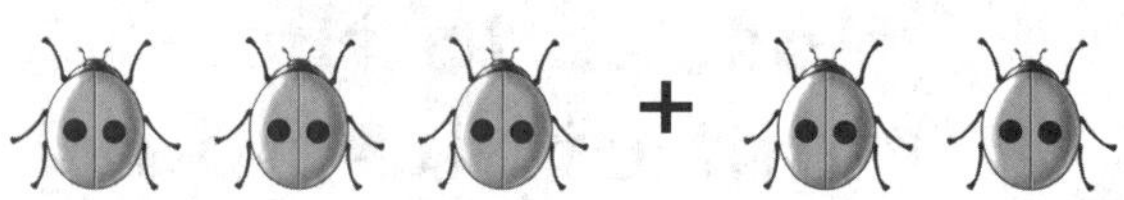

_____ + _____ = _____

3. Color the triangles. What color will come next?

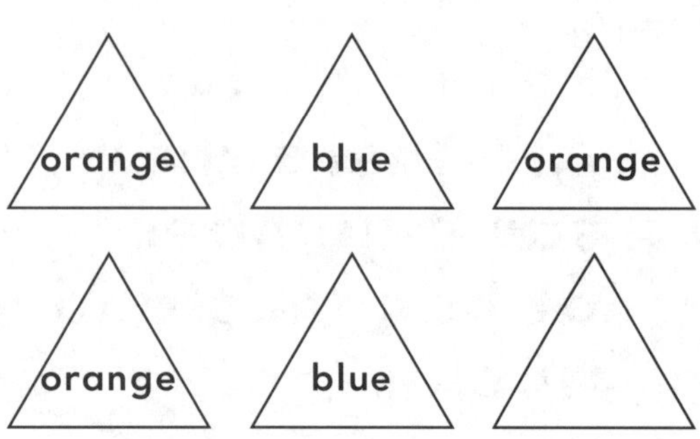

4. Circle the container that holds more.

5. Does the picture have symmetry? Circle the answer.

yes no

6. Circle the smallest square.

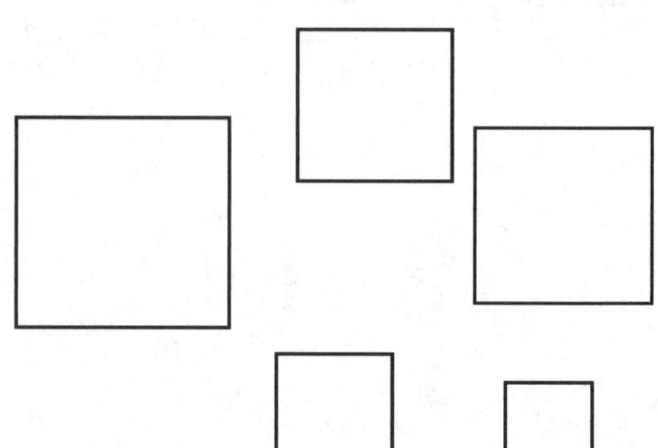

NAME: ______________________

DIRECTIONS Solve each problem.

1. Color 13 balls.

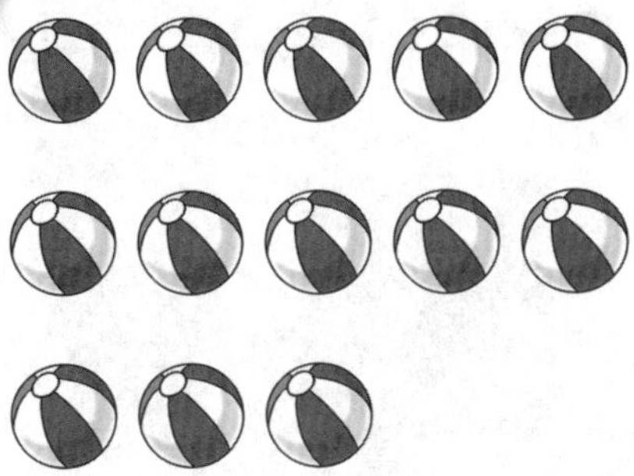

2. Write the number sentence.

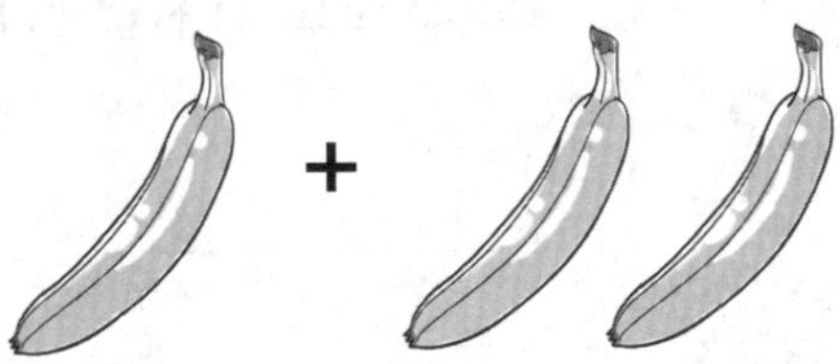

_____ + _____ = _____

3. Circle the part that repeats.

4. What time is it?

_____ o'clock

5. Circle the shape with 3 sides.

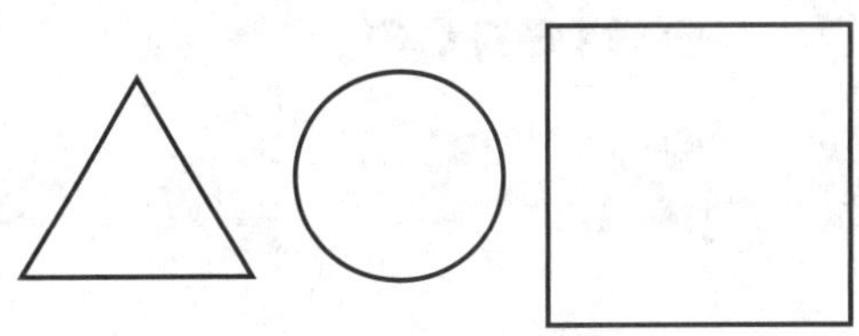

6. How many legs are on 4 snakes?

____

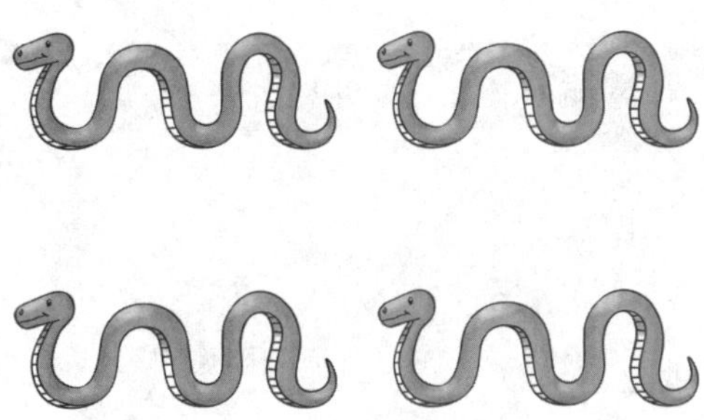

SCORE

1. ☺ 😐

2. ☺ 😐

3. ☺ 😐

4. ☺ 😐

5. ☺ 😐

6. ☺ 😐

____ / 6

Total

DAY 62

NAME: ____________________

DIRECTIONS Solve each problem.

SCORE

1. ☺ 😐
2. ☺ 😐
3. ☺ 😐
4. ☺ 😐
5. ☺ 😐
6. ☺ 😐

____ / 6 Total

1. Write what number comes next.

11 12 13 ______

2. Write the number sentence.

______ – ______ = ______

3. Circle what will come next.

4. Circle the taller object.

5. Circle the solid that looks like the object.

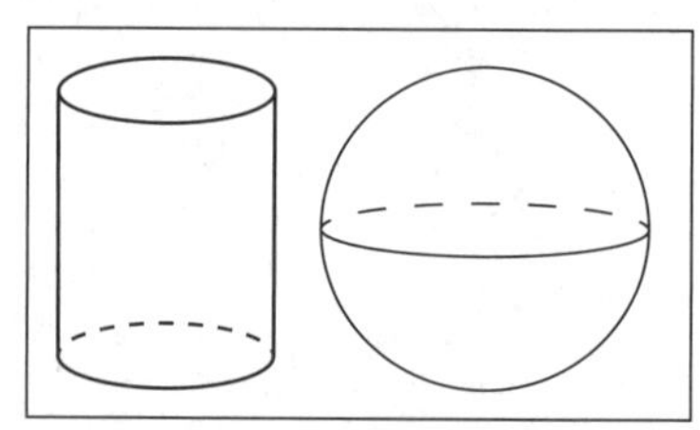

6. A man is walking 2 dogs. A woman is walking 1 dog. How many dogs are there?

____

NAME: ____________________________

DIRECTIONS Solve each problem.

1. Draw more cookies to make 10.

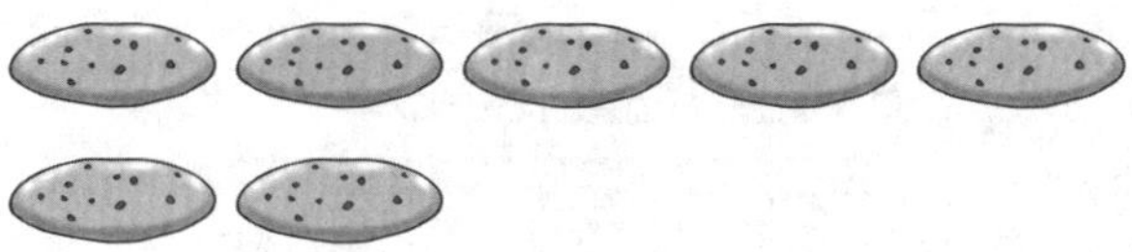

2. Add.

2 + 4 = ______

3. Circle what will come next.

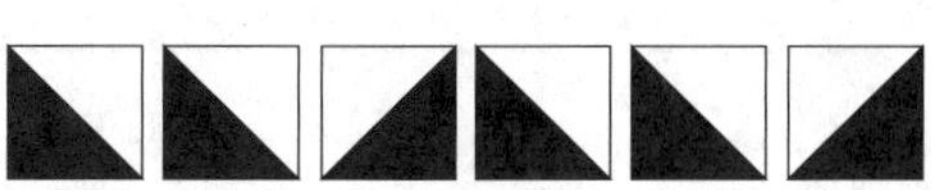 ?

4. Circle about how many buttons are on a phone.

10 100

5. Draw a present in the wagon.

6. Draw a shape with the same number of sides as the shape below.

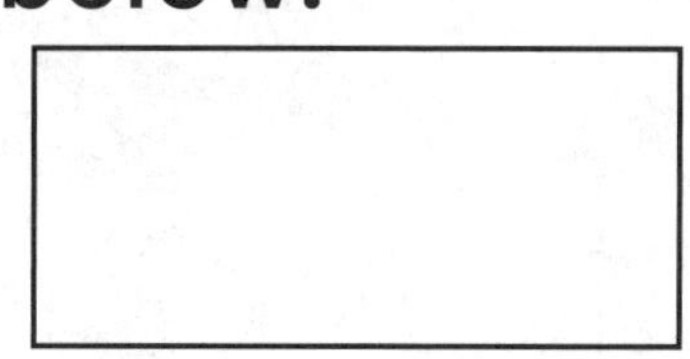

SCORE

1. ☺ 😐

2. ☺ 😐

3. ☺ 😐

4. ☺ 😐

5. ☺ 😐

6. ☺ 😐

___ / 6

Total

DAY
64

NAME: ______________________

DIRECTIONS Solve each problem.

SCORE

1. ☺ ☹
2. ☺ ☹
3. ☺ ☹
4. ☺ ☹
5. ☺ ☹
6. ☺ ☹

___ / 6
Total

1. Circle the set with more bananas.

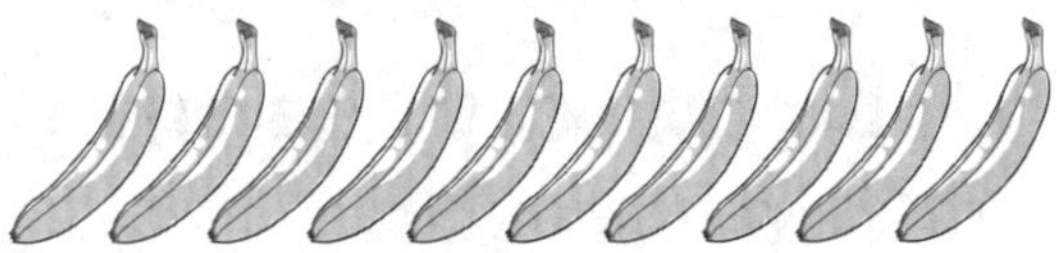

2. Subtract.

5 – 4 = ______

3. Circle what will come next.

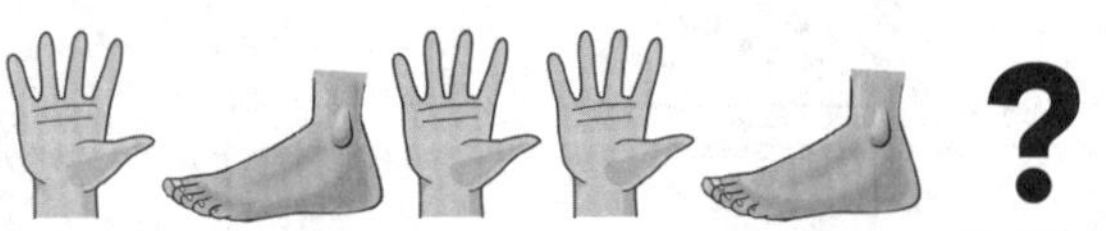

4. How long is the pen?

______ cubes

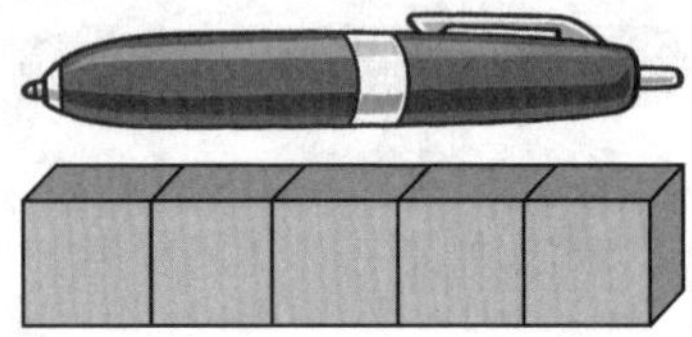

5. Draw a hexagon.

6. I am the number that comes after 5. What number am I?

____

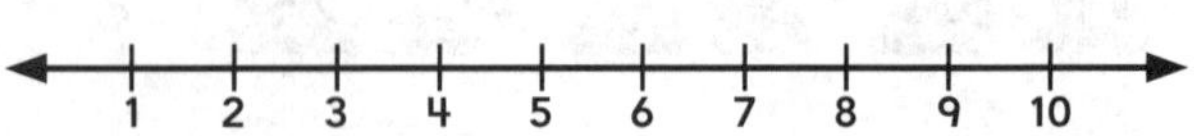

NAME: ____________________

DIRECTIONS Solve each problem.

1. How many ants are there? Circle the answer.

19 20 21

2. Add.

1 + 2 = ______

3. Circle the part that repeats.

4. Circle a good time to go to a park.

3:00 in the morning

3:00 in the afternoon

5. How many sides does a rectangle have?

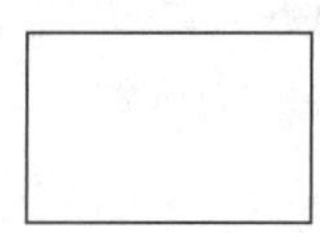 ______

6. Circle groups of 10.

How many groups of 10 are there?

____

How many are left over?

____

SCORE

1.

2.

3.

4.

5.

6.

____ / 6

Total

DAY 66

NAME: ______________________________

DIRECTIONS Solve each problem.

SCORE

1. ☺ 😐
2. ☺ 😐
3. ☺ 😐
4. ☺ 😐
5. ☺ 😐
6. ☺ 😐

____ / 6 Total

1. Will every cupcake get a cherry? Circle the answer.

yes no

2. Subtract.

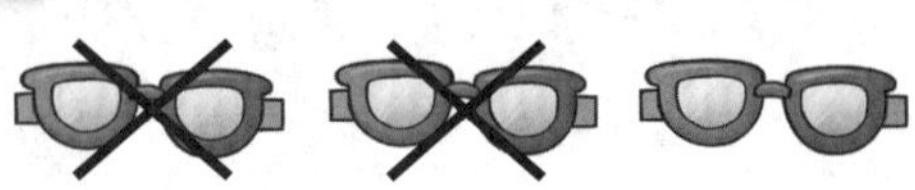

3 – 2 = ____

3. Color the squares. What color will come next?

green	green	blue	green	green	blue	

4. Circle the tool you use to measure your weight.

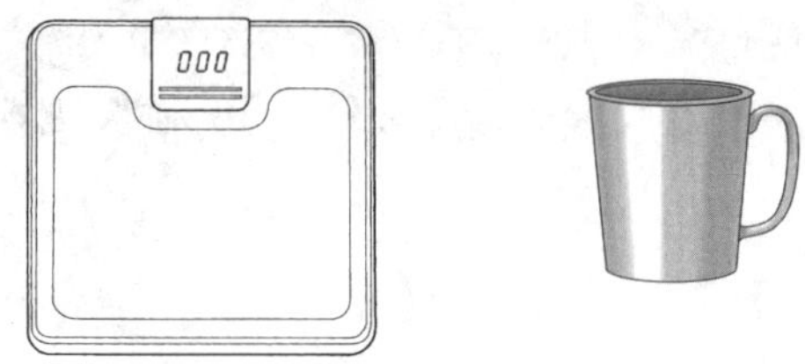

5. Draw a plate under the cookie.

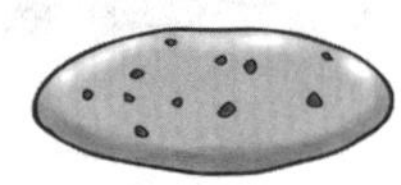

6. Count the fish. How many more fish are needed to make 10?

____

NAME: ______________________________

DIRECTIONS Solve each problem.

SCORE

1. Count the round buttons. Draw an equal set of circles.

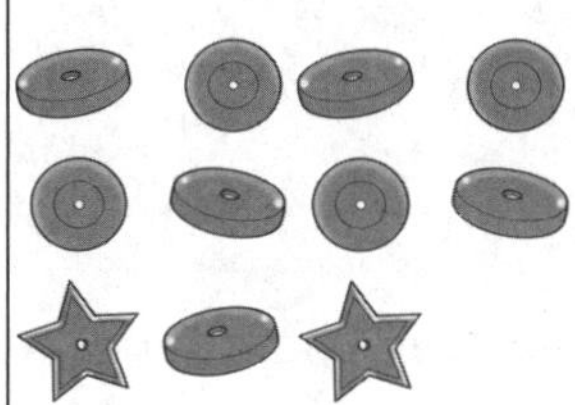

2. Add.

1 + 3 = ______

3. Circle what will come next.

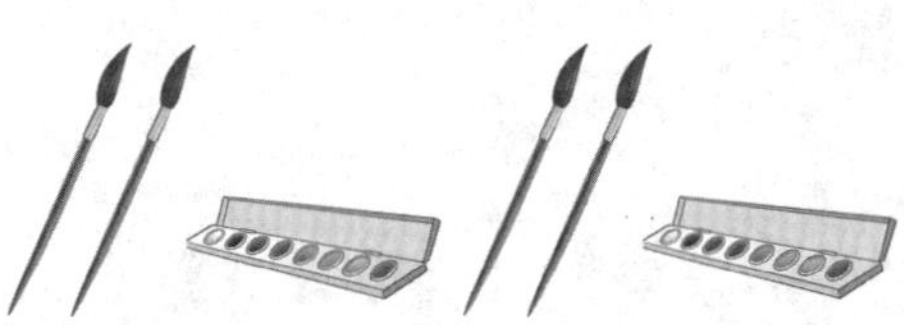

?

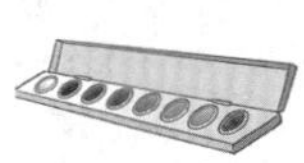

4. Circle the object that weighs more.

5. Is this figure open or closed? Circle the answer.

open closed

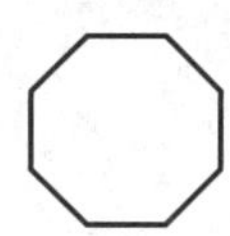

6. Sabrina saw 2 rabbits. Both of the rabbits hopped away. How many rabbits are left?

____

1. ☺ 😐
2. ☺ 😐
3. ☺ 😐
4. ☺ 😐
5. ☺ 😐
6. ☺ 😐

____ / 6
Total

NAME: ______________________________

DIRECTIONS Solve each problem.

SCORE

1. ☺ 😐
2. ☺ 😐
3. ☺ 😐
4. ☺ 😐
5. ☺ 😐
6. ☺ 😐

____ / 6 Total

1. Draw 4 legs on the dog.

2. Write the number sentence.

______ – ______ = ______

3. Circle what will come next.

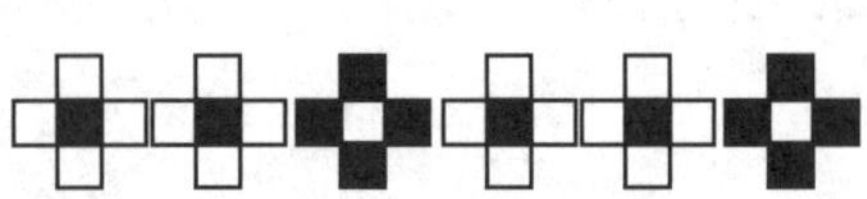 ?

4. Circle what day comes after Wednesday.

Thursday   Saturday

5. Will the object roll? Circle the answer.

yes   no

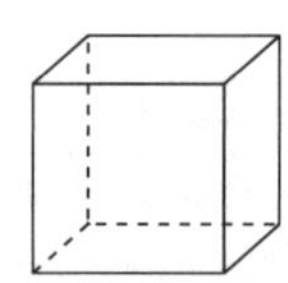

6. Circle the third dog.

NAME: ____________________

DIRECTIONS Solve each problem.

1. Circle the box with 8 dots.

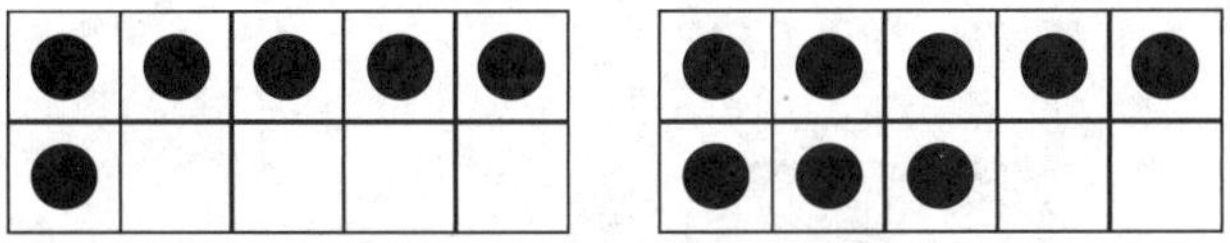

2. Add.

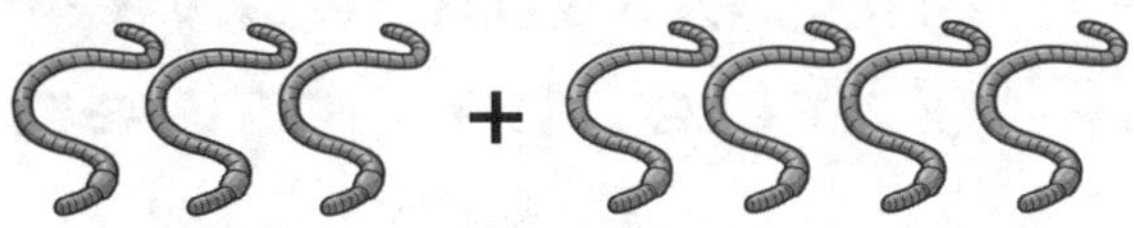

3 + 4 = ______

3. Circle what will come next.

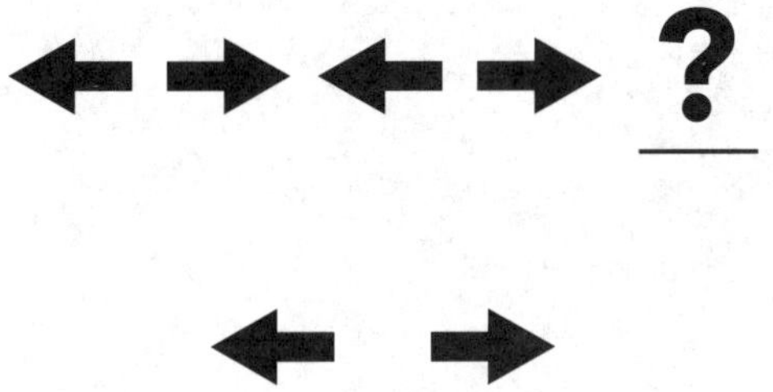

4. Circle how long it takes to go on a long drive.

1 minute 1 hour

5. Circle where the toys are.

next to the rug

on the rug

6. Circle the shape you would put in a group with straight sides.

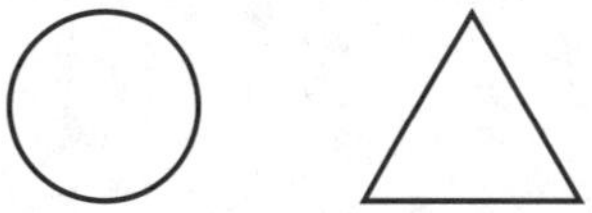

SCORE

1. ☺ 😐

2. ☺ 😐

3. ☺ 😐

4. ☺ 😐

5. ☺ 😐

6. ☺ 😐

___ / 6

Total

NAME: ______________________________

DIRECTIONS Solve each problem.

1. How many sunflowers are there?

____

2. Subtract.

5 – 4 = ______

3. Circle what will come next.

4. Circle the container that holds less.

5. Does the shape have symmetry? Circle the answer.

yes no

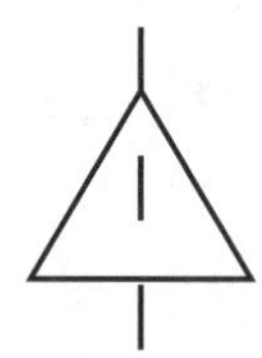

6. Show 10 bananas. Add or cross out bananas if needed.

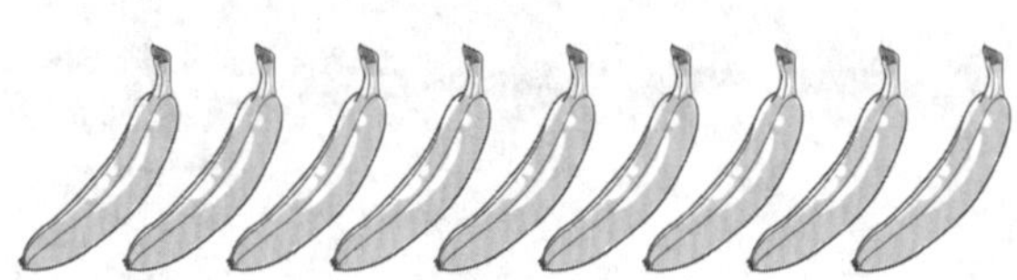

SCORE

1. ☺ 😐
2. ☺ 😐
3. ☺ 😐
4. ☺ 😐
5. ☺ 😐
6. ☺ 😐

____ / 6
Total

NAME: ____________________

DIRECTIONS Solve each problem.

1. Circle 14 bees.

2. Add.

3 + 4 = _____

3. Color the squares. What will come next?

purple	red	purple	red	purple	

4. What time is it?

_____ o'clock

5. Color the shapes with 3 corners.

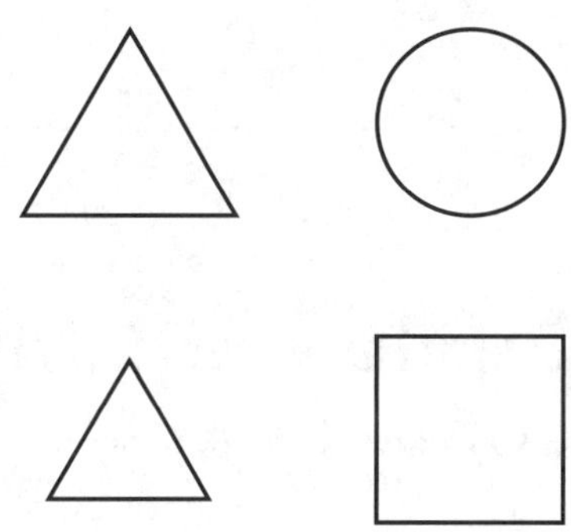

6. How many points are on 3 stars?

____

SCORE

1. ☺ 😐

2. ☺ 😐

3. ☺ 😐

4. ☺ 😐

5. ☺ 😐

6. ☺ 😐

____ / 6 Total

DAY 72

NAME: ____________________

DIRECTIONS Solve each problem.

SCORE

1. ☺ 😐
2. ☺ 😐
3. ☺ 😐
4. ☺ 😐
5. ☺ 😐
6. ☺ 😐

____ / 6 Total

1. Write what number comes next.

12 13 14 ______

2. Write the number sentence.

______ – ______ = ______

3. Circle what will come next.

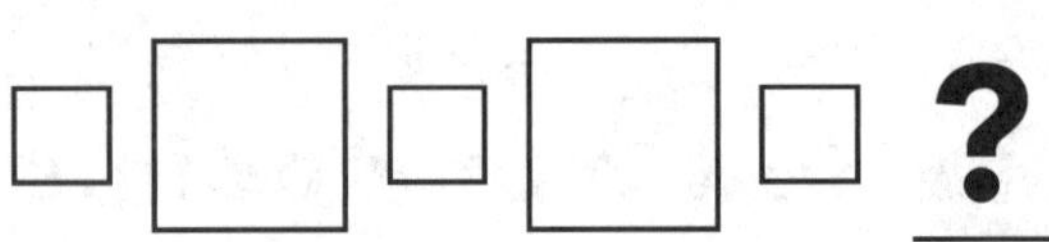

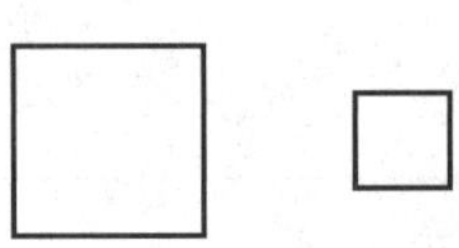

4. Circle the shorter object.

5. Circle the solid that looks like the object.

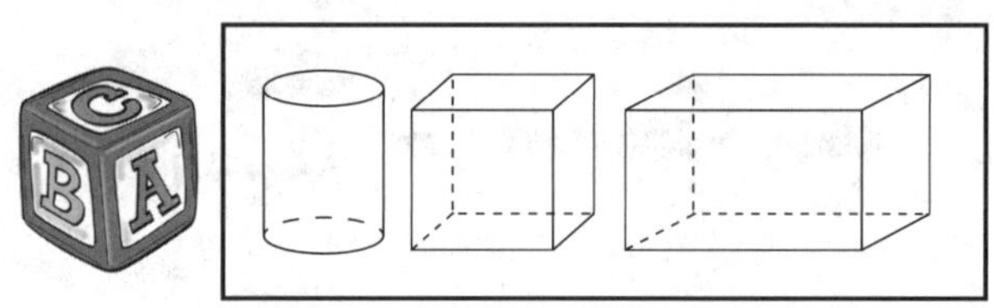

6. Three ants are crawling on a rock. Three more ants come. How many ants are there in all?

____

NAME: ____________________

DIRECTIONS Solve each problem.

1. Draw more Xs to make 10.

2. Write the number sentence.

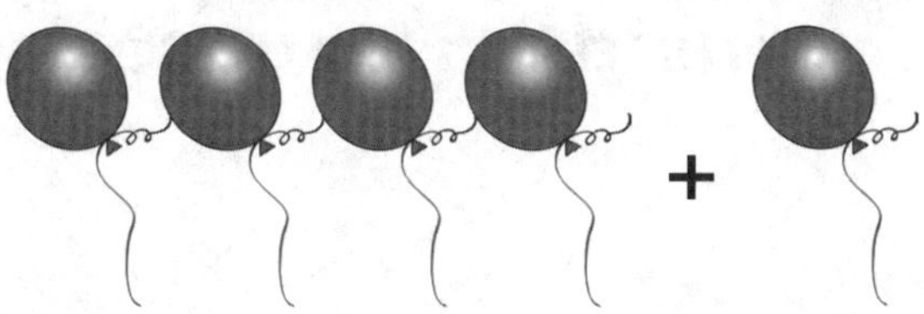

_____ + _____ = _____

3. Circle the part that repeats.

4. Circle how many fingers are on 3 people.

3 30

5. Draw a star to the left of the sun.

6. Circle the numbers that have only curved lines.

0 1 2 3 4

5 6 7 8 9

SCORE

1. ☺ 😐

2. ☺ 😐

3. ☺ 😐

4. ☺ 😐

5. ☺ 😐

6. ☺ 😐

____ / 6 Total

NAME: ____________________

DIRECTIONS Solve each problem.

SCORE

1. ☺ 😐
2. ☺ 😐
3. ☺ 😐
4. ☺ 😐
5. ☺ 😐
6. ☺ 😐

____ / 6 Total

1. Put these numbers in order.

4 2 3 5 1

____

2. Add.

3 + 4 = ______

3. Circle what will come next.

4. How tall is the toy car?

______ cubes

5. Draw a circle inside a square.

6. Circle groups of 2. How many groups of 2 can you make?

____

NAME: ______________________

DIRECTIONS Solve each problem.

1. Write how many penguins there are.

____

2. Subtract.

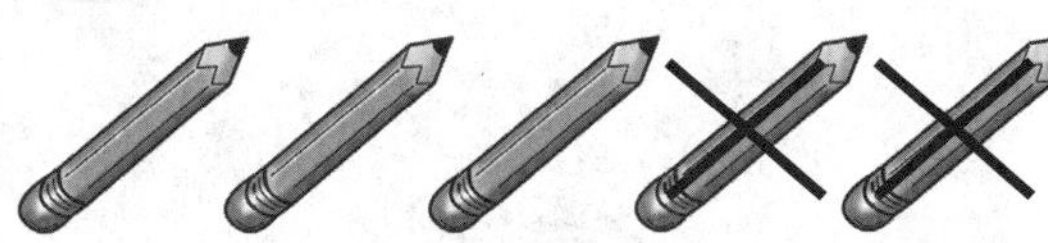

5 – 2 = ______

3. Circle what will come next.

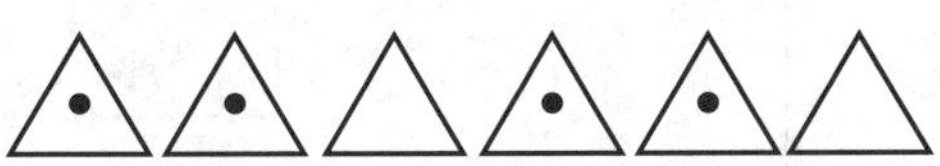

?

4. When is the best time to go to a friend's house?

2:00 in the morning

2:00 in the afternoon

5. Does the solid have any curved surfaces? Circle the answer.

yes no

6. How many boys are there?

____

Boys	12
Girls	8

SCORE

1.

2.

3.

4.

5.

6.

___ / 6
Total

DAY **76**

NAME: ____________________________

DIRECTIONS Solve each problem.

SCORE

1. ☺ 😐
2. ☺ 😐
3. ☺ 😐
4. ☺ 😐
5. ☺ 😐
6. ☺ 😐

____ / 6
Total

1. Will every lock get a key? Circle the answer.

yes no

2. Add.

1 + 0 = ______

3. Draw what will come next.

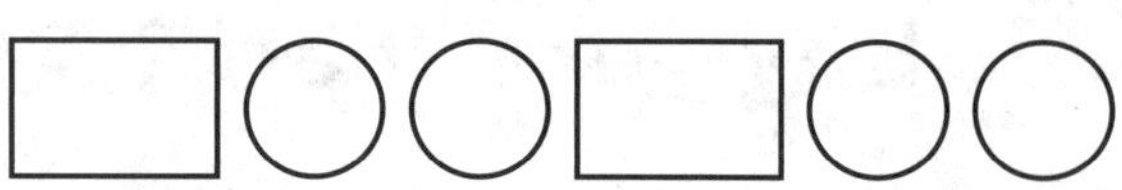

4. Circle what tool is best to measure how long a movie is.

5. The fruit is ______ the bowl.

in under

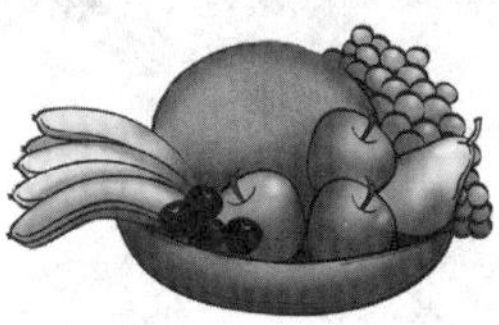

6. Cross out the shape that does not belong.

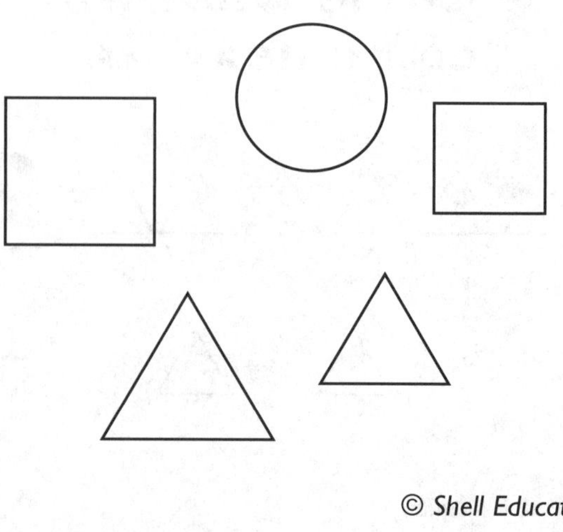

DAY 77

NAME: ____________________

DIRECTIONS Solve each problem.

1. Count the pretzels. Draw an equal set of circles.

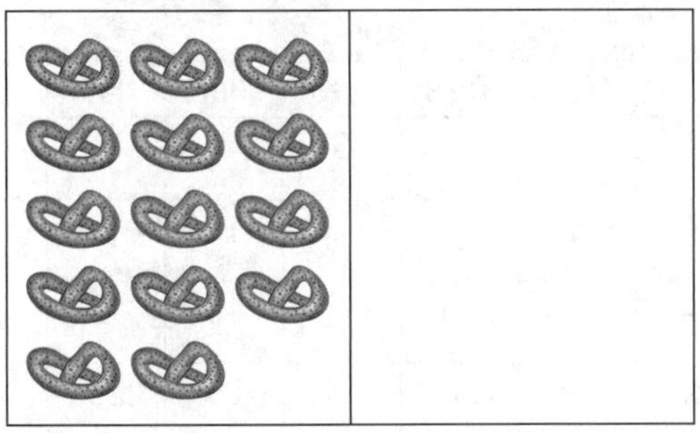

2. Subtract.

5 – 1 = _____

3. Write what will come next.

A B B A B B **?**

____

4. Circle the object that weighs less.

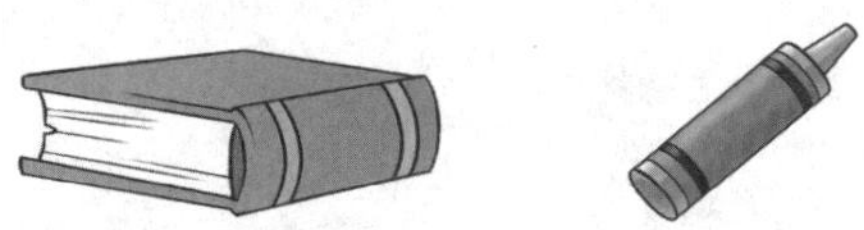

5. Is this figure open or closed? Circle the answer.

open closed

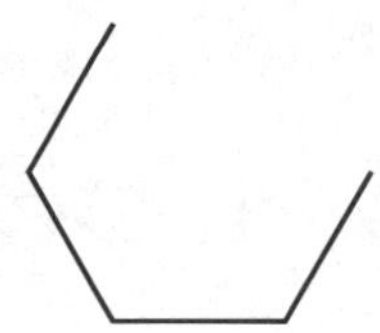

6. Eric had 5 marbles. He gave 3 marbles away. How many marbles does Eric have now?

____

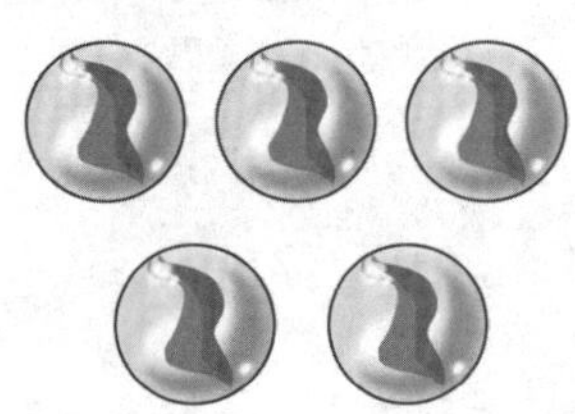

SCORE

1.

2.

3.

4.

5.

6.

___ / 6

Total

DAY
78

NAME: ______________________

DIRECTIONS Solve each problem.

SCORE

1. ☺ 😐
2. ☺ 😐
3. ☺ 😐
4. ☺ 😐
5. ☺ 😐
6. ☺ 😐

____ / 6
Total

1. Draw 10 squares.

2. Add.

2 + 2 = ______

3. Color the circles. What will come next?

(red) (red) (green) (red) (red) (green) ( )

4. What day of the week is May 13th?

____

May						
Sun	Mon	Tues	Wed	Thurs	Fri	Sat
	1	2	3	4	5	6
7	8	9	10	11	12	13
14	15	16	17	18	19	20
21	22	23	24	25	26	27
28	29	30	31			

5. Will the solid stack? Circle the answer.

yes no

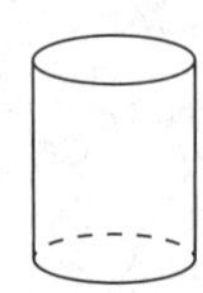

6. Draw lines to match the number to the word.

1 two

2 one

3 four

4 three

DAY 79

NAME: ____________________

DIRECTIONS Solve each problem.

1. Circle the group that has 12.

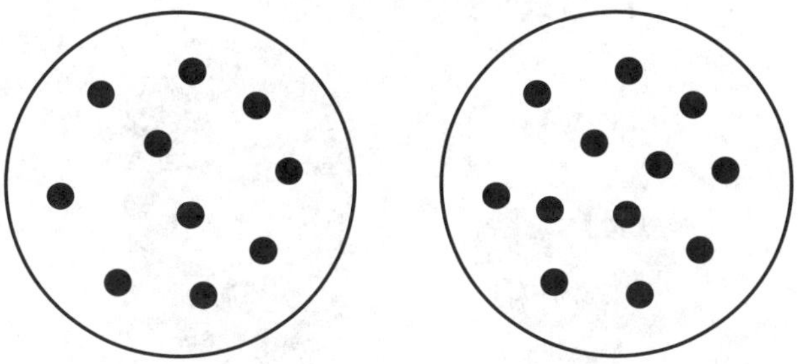

2. Subtract.

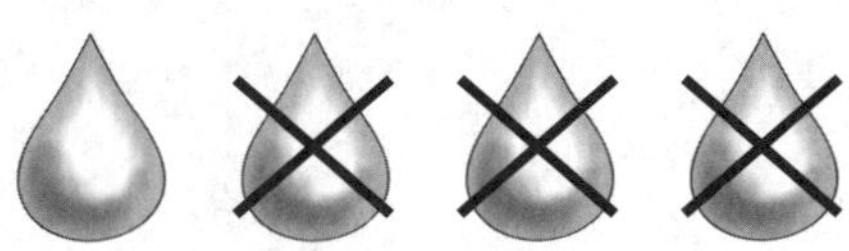

4 – 3 = ______

3. Circle who will come next.

? ______

4. Circle how long it takes to wink.

1 second

1 minute

1 hour

5. Circle the picture that shows the pencil in the box.

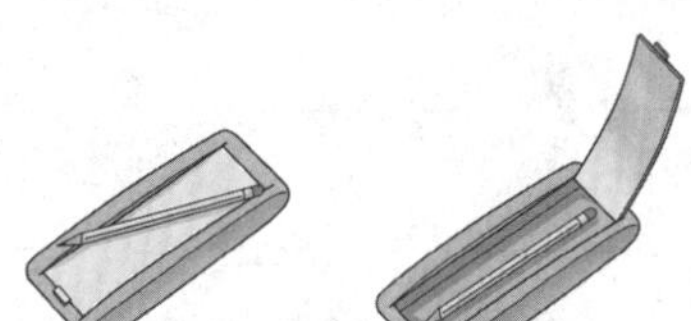

6. There are 4 buckets and 3 shovels. Does each bucket have a shovel?

____

SCORE

1.

2.

3.

4.

5.

6.

____ / 6

Total

DAY
80

NAME: ____________________

DIRECTIONS Solve each problem.

SCORE

1. ☺ 😐
2. ☺ 😐
3. ☺ 😐
4. ☺ 😐
5. ☺ 😐
6. ☺ 😐

____ / 6
Total

1. Write how many lizards there are.

____

2. Write the number sentence.

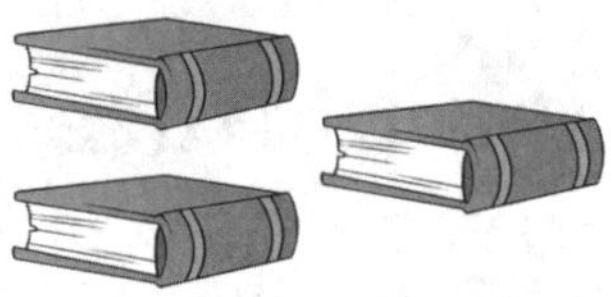 + 

______ + ______ = ______

3. Draw what will come next.

 ?
______

4. Circle the container that holds less.

5. Does the picture have symmetry? Circle the answer.

yes   no

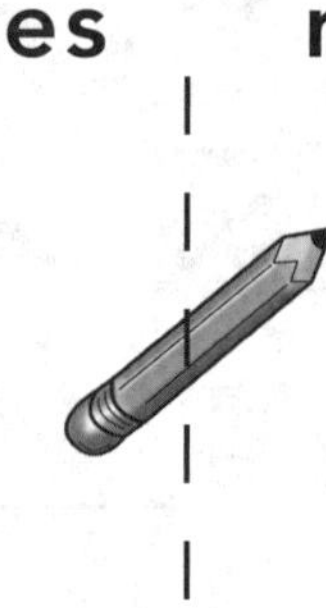

6. I have no sides.

I have no corners.

I am round all over.

What shape am I?

____

NAME: ______________________

DIRECTIONS Solve each problem.

1. Circle 16 fish.

2. Subtract.

3 – 2 = ______

3. Circle the part that repeats.

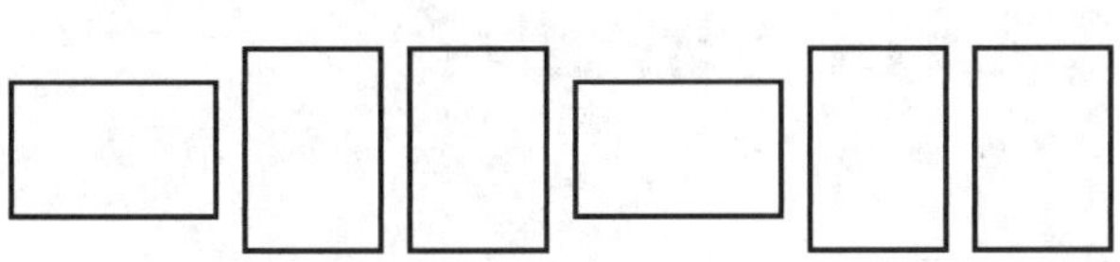

4. What time is it?

_____ : _____

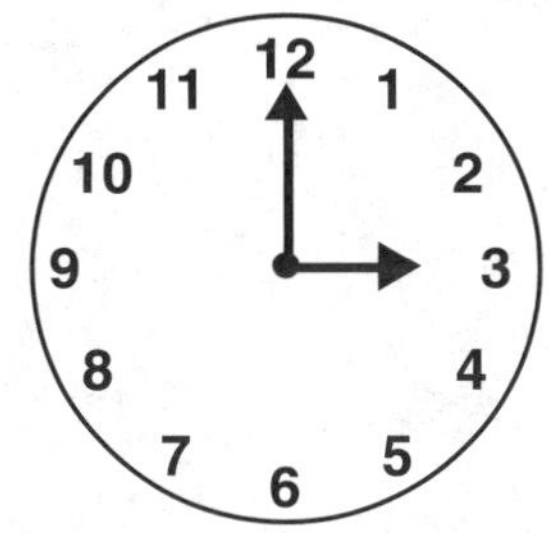

5. Color the shapes with 4 corners.

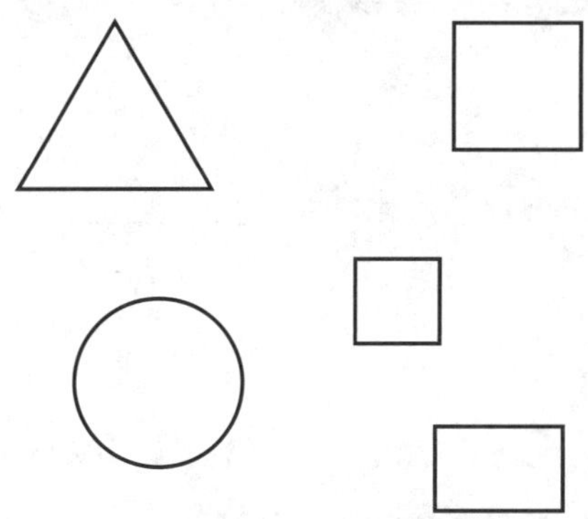

6. How many wheels are on 4 bicycles?

____

SCORE

1.

2.

3.

4.

5.

6.

____ / 6
Total

DAY 82

NAME: ______________________________

DIRECTIONS Solve each problem.

SCORE

1. ☺ 😐
2. ☺ 😐
3. ☺ 😐
4. ☺ 😐
5. ☺ 😐
6. ☺ 😐

____ / 6 Total

1. Write what comes next.

14 15 16 17 ______

2. Add.

2 + 1 = ______

3. Circle what will come next.

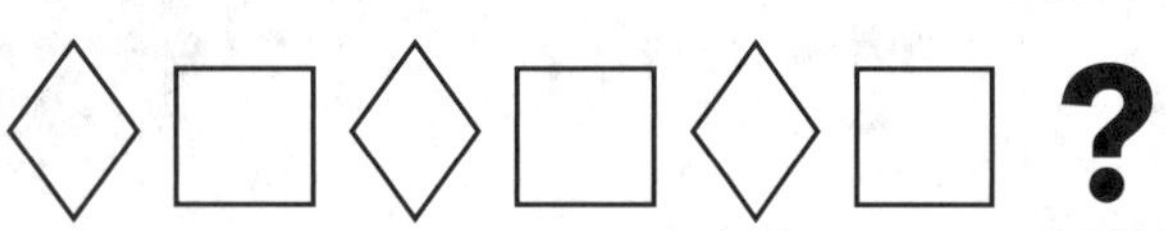

4. Draw an object that is taller than the book.

5. Circle the solid that looks like the object.

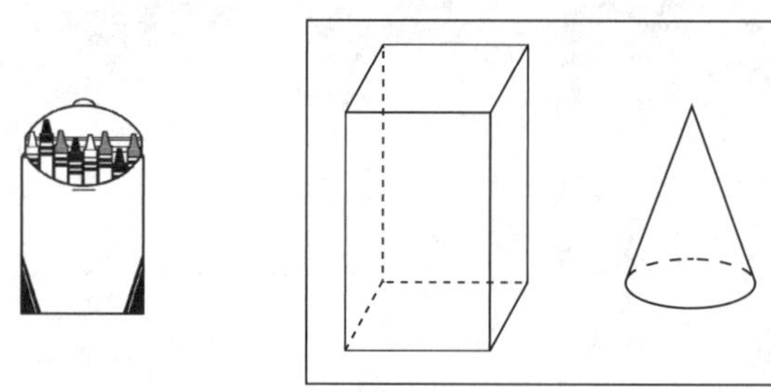

6. Mike eats 3 peas. Then he eats 3 more. How many peas does Mike eat in all?

____

NAME: ______________________

DIRECTIONS Solve each problem.

1. Draw more triangles to make a set of 10.

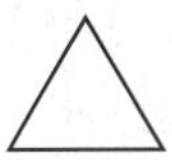

2. Subtract.

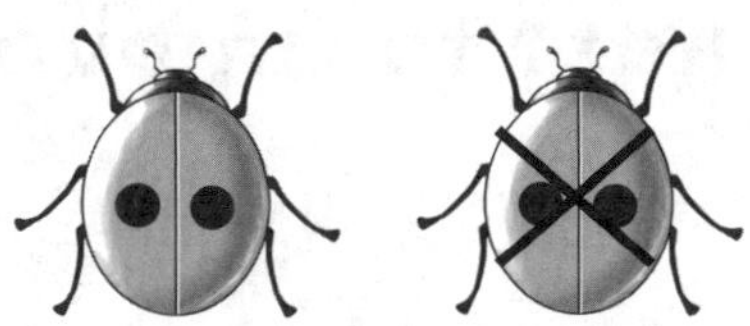

2 – 1 = ______

3. Circle what will come next.

?
___

4. Circle about how many glasses of water you drink every day.

100 10

5. Draw a ball outside the box.

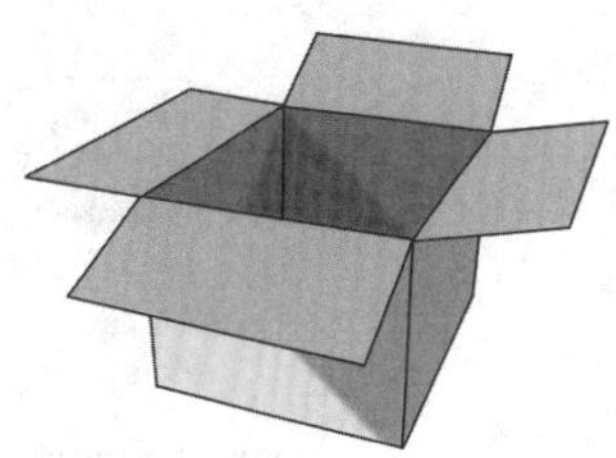

6. I am the number that comes before 7. What number am I?

____

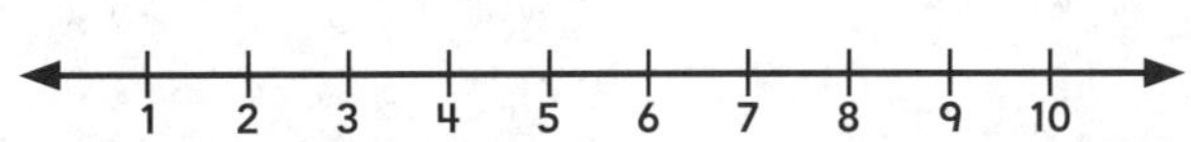

SCORE

1. ☺ 😐

2. ☺ 😐

3. ☺ 😐

4. ☺ 😐

5. ☺ 😐

6. ☺ 😐

____ / 6
Total

DAY 84

NAME: ______________________

DIRECTIONS Solve each problem.

SCORE

1. ☺ 😐
2. ☺ 😐
3. ☺ 😐
4. ☺ 😐
5. ☺ 😐
6. ☺ 😐

____ / 6 Total

1. Put these numbers in order.

9 7 8 6 5

____

2. Add.

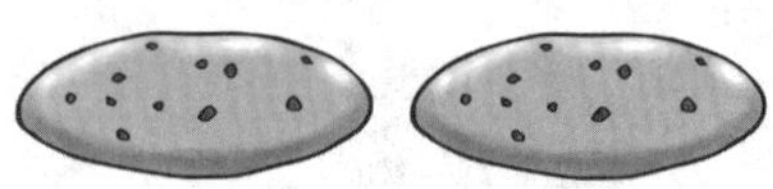

2 + 0 = ______

3. Color the triangles. What color will come next?

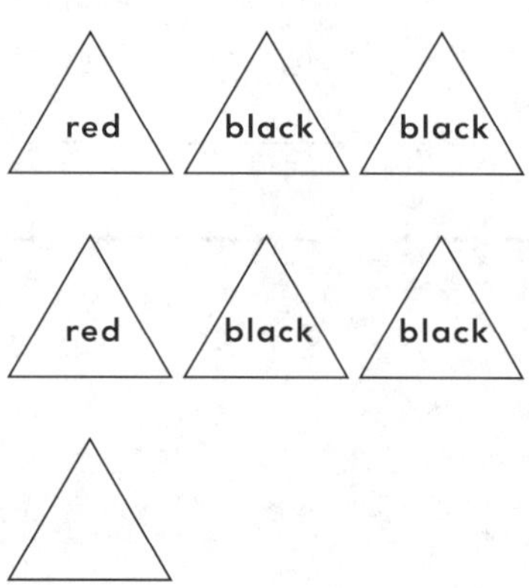

4. Circle how long the ring is.

1 cube 2 cubes

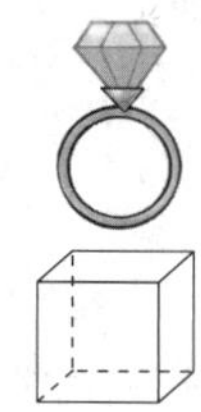

5. Draw a triangle next to an oval.

6. Julia started counting like this:

13 14 15 16 17

How is she counting? Circle the answer.

forward backward

NAME: ______________________

DIRECTIONS Solve each problem.

1. How many monkeys are there?

____

2. Subtract.

4 – 2 = ______

3. Circle who will come next.

 ?

4. Circle the best time to do homework.

5:00 in the afternoon

5:00 in the morning

5. How many sides does a pentagon have?

____

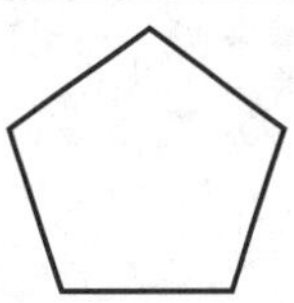

6. Circle groups of 10 buttons.

How many are left over?

____

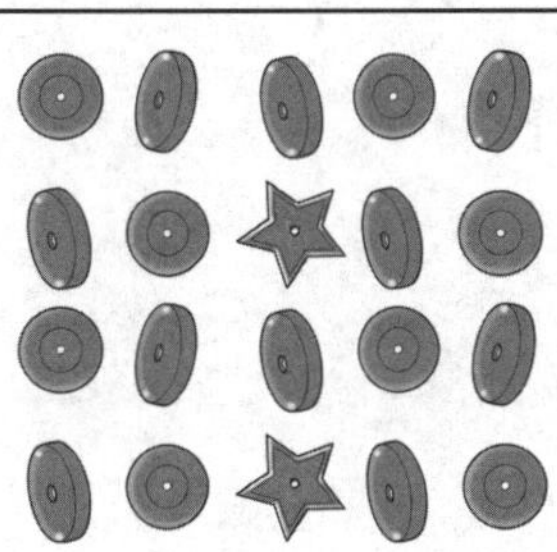

SCORE

1.

2.

3.

4.

5.

6.

____ / 6

Total

DAY
86

NAME: ____________________

DIRECTIONS Solve each problem.

SCORE

1. ☺ 😐

2. ☺ 😐

3. ☺ 😐

4. ☺ 😐

5. ☺ 😐

6. ☺ 😐

____ / 6
Total

1. Will every girl get an umbrella? Circle the answer.

yes no

2. Add.

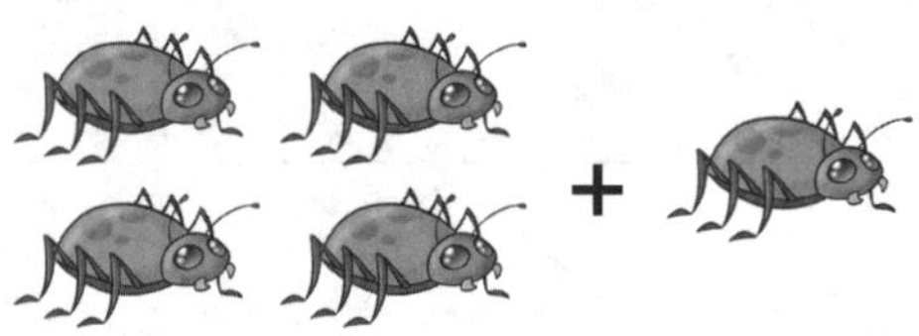

4 + 1 = ______

3. Circle what will come next.

 **?**

4. Circle which tool is best to measure milk.

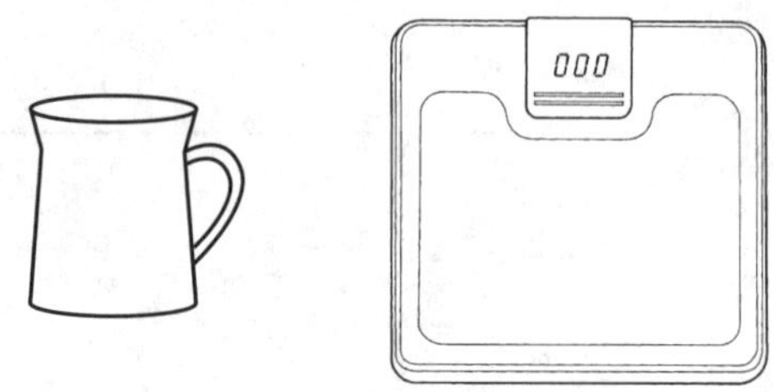

5. On which shelf is the ball? Circle the answer.

top middle bottom

6. Look at the shape below. Draw a shape with fewer sides.

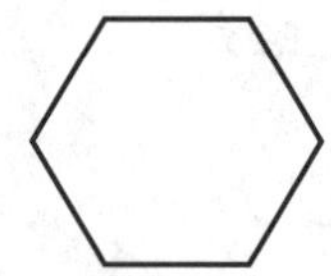

DAY 87

NAME: ______________________

DIRECTIONS Solve each problem.

1. Count the rings. Draw an equal set of circles.

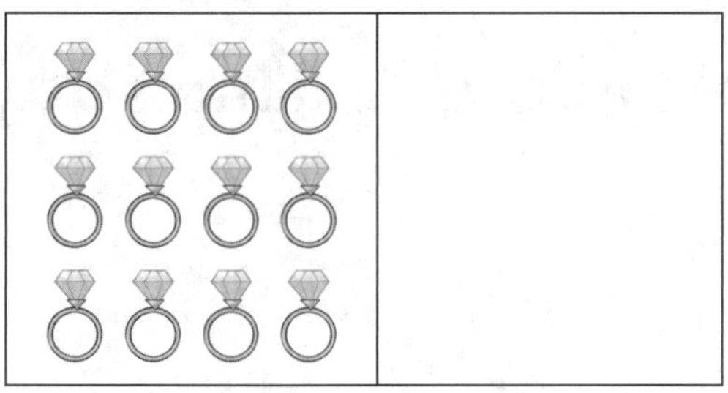

2. Write the number sentence.

_____ – _____ = _____

3. Circle what will come next.

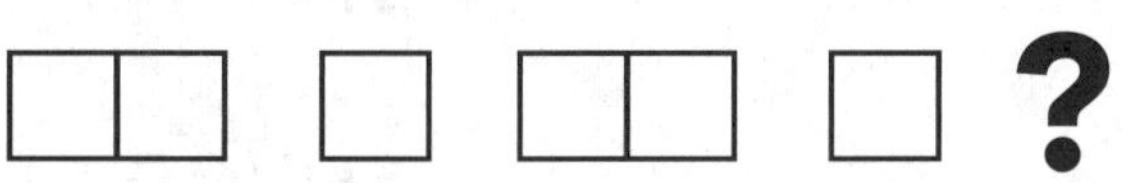

4. Circle the object that weighs more.

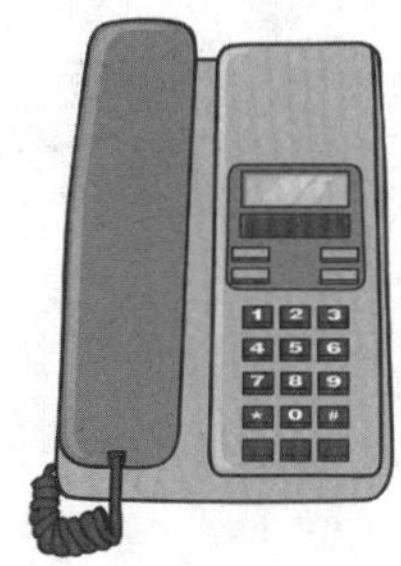

5. How many corners does a circle have?

____

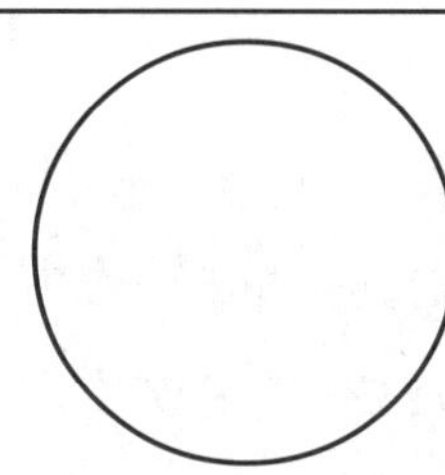

6. Simi has 8 crayons. He loses 3 crayons. How many crayons does he have now?

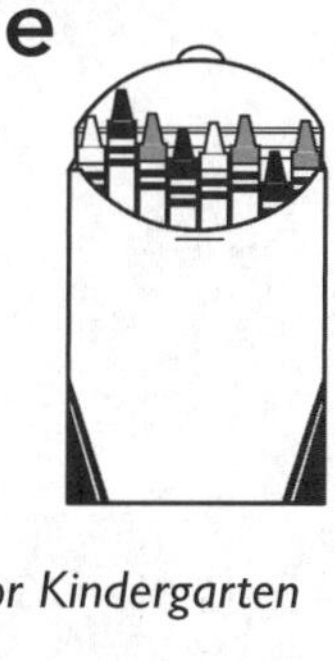

____

SCORE

1. ☺ 😐

2. ☺ 😐

3. ☺ 😐

4. ☺ 😐

5. ☺ 😐

6. ☺ 😐

____ / 6
Total

DAY 88

NAME: ____________________

DIRECTIONS Solve each problem.

SCORE

1. ☺ 😐

2. ☺ 😐

3. ☺ 😐

4. ☺ 😐

5. ☺ 😐

6. ☺ 😐

____ / 6
Total

1. Draw 3 legs on the stool.

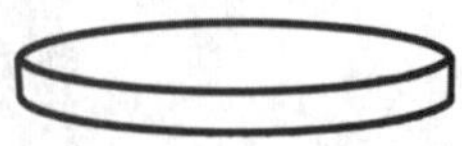

2. Add.

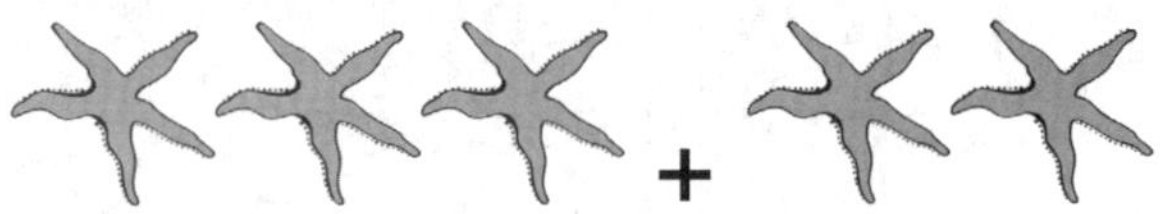

3 + 2 = ______

3. Circle what will come next.

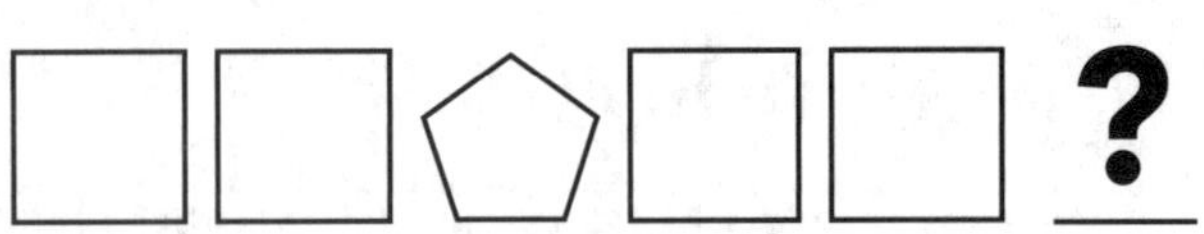

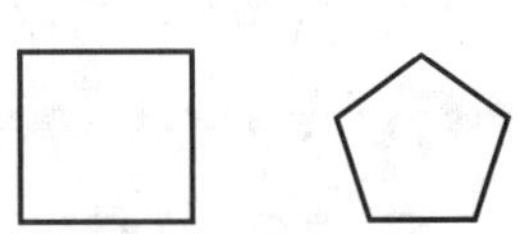

4. Circle the day that comes before Friday.

Monday Thursday

5. Will the solid slide? Circle the answer.

yes no

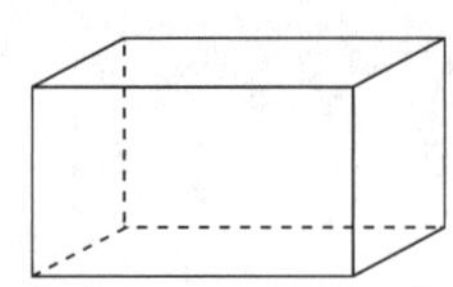

6. Draw lines to match the number to the word.

6	eight
7	six
8	seven
9	ten
10	nine

NAME: ______________________

DIRECTIONS Solve each problem.

1. Circle the group that has 14.

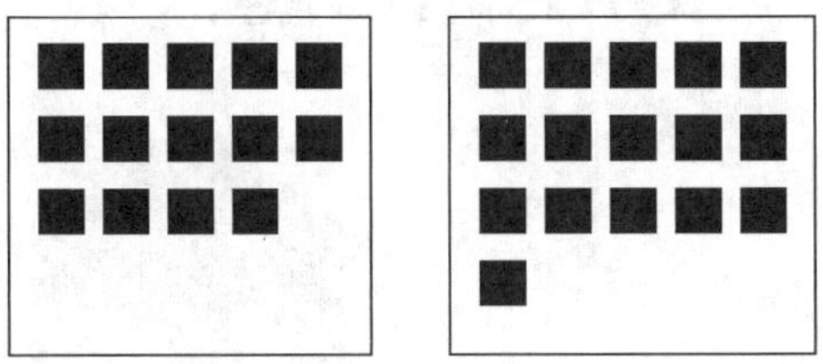

2. Subtract.

5 – 3 = ______

3. Write what will come next in this pattern.

A A B A A B ☐

4. Circle the time it takes to tie your shoes.

1 minute   1 hour

5. Where is the car? Circle the answer.

on the road

in the road

6. Circle the number that has straight lines.

7   8

SCORE

1. ☺ 😐

2. ☺ 😐

3. ☺ 😐

4. ☺ 😐

5. ☺ 😐

6. ☺ 😐

___ / 6 Total

NAME: ____________________

DIRECTIONS Solve each problem.

SCORE

1. ☺ 😐

2. ☺ 😐

3. ☺ 😐

4. ☺ 😐

5. ☺ 😐

6. ☺ 😐

___ / 6 Total

1. How many carrots are there?

____

2. Add.

1 + 3 = ______

3. Color the rhombuses. What color will come next?

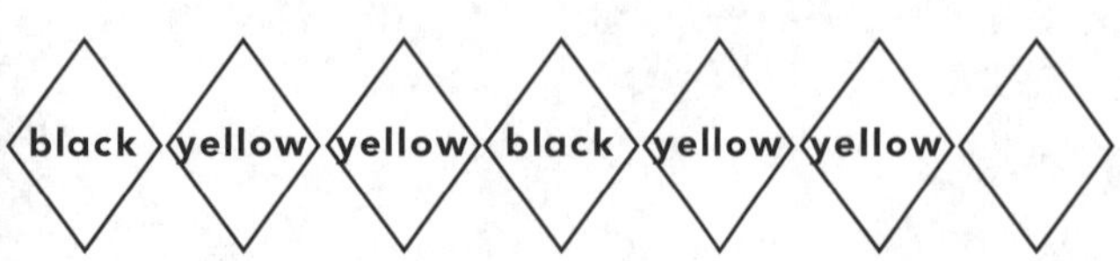

4. Circle the container that holds more.

5. Does the picture have symmetry? Circle the answer.

yes   no

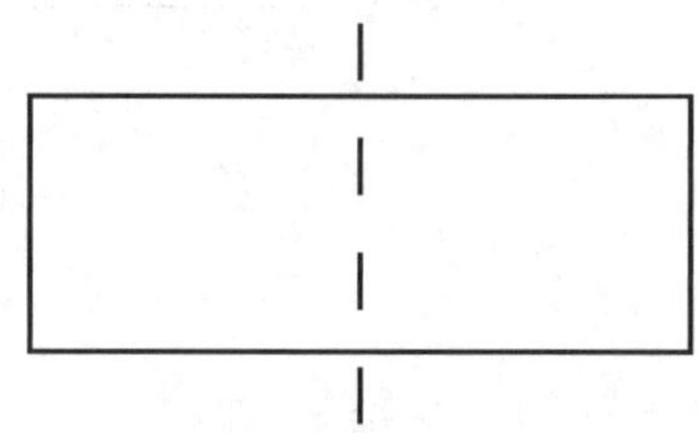

6. Show 7 worms. Add or cross out worms.

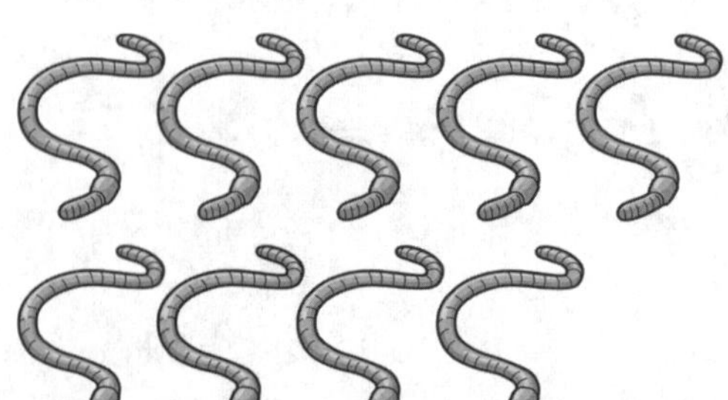

NAME: ____________________

DIRECTIONS Solve each problem.

1. Circle an equal number of squares.

2. Subtract.

5 – 2 = ______

3. Make the same pattern using letters.

A B ___ ___ ___ ___

4. What time is it?

______ o'clock

5. Color the shapes with no corners.

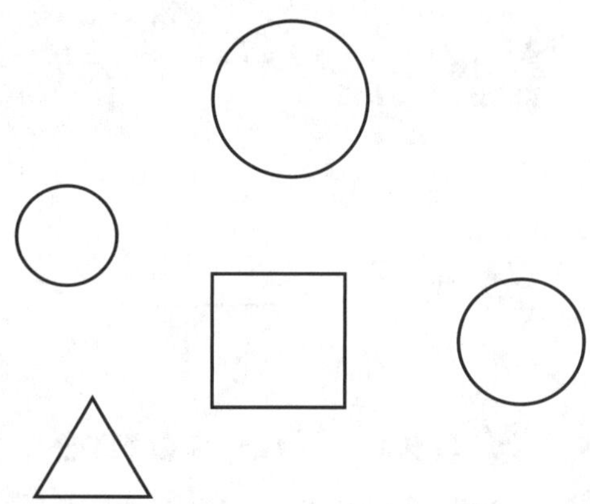

6. How many toes are on 2 feet?

____

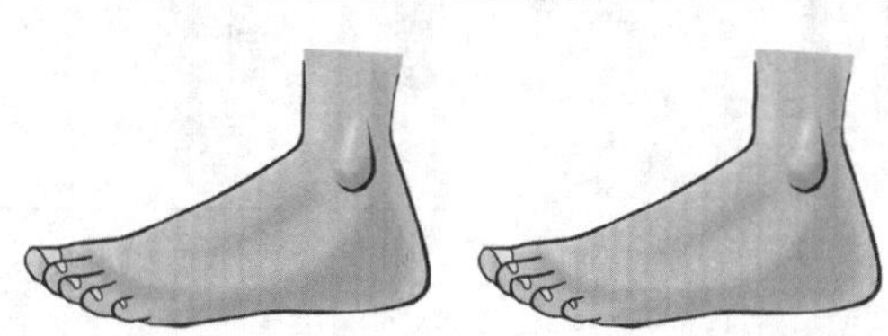

SCORE

1.

2.

3.

4.

5.

6.

___ / 6
Total

DAY

92

NAME: ______________________________

DIRECTIONS Solve each problem.

SCORE

1. ☺ 😐

2. ☺ 😐

3. ☺ 😐

4. ☺ 😐

5. ☺ 😐

6. ☺ 😐

____ / 6

Total

1. Write what number comes next.

16 17 18 19 ______

2. Add.

2 + 3 = ______

3. Make the same pattern using letters.

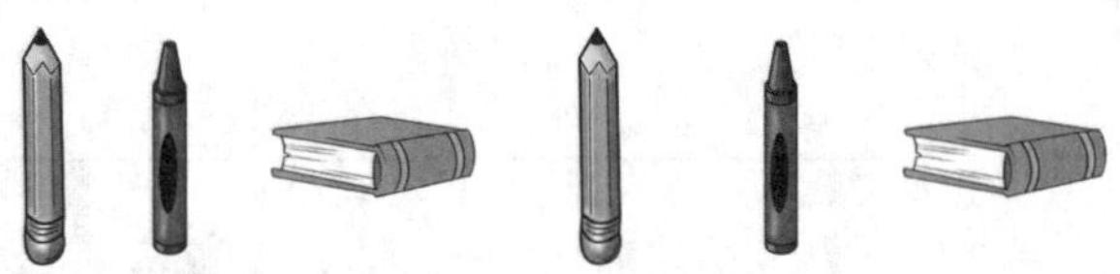

A B C ___ ___ ___

4. Circle the taller animal.

5. Circle the solid that looks like the object.

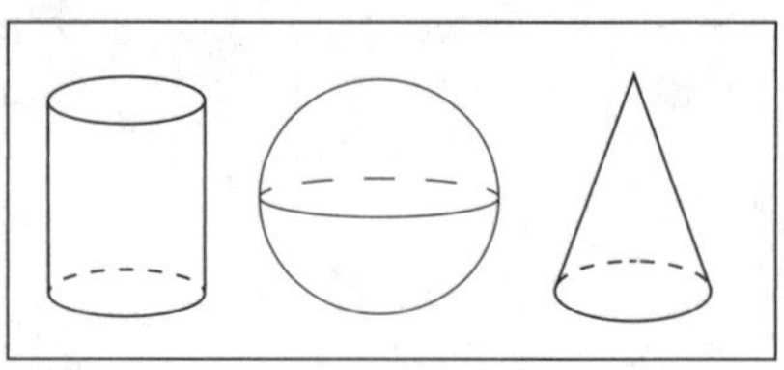

6. Tran has 2 sisters and 1 brother. How many sisters and brothers does he have in all?

____

NAME: ____________________

DIRECTIONS Solve each problem.

1. Draw more pumpkins to make a set of 10.

2. Subtract.

2 – 0 = ______

3. Circle what will come next.

?

4. Circle about how many pots are on a stove.

3 30

5. Draw a ball in the mitt.

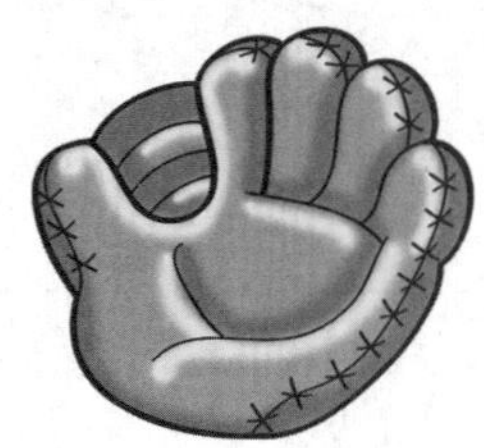

6. Circle the second cat.

SCORE

1.

2.

3.

4.

5.

6.

___ / 6

Total

DAY 94

NAME: ____________________

DIRECTIONS Solve each problem.

SCORE

1.
2.
3.
4.
5.
6.

___ / 6
Total

1. Circle the largest number.

12 14 11 13 15 10

2. Write the number sentence.

 + 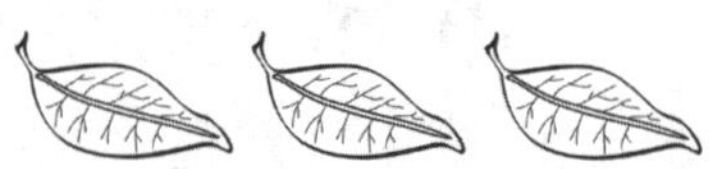

______ + ______ = ______

3. Circle the part that repeats.

4. How tall are the books?

______ cubes

5. Draw a circle with a diamond in the middle.

6. Count Aidan's and Karla's pennies. Who has more?

____

Aidan's 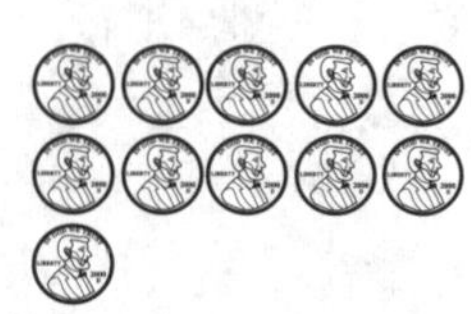

Karla's 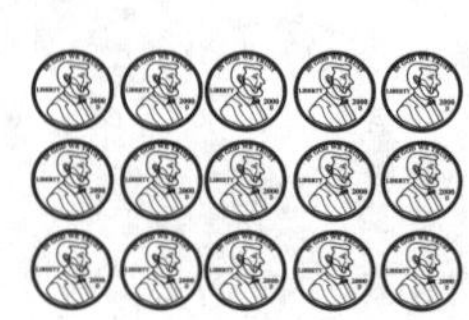

NAME: ______________________

DIRECTIONS Solve each problem.

1. How many spiders are there?

____

2. Subtract.

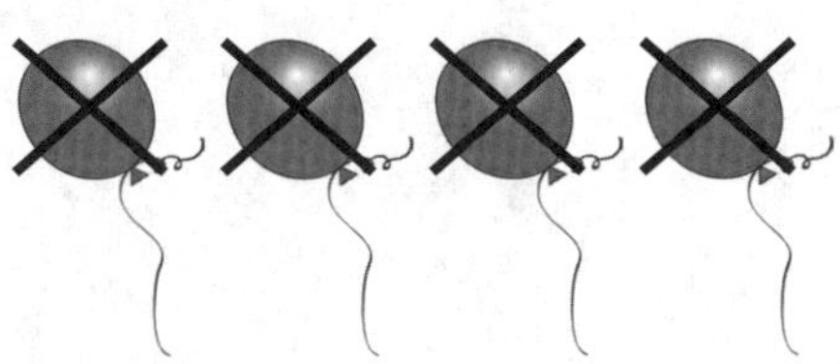

4 – 4 = ______

3. Make the same pattern using letters.

A B C ___ ___ ___

4. Circle the best time to call your grandmother.

6:00 in the morning

6:00 in the evening

5. Does the solid have any curved surfaces? Circle the answer.

yes no

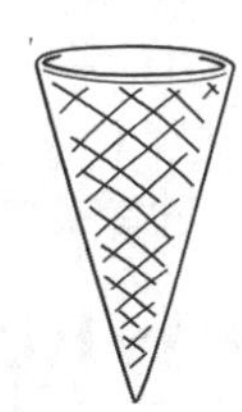

6. Draw 2 squares. Color half of each square orange.

SCORE

1.

2.

3.

4.

5.

6.

___ / 6 Total

DAY
96

NAME: ____________________

DIRECTIONS Solve each problem.

SCORE

1. ☺ 😐
2. ☺ 😐
3. ☺ 😐
4. ☺ 😐
5. ☺ 😐
6. ☺ 😐

____ / 6
Total

1. Circle the larger number.

4 7

2. Add.

3 + 0 = ______

3. Circle what will come next.

 **?** ___

4. Circle the tool to tell what day it is.

5. Is the boy on the right or on the left?

____

6. What time will it be 1 hour from now?

____

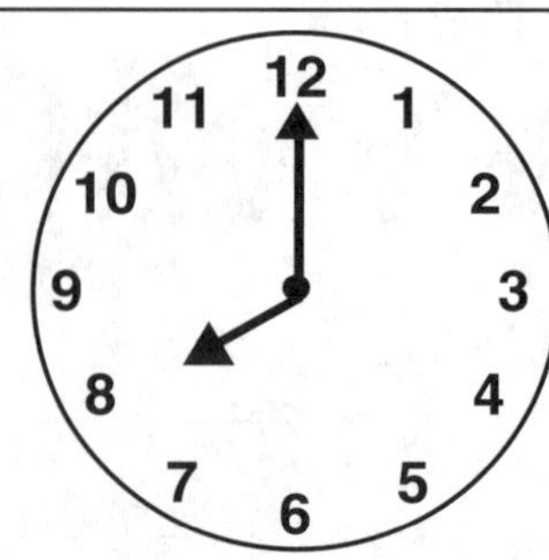

DAY 97

NAME: ____________________

DIRECTIONS Solve each problem.

1. Count the socks. Draw an equal set of circles.

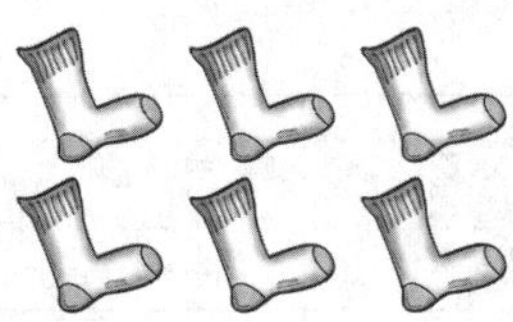

2. Subtract.

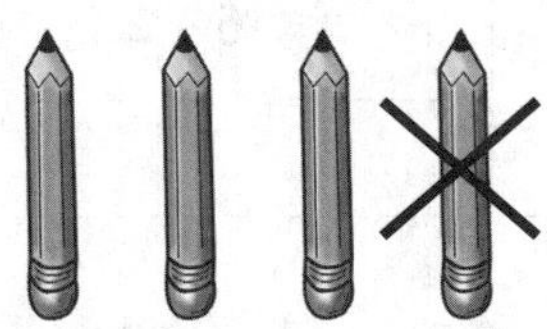

4 – 1 = ______

3. Draw what will come next.

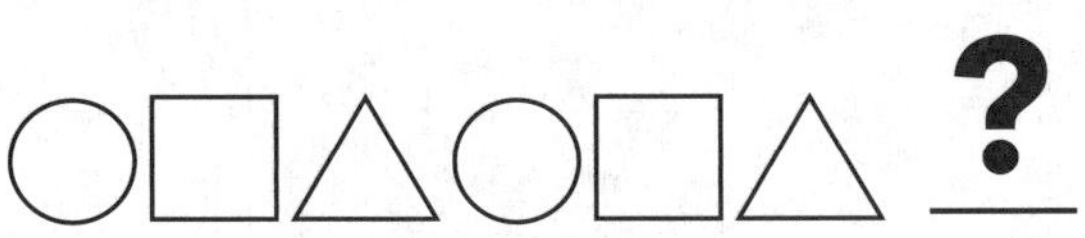

4. Circle the object that weighs less.

5. How many sides does a hexagon have?

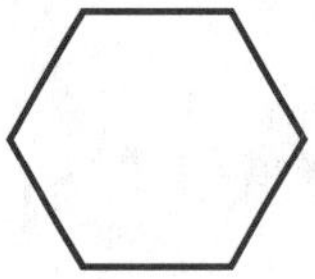

____

6. Max picks 2 apples from the tree. He gives one to his mom. How many apples does he have left?

____

SCORE

1. ☺ 😐

2. ☺ 😐

3. ☺ 😐

4. ☺ 😐

5. ☺ 😐

6. ☺ 😐

____ / 6 Total

DAY
98

NAME: ____________________

DIRECTIONS Solve each problem.

SCORE

1.

2.

3.

4.

5.

6.

___ / 6
Total

1. Draw 7 circles.

2. Add.

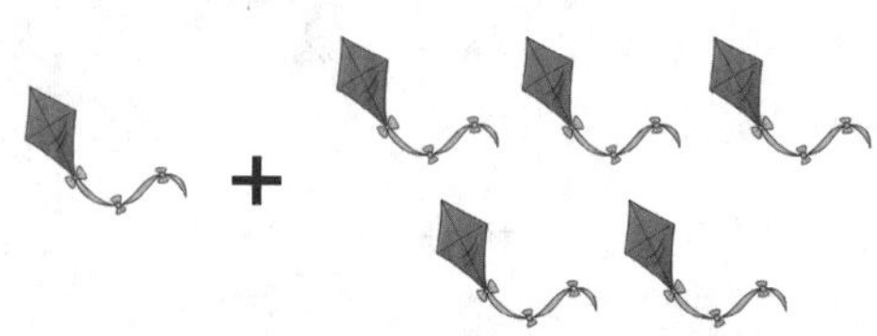

1 + 5 = ______

3. Make the same pattern using letters.

A A B ___ ___ ___

4. What day of the week is November 4th?

____

November						
Sun	Mon	Tues	Wed	Thurs	Fri	Sat
1	2	3	4	5	6	7
8	9	10	11	12	13	14
15	16	17	18	19	20	21
22	23	24	25	26	27	28
29	30					

5. Will the object roll? Circle the answer.

yes no

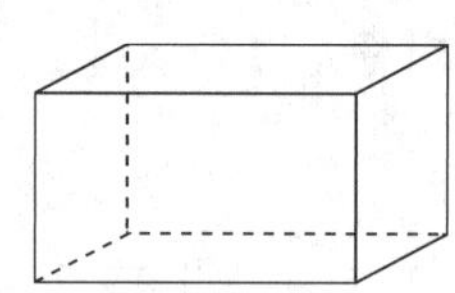

6. Circle the number that is equal to 7.

0 1 2 3 4

5 6 7 8 9

NAME: ____________________

DIRECTIONS Solve each problem.

1. Circle the hive with more than 3 bees.

2. Subtract.

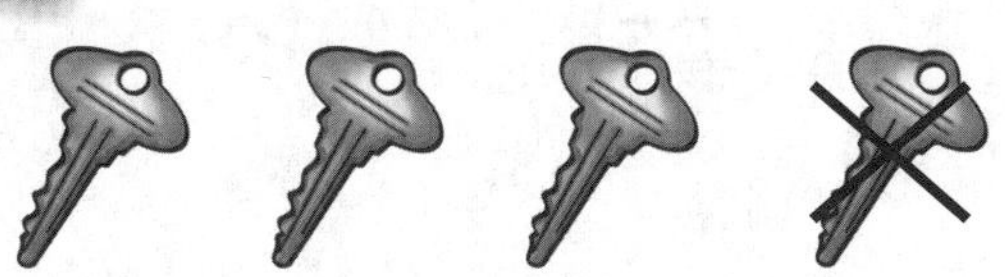

4 – 1 = ______

3. Circle what will come next.

4. Circle the time it takes to read your name.

1 second   1 hour

5. Circle the picture that shows the block to the left of the top.

6. Draw 4 apples. Mike eats one apple. How many are left?

____

SCORE

1. ☺ 😐
2. ☺ 😐
3. ☺ 😐
4. ☺ 😐
5. ☺ 😐
6. ☺ 😐

____ / 6 Total

NAME: ______________________

DIRECTIONS Solve each problem.

SCORE

1. ☺ 😐

2. ☺ 😐

3. ☺ 😐

4. ☺ 😐

5. ☺ 😐

6. ☺ 😐

___ / 6 Total

1. Count how many.

____

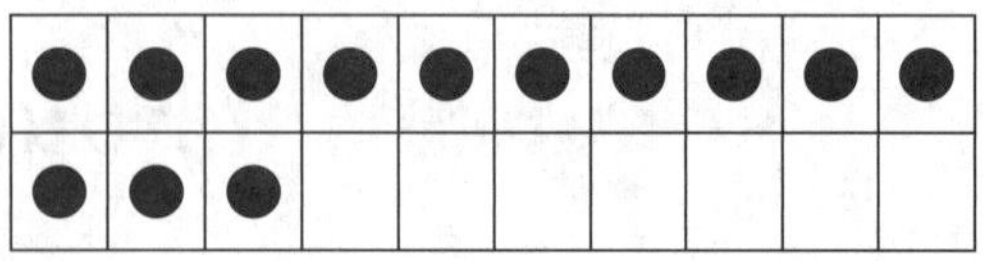

2. Write the number sentence.

_____ + _____ = _____

3. Circle what will come next.

 ?

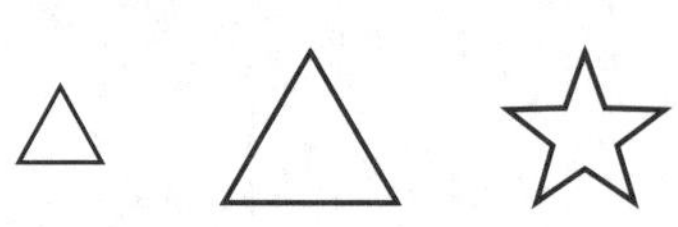

4. Draw a container that holds less than a bucket.

5. Does the picture have symmetry? Circle the answer.

yes no

6. I have 4 sides.

I have 4 corners.

All my sides are equal.

What shape am I?

____

NAME: ____________________

DIRECTIONS Solve each problem.

SCORE

1. Draw an equal number of squares.

2. Circle the number sentence that matches the picture.

3 – 3 = 0

3 + 2 = 5

3 – 2 = 1

3. Circle the part that repeats.

4. What time is it?

_____ : _____

5. Color the shapes with straight sides.

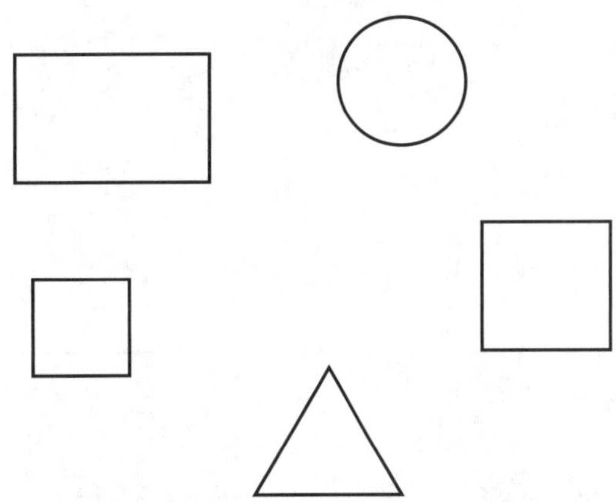

6. How many legs are on 4 turtles?

____

1. ☺ 😐
2. ☺ 😐
3. ☺ 😐
4. ☺ 😐
5. ☺ 😐
6. ☺ 😐

____ / 6
Total

DAY 102

NAME: ____________________

DIRECTIONS Solve each problem.

SCORE

1. ☺ 😐
2. ☺ 😐
3. ☺ 😐
4. ☺ 😐
5. ☺ 😐
6. ☺ 😐

____ /6 Total

1. Write the missing number.

3 4 ______ 6

2. Write a number sentence.

______ – ______ = ______

3. Make the same pattern using letters.

A A B ___ ___ ___

4. Circle the shortest person.

5. Circle the solid that looks like the object.

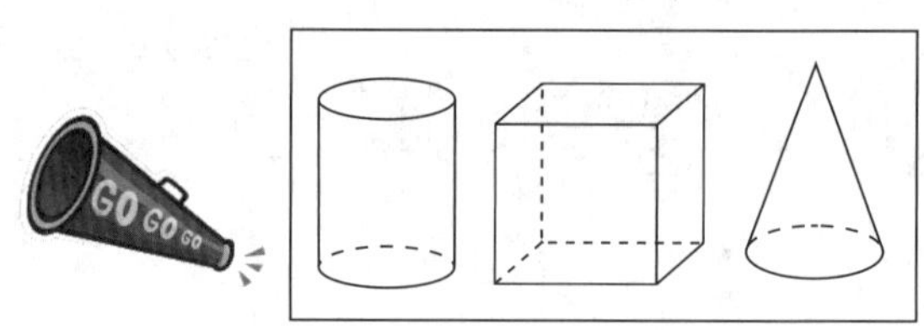

6. Kelly has 3 pairs of shoes. Her mother buys her one more pair. Now, how many pairs of shoes does she have?

____

NAME: ______________________________

DIRECTIONS Solve each problem.

SCORE

1. Draw a set of 2 triangles. Draw a set of more than 2 circles.

2	more than 2

2. Circle the number sentence that matches the picture.

2 + 2 = 4

2 + 1 = 3

3. Circle what will come next.

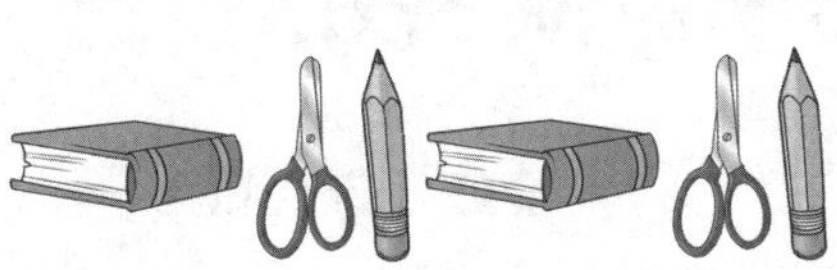

?

4. Circle about how many pieces of paper are in a notebook.

10   100

5. Draw some eggs in the basket.

6. I am the number that comes before 3. What number am I?

____

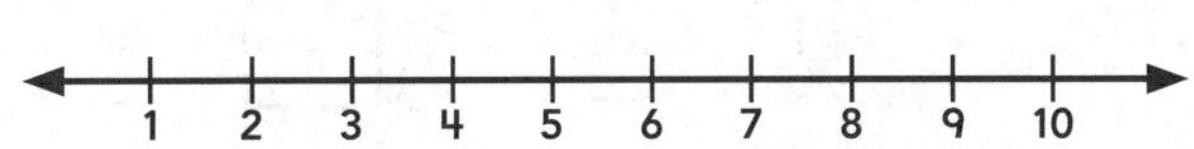

1. ☺ 😐
2. ☺ 😐
3. ☺ 😐
4. ☺ 😐
5. ☺ 😐
6. ☺ 😐

____ / 6
Total

DAY
104

NAME: ____________________

DIRECTIONS Solve each problem.

SCORE

1.

2.

3.

4.

5.

6.

____ / 6

Total

1. Put these numbers in order.

19 18 20

______ ______ ______

2. Add.

1 + 1 = ______

1 + 2 = ______

1 + 3 = ______

3. Circle what shape will come next.

4. How long is the marker?

______ paperclips

5. Draw a square with an oval in it.

6. Draw lines to match the number to the word.

1	second
2	third
3	first

NAME: ______________________________

DIRECTIONS Solve each problem.

1. How many dots are there?

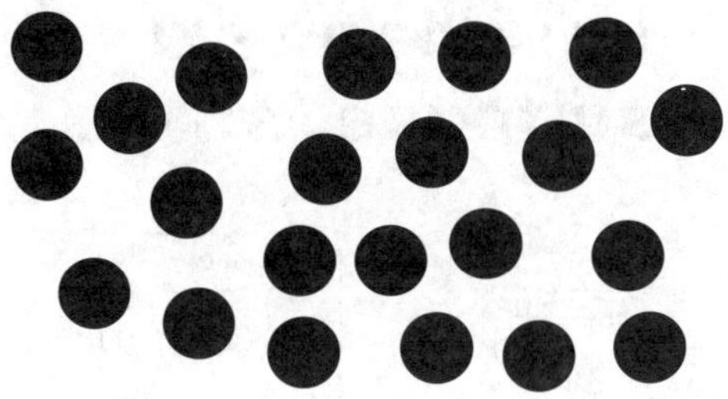

____

2. Circle the number sentence that matches the picture.

5 – 3 = 2

5 – 2 = 3

3 + 2 = 5

3. Circle the part that repeats.

4. Circle the best time to eat lunch.

12:00 A.M.

12:00 P.M.

5. How many sides does a diamond have?

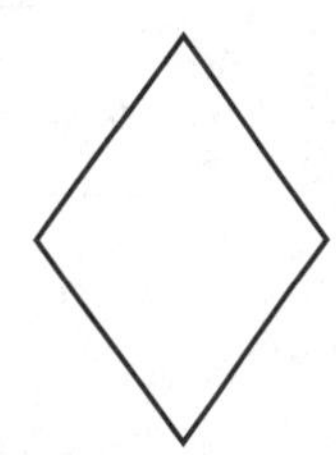

____

6. How many people like bananas?

____

Apples	|||
Bananas	~~||||~~ ||
Oranges	||||

SCORE

1.

2.

3.

4.

5.

6.

____ / 6 Total

DAY 106

NAME: ____________________

DIRECTIONS Solve each problem.

SCORE

1.
2.
3.
4.
5.
6.

____ / 6 Total

1. Circle the smaller number.

6 3

2. Subtract.

5 – 1 = ______

5 – 2 = ______

5 – 3 = ______

3. Make the same pattern using letters.

A B B ___ ___ ___

4. Circle what tool is best to measure how heavy a suitcase is.

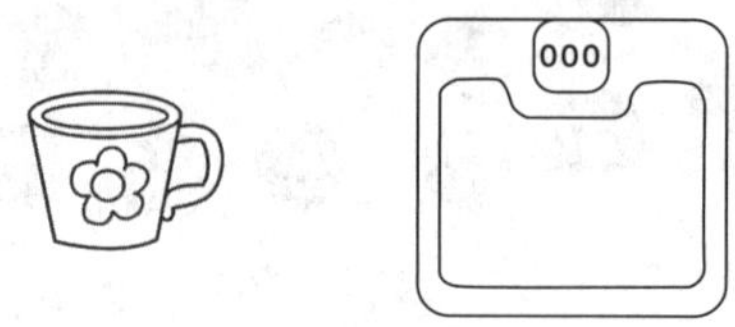

5. The clock is ______ the chair.

on below above

6. Count the dots.

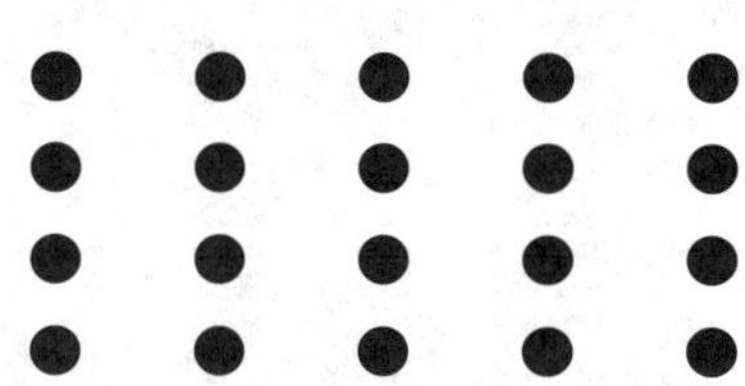

How many groups of 10 are there?

____

DAY
107

NAME: ____________________

DIRECTIONS Solve each problem.

SCORE

1. Count the balls. Draw an equal set of circles.

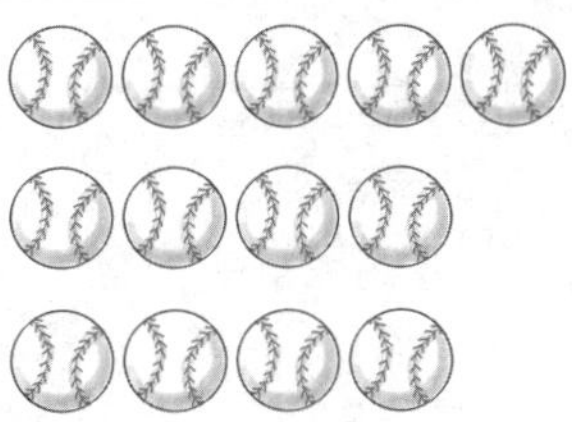

2. Add.

2 + 1 = ______

2 + 2 = ______

2 + 3 = ______

3. Circle what will come next.

?

4. Circle the object that weighs the most.

5. How many corners does a square have?

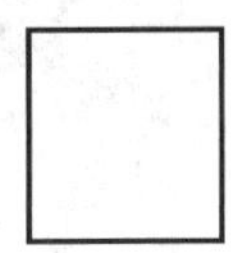

____

6. Tyrone made 2 peanut butter sandwiches. He gave one to his brother. How many sandwiches does Tyrone have now?

____

1. ☺ 😐

2. ☺ 😐

3. ☺ 😐

4. ☺ 😐

5. ☺ 😐

6. ☺ 😐

___ / 6
Total

NAME: ______________________

DIRECTIONS Solve each problem.

SCORE

1. ☺ 😐
2. ☺ 😐
3. ☺ 😐
4. ☺ 😐
5. ☺ 😐
6. ☺ 😐

___ / 6 Total

1. Draw 5 squares.

2. Circle the number sentence that matches the picture.

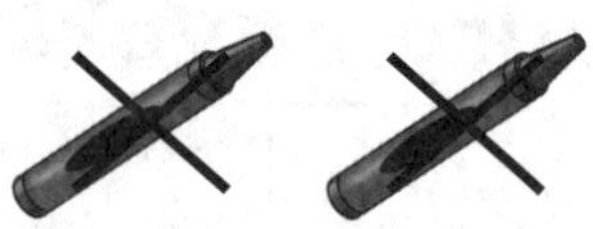

2 + 2 = 4

2 − 0 = 2

2 − 2 = 0

3. Circle what will come next.

? ___

4. Circle what day comes after Sunday.

Monday Thursday

5. Will the solid roll?

Circle the answer.

yes no

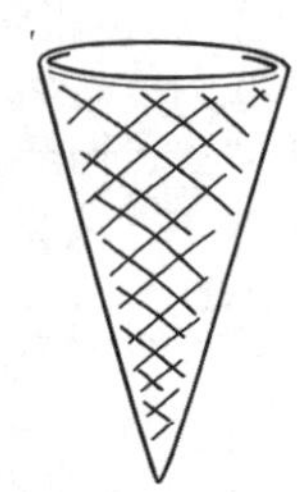

6. Circle the numbers that are larger than 8.

0 1 2 3 4

5 6 7 8 9

NAME: ________________________________

DIRECTIONS Solve each problem.

1. Circle the log with less than 4 frogs.

2. Add.

1 + 3 = ______

1 + 4 = ______

1 + 5 = ______

3. Circle the part that repeats.

4. Circle about how long it takes to eat breakfast.

15 seconds

15 minutes

15 hours

5. Circle where the clouds are in the picture.

at the top

in the middle

at the bottom

6. Circle the solid that can roll.

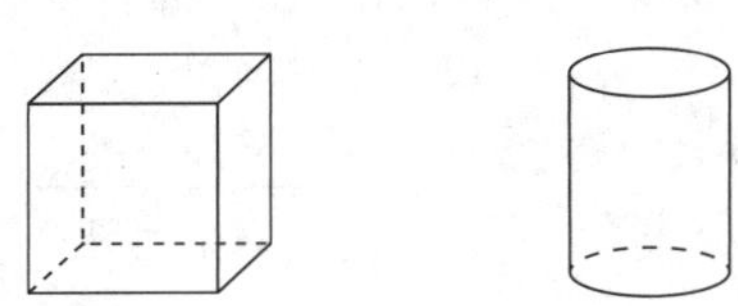

SCORE

1.

2.

3.

4.

5.

6.

____ / 6

Total

DAY
110

NAME: ____________________

DIRECTIONS Solve each problem.

SCORE

1. ☺ 😐
2. ☺ 😐
3. ☺ 😐
4. ☺ 😐
5. ☺ 😐
6. ☺ 😐

___ / 6
Total

1. Count how many.

____

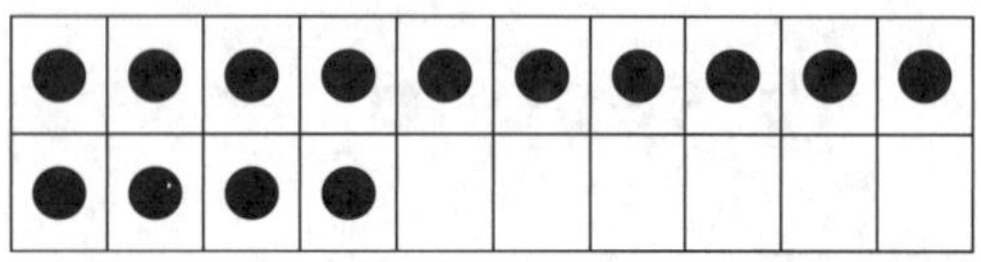

2. Add.

3 + 1 = ______

1 + 3 = ______

3. Make the same pattern using letters.

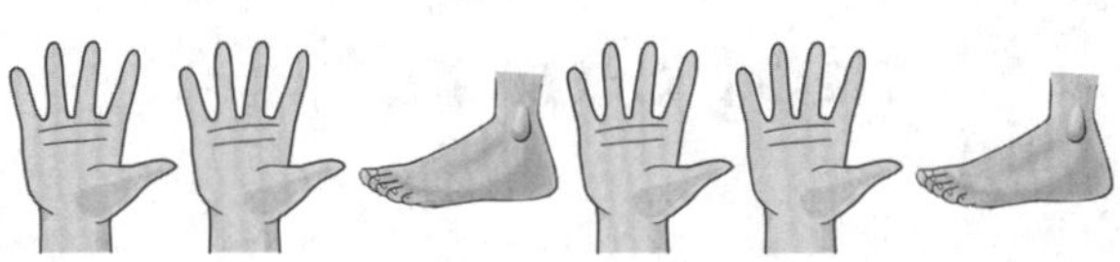

A A B ___ ___ ___

4. Circle the object that holds the most.

5. Does the object have symmetry? Circle the answer.

yes no

6. Show 5 apples. Add or cross out apples.

NAME: ____________________

DIRECTIONS Solve each problem.

1. Circle an equal number of triangles.

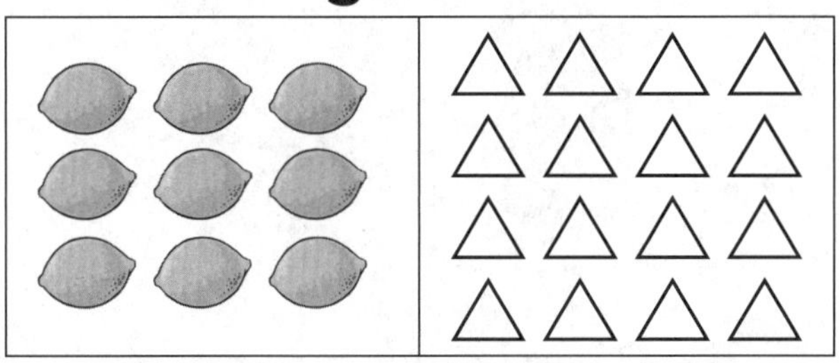

2. Subtract.

$4 - 1 =$ ______

$4 - 2 =$ ______

$4 - 3 =$ ______

3. Circle what will come next.

4. What time is it?

______ o'clock

5. Circle the shapes with five sides.

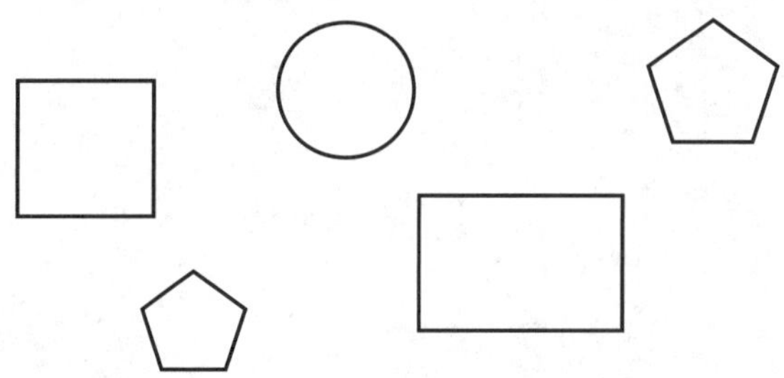

6. How many wheels are on 2 bicycles and 1 tricycle?

____

SCORE

1. ☺ 😐

2. ☺ 😐

3. ☺ 😐

4. ☺ 😐

5. ☺ 😐

6. ☺ 😐

___ / 6 Total

DAY
112

NAME: ______________________

DIRECTIONS Solve each problem.

SCORE

1. ☺ 😐
2. ☺ 😐
3. ☺ 😐
4. ☺ 😐
5. ☺ 😐
6. ☺ 😐

____ / 6
Total

1. Write the missing number.

7 ______ 9 10

2. Circle the number sentence that matches the picture.

4 – 2 = 2

2 + 2 = 4

2 + 0 = 2

3. Draw what will come next.

 ?
___

4. Circle the tallest object.

5. Circle the solid that looks like the object.

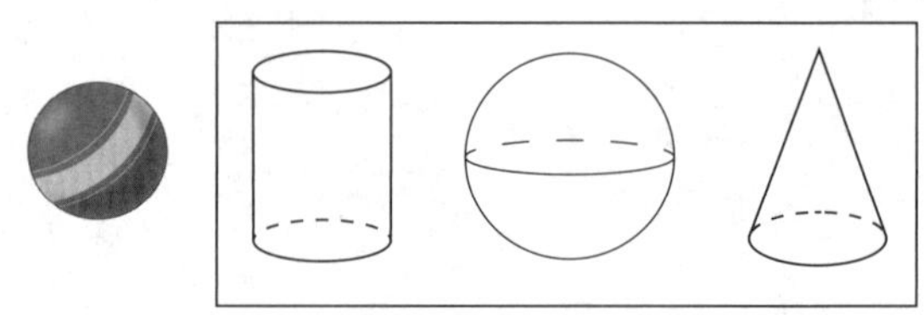

6. There are 5 children riding bikes. No more children come out to play. How many children are riding bikes?

____

NAME: ______________________________

DIRECTIONS Solve each problem.

1. Draw a set of 4 circles. Draw a set of fewer than 4 squares.

4	fewer than 4

2. Add.

2 + 3 = ______

3 + 2 = ______

3. Circle the part that repeats.

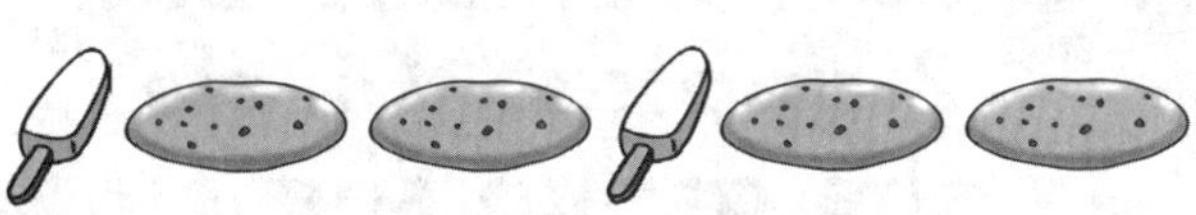

4. Circle how many spoons of water will fit in a cup.

2 20

5. Draw a toy outside the bathtub.

6. Jenny puts 2 stickers on each page of her sticker book. She has 4 pages in her book. How many stickers does she have?

____

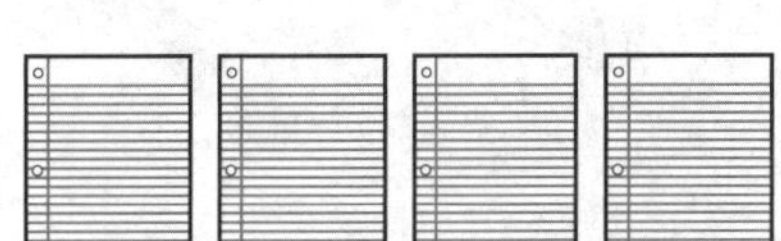

SCORE

1.

2.

3.

4.

5.

6.

____ / 6

Total

DAY
114

NAME: ____________________

DIRECTIONS Solve each problem.

SCORE

1. ☺ 😐
2. ☺ 😐
3. ☺ 😐
4. ☺ 😐
5. ☺ 😐
6. ☺ 😐

____ / 6
Total

1. Write these numbers in order.

22 23 21

______ ______ ______

2. Add.

2 + 0 = ______

2 + 1 = ______

2 + 2 = ______

3. Circle what will come next.

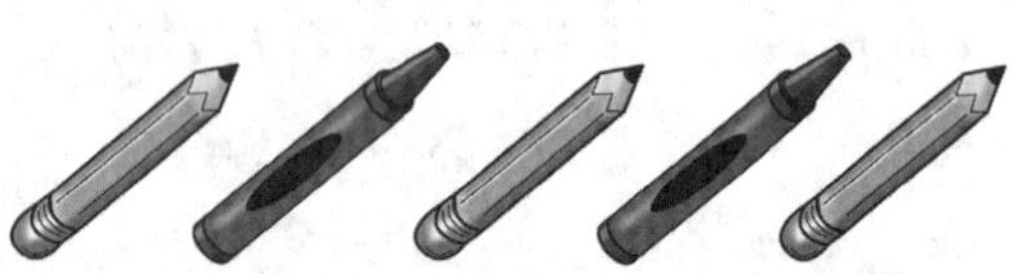

?
___

4. How tall is the glass?

______ cubes

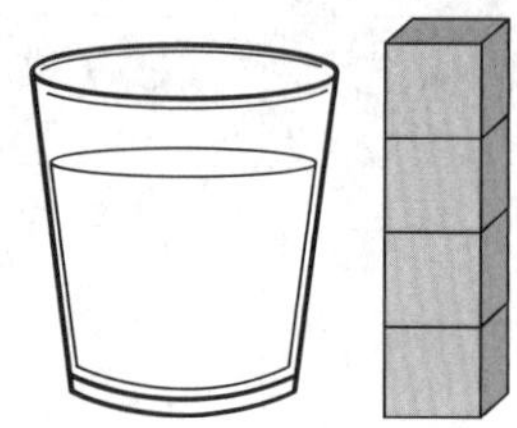

5. Draw a rectangle to the right of an oval.

6. Suri wants to buy 2 apples. Circle the group she should buy.

NAME: ____________________

DIRECTIONS Solve each problem.

1. How many socks are there?

____

2. Circle the number sentence that matches the picture.

4 + 1 = 5

4 – 0 = 4

4 – 4 = 0

3. Make the same pattern using letters.

___ ___ ___ ___ ___ ___

4. Circle the best time to go to school.

8:00 A.M. 8:00 P.M.

5. Does the solid have any curved surfaces? Circle the answer.

yes no

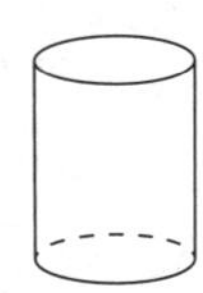

6. How many scoops of ice cream are on the cone?

____

SCORE

1.

2.

3.

4.

5.

6.

___ / 6

Total

DAY
116

NAME: ____________________________

DIRECTIONS Solve each problem.

SCORE

1. ☺ 😐
2. ☺ 😐
3. ☺ 😐
4. ☺ 😐
5. ☺ 😐
6. ☺ 😐

____ / 6
Total

1. Circle the larger number.

5 9

2. Subtract.

3 – 1 = ______

3 – 2 = ______

3 – 3 = ______

3. Circle who will come next.

4. Circle the tool to measure how long a worm is.

5. The milk is ______ the plate.

on below next to

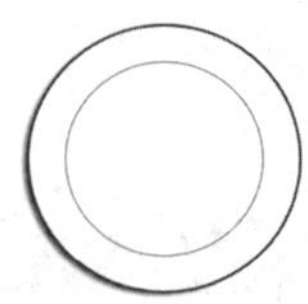

6. Draw a picture to match.

Mom gave me 2 cookies. Then she gave me 1 more.

DAY 117

NAME: ____________________

DIRECTIONS Solve each problem.

1. Count the hats. Draw a set of circles that is less than the hats.

2. Circle the number sentence that matches the picture.

6 – 5 = 1

1 + 5 = 6

5 + 6 = 11

3. Circle what will come next.

?

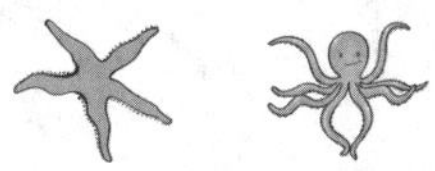

4. Circle the object that weighs the least.

5. How many sides does a rectangle have?

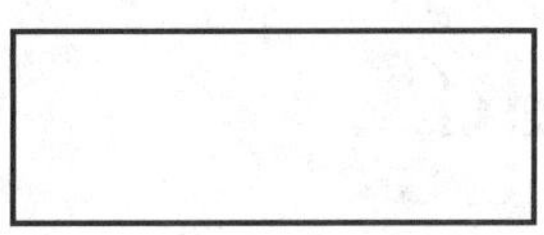

____

6. Five pieces of watermelon were on a plate. Tracy ate 3 pieces. How many pieces are left?

________ 

SCORE

1. ☺ 😐

2. ☺ 😐

3. ☺ 😐

4. ☺ 😐

5. ☺ 😐

6. ☺ 😐

____ / 6 Total

DAY
118

NAME: ____________________

DIRECTIONS Solve each problem.

SCORE

1. ☺☹
2. ☺☹
3. ☺☹
4. ☺☹
5. ☺☹
6. ☺☹

____ / 6
Total

1. Draw 12 eggs in the basket.

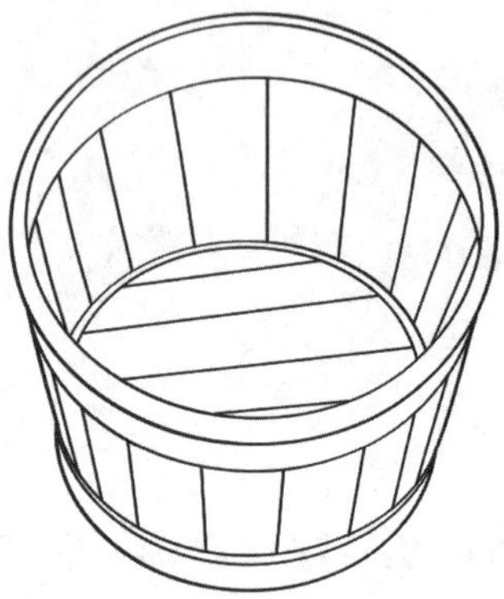

2. Add.

1 + 4 = ______

4 + 1 = ______

3. Circle the part that repeats.

4. What day of the week is May 1st?

____

May						
Sun	Mon	Tues	Wed	Thurs	Fri	Sat
	1	2	3	4	5	6
7	8	9	10	11	12	13
14	15	16	17	18	19	20
21	22	23	24	25	26	27
28	29	30	31			

5. Will the object slide? Circle the answer.

yes   no

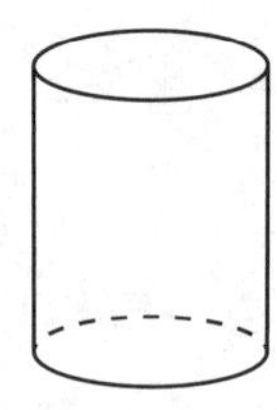

6. Circle the numbers that are smaller than 3.

0 1 2 3 4

5 6 7 8 9

DAY 119

NAME: ______________________

DIRECTIONS Solve each problem.

1. Circle the animal with more than 4 legs.

2. Subtract.

4 – 0 = ______

4 – 1 = ______

4 – 2 = ______

3. Make the same pattern using letters.

___ ___ ___ ___ ___ ___

4. Circle about how long it takes to draw a picture.

15 seconds

15 minutes

15 hours

5. Circle the picture that shows the airplane above the clouds.

6. I have 3 equal sides.

I have 3 corners.

What shape am I?

____

SCORE

1. ☺ 😐

2. ☺ 😐

3. ☺ 😐

4. ☺ 😐

5. ☺ 😐

6. ☺ 😐

___ / 6 Total

DAY 120

NAME: ______________________

DIRECTIONS Solve each problem.

SCORE

1. ☺ 😐
2. ☺ 😐
3. ☺ 😐
4. ☺ 😐
5. ☺ 😐
6. ☺ 😐

___ / 6 Total

1. Count how many.

____

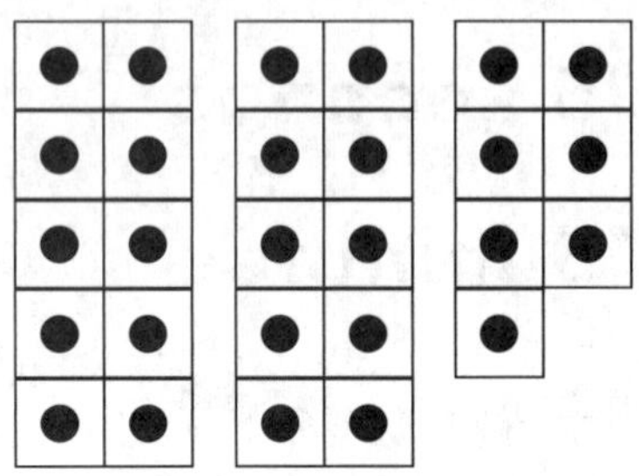

2. Add.

2 + 1 = ______

1 + 2 = ______

3. Circle what will come next.

 **?** ____

4. Draw a container that holds less than a carton of milk.

5. Does the picture have symmetry? Circle the answer.

yes no

6. Kent started counting like this:

17 16 15 14 13

How was Kent counting? Circle the answer.

forward backward

NAME: ____________________

DIRECTIONS Solve each problem.

1. Color an equal number of circles.

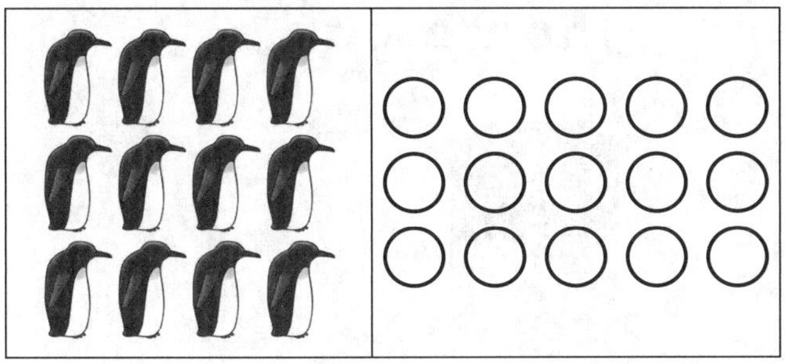

2. Circle the number sentence that matches the picture.

3 + 0 = 3

3 – 3 = 0

3 – 0 = 3

3. Circle what will come next.

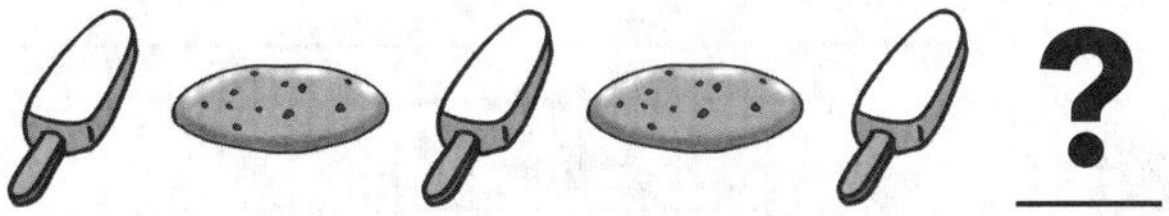

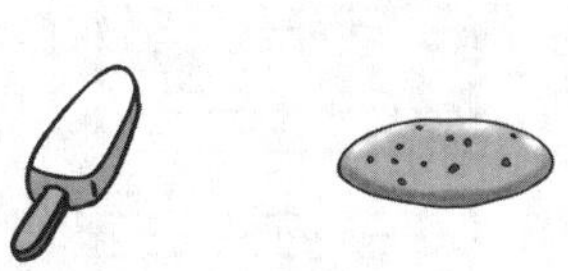

4. What time is it?

_____ : _____

5. Circle the name of the shapes.

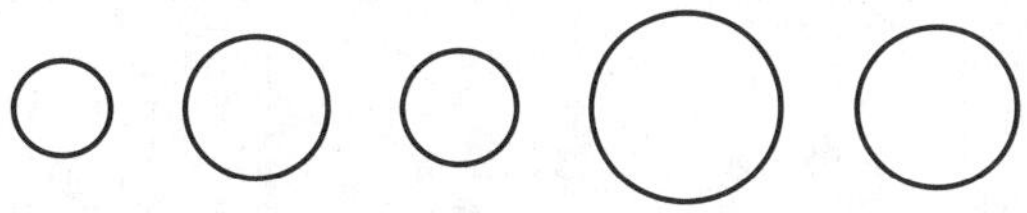

triangle

circle

square

6. How many groups of 5 are there?

____

SCORE

1. ☺ 😐

2. ☺ 😐

3. ☺ 😐

4. ☺ 😐

5. ☺ 😐

6. ☺ 😐

____ / 6 Total

DAY 122

NAME: ____________________

DIRECTIONS Solve each problem.

SCORE

1. ☺ 😐
2. ☺ 😐
3. ☺ 😐
4. ☺ 😐
5. ☺ 😐
6. ☺ 😐

____ / 6 Total

1. Write the missing number.

12 13 ______ 15

2. Add.

2 + 2 = ______

2 + 1 = ______

2 + 0 = ______

3. Circle the part that repeats.

4. Draw an object that is shorter than a can.

5. Circle the solid that looks like the object.

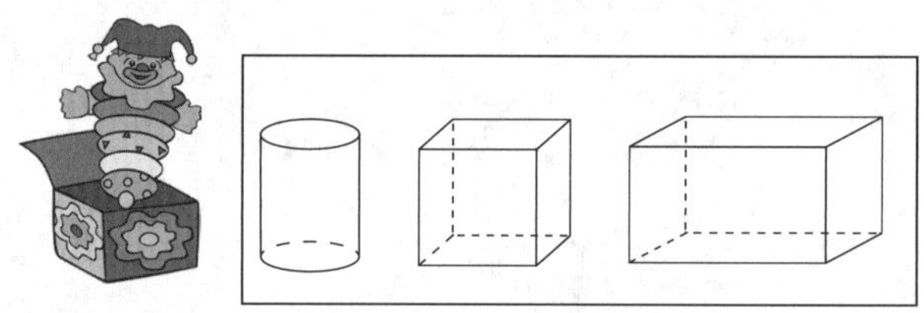

6. Eli drew 3 hearts. Then she drew 2 more. How many hearts did Eli draw?

____

NAME: ____________________

DIRECTIONS Solve each problem.

1. Draw a set of 5 squares. Draw a set of more than 5 circles.

5	more than 5

2. Add.

3 + 0 = ______

0 + 3 = ______

3. Make the same pattern using letters.

___ ___ ___ ___ ___ ___

4. Circle about how many lightbulbs will fit in a lunchbox.

5 50

5. Draw a person in the tent.

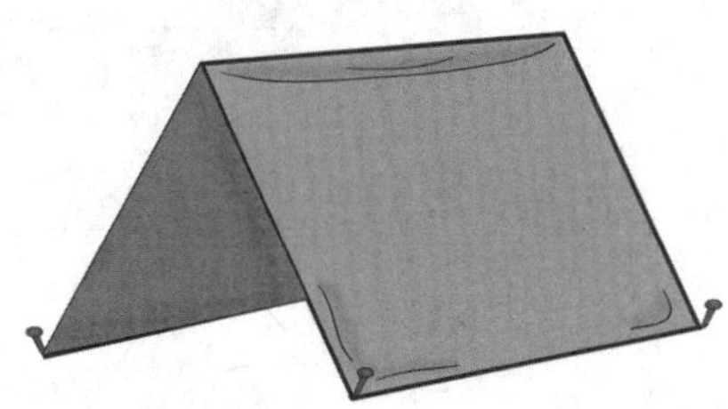

6. I am the number that is one more than 7. What number am I?

____

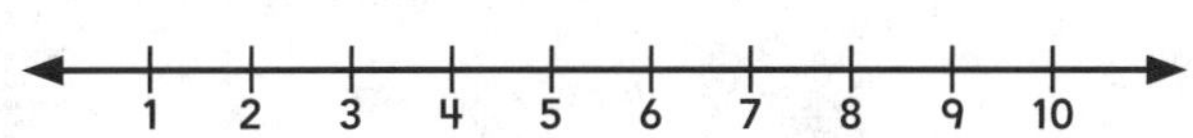

SCORE

1. ☺ 😐

2. ☺ 😐

3. ☺ 😐

4. ☺ 😐

5. ☺ 😐

6. ☺ 😐

___ / 6

Total

DAY

124

NAME: ____________________

DIRECTIONS Solve each problem.

SCORE

1. ☺ 😐
2. ☺ 😐
3. ☺ 😐
4. ☺ 😐
5. ☺ 😐
6. ☺ 😐

____ / 6

Total

1. Put these numbers in order.

29 27 28 25 26

______ ______ ______

______ ______

2. Subtract.

5 – 4 = ______

5 – 3 = ______

5 – 2 = ______

3. Circle what will come next.

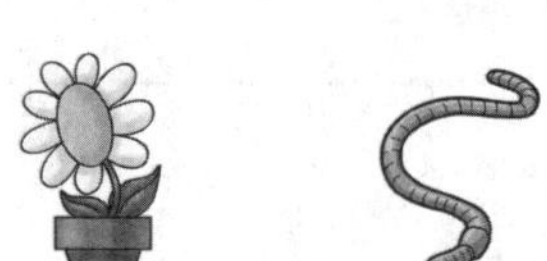

4. How long is the worm?

______ cubes

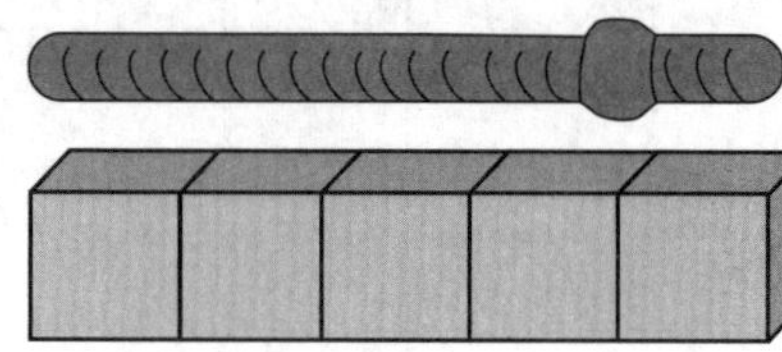

5. Draw a circle to the left of a diamond.

6. Nia has homework every school day except Friday. How many days does Nia have homework?

____

NAME: ____________________

DIRECTIONS Solve each problem.

1. How many snails are there?

______

2. Circle the number sentence that matches the picture.

3 – 2 = 1

1 + 2 = 3

3. Circle what will come next.

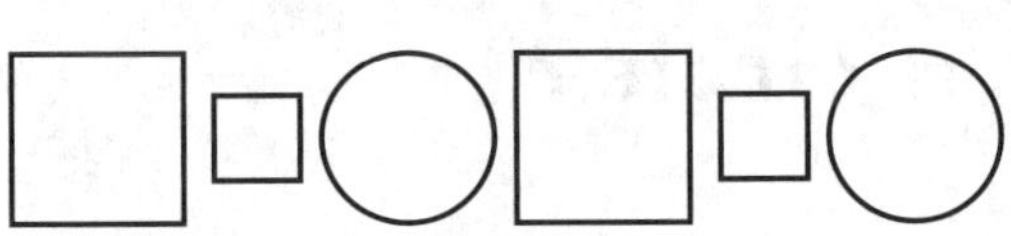

?

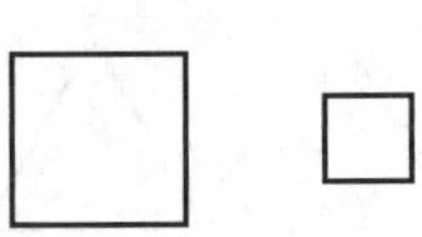

4. Circle the best time to eat lunch.

12:00 A.M. 12:00 P.M.

5. How many sides does a hexagon have?

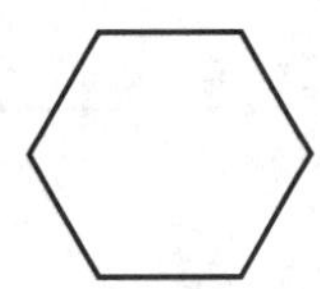

____

6. Maria starts on the number 2. She counts forward 2. What number is she on now?

____

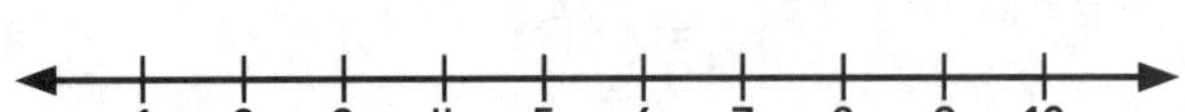

SCORE

1. ☺ 😐

2. ☺ 😐

3. ☺ 😐

4. ☺ 😐

5. ☺ 😐

6. ☺ 😐

____ / 6

Total

NAME: ____________________

DIRECTIONS Solve each problem.

SCORE

1. ☺ 😐
2. ☺ 😐
3. ☺ 😐
4. ☺ 😐
5. ☺ 😐
6. ☺ 😐

____ / 6
Total

1. Circle the smaller number.

10 8

2. Add.

1 + 5 = ______

5 + 1 = ______

3. Circle the part that repeats.

4. Circle the tool you use to tell when it will be Halloween.

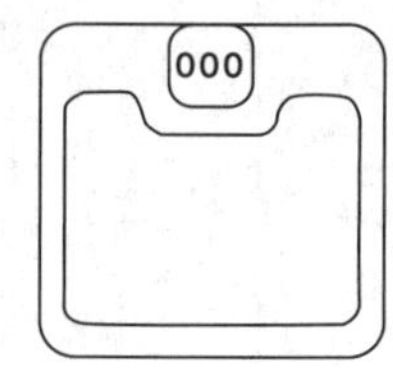

5. The glass is _____ the book. Circle the answer.

under on below

6. The shapes below are in a bag. Are you more likely to grab a triangle or a circle?

____

NAME: ____________________

DIRECTIONS Solve each problem.

1. Count the pencils. Draw a set of circles that is more than the pencils.

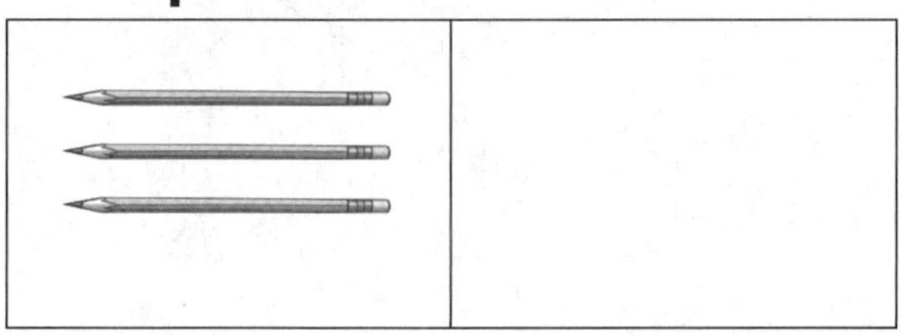

2. Add.

1 + 3 = ______

1 + 2 = ______

1 + 1 = ______

3. Make the same pattern using letters.

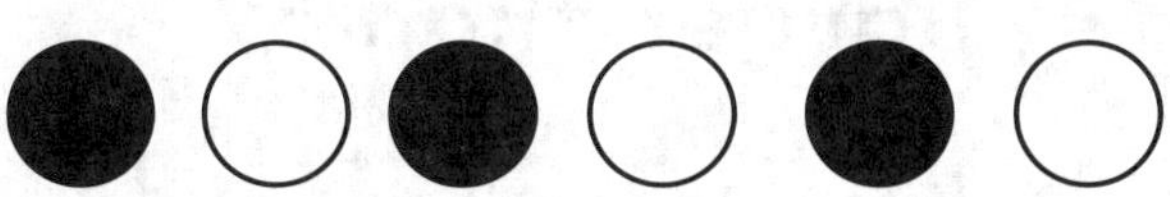

___ ___ ___ ___ ___ ___

4. Circle the object that weighs the most.

5. How many corners does a triangle have?

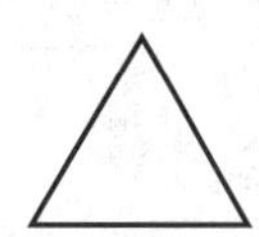

____

6. Miguel saw 6 birds on the roof. Five of them flew away. How many birds are still on the roof?

____

SCORE

1. ☺ 😐
2. ☺ 😐
3. ☺ 😐
4. ☺ 😐
5. ☺ 😐
6. ☺ 😐

___ / 6

Total

DAY 128

NAME: ____________________

DIRECTIONS Solve each problem.

SCORE

1. ☺ 😐
2. ☺ 😐
3. ☺ 😐
4. ☺ 😐
5. ☺ 😐
6. ☺ 😐

____ / 6 Total

1. Draw 4 legs on each tiger. How many legs are on 2 tigers?

____

2. Add.

1 + 0 = ______

0 + 1 = ______

3. Circle what will come next.

? ____

4. Circle the day that comes before Wednesday.

Sunday   Tuesday

5. Will the object roll? Circle the answer.

yes   no

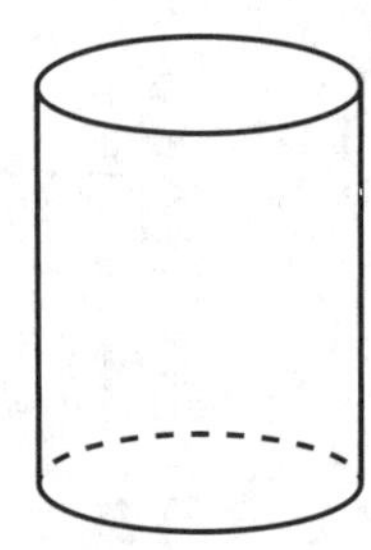

6. Circle the numbers that are larger than 5.

0 1 2 3 4

5 6 7 8 9

NAME: ____________________

DIRECTIONS Solve each problem.

1. Circle the plate with more than 6 strawberries.

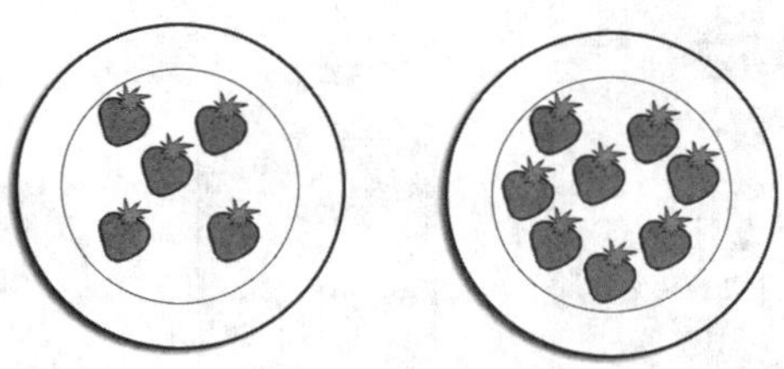

2. Circle the number sentence that matches.

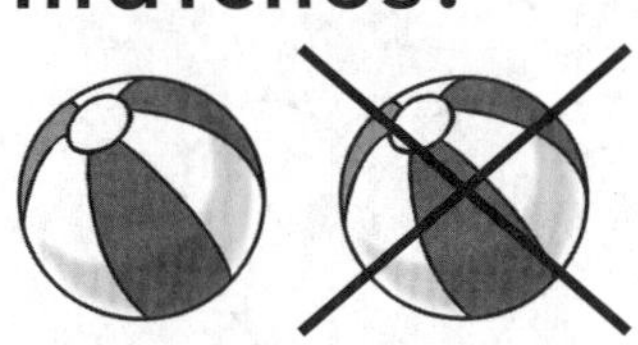

2 – 1 = 1

2 + 1 = 3

3 – 1 = 2

3. Draw what will come next.

□ □ # □ □ ?

4. Draw something that takes longer than building a tower of blocks.

5. Circle where the worm is.

left of the apple

right of the apple

6. Sam saves 2 pennies each day. How many pennies does he have after 4 days?

____

SCORE

1. ☺ 😐

2. ☺ 😐

3. ☺ 😐

4. ☺ 😐

5. ☺ 😐

6. ☺ 😐

___ / 6 Total

NAME: ____________________

DIRECTIONS Solve each problem.

SCORE

1. ☺ 😐
2. ☺ 😐
3. ☺ 😐
4. ☺ 😐
5. ☺ 😐
6. ☺ 😐

___ / 6 Total

1. Count how many.

____

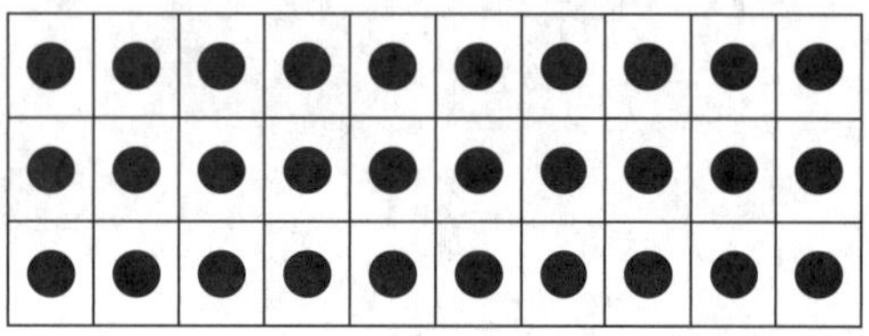

2. Add.

1 + 3 = ______

3 + 1 = ______

3. Circle the part that repeats.

4. Circle the container that holds the least.

5. Draw a line of symmetry.

6. Lily has 3 crayons. She gives 1 to her friend. How many does she have left?

____

NAME: ______________________________

DIRECTIONS Solve each problem.

1. Circle an equal number of triangles.

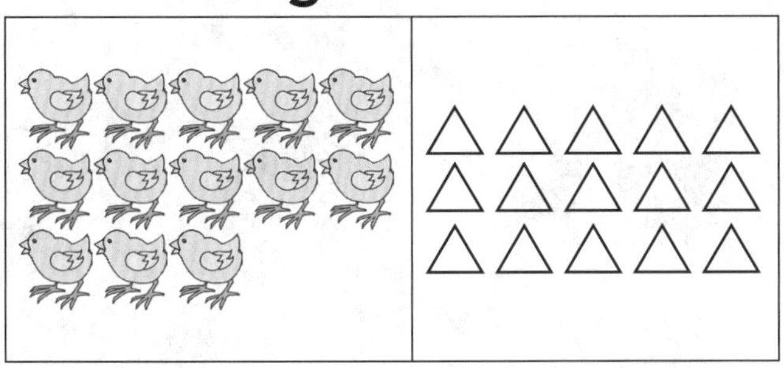

2. Circle the number sentence that matches the picture.

4 - 3 = 1

3 - 1 = 2

1 + 3 = 4

3. Make the same pattern using letters.

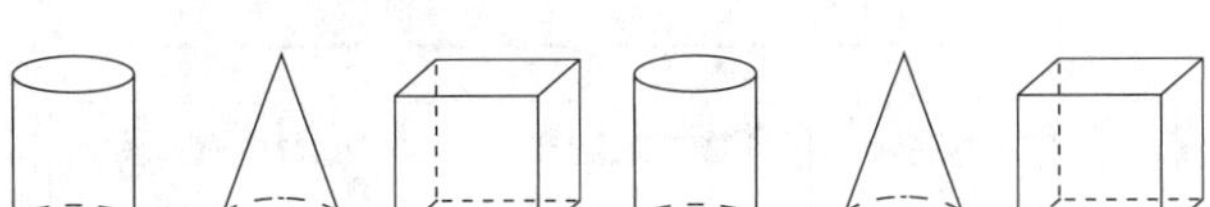

____ ____ ____ ____ ____ ____

4. What time is it?
_____ o'clock

5. Circle the name of the shapes.

triangles

circles

squares

6. How many legs are on 2 birds, 1 dog, and 1 snake?

____

SCORE

1.

2.

3.

4.

5.

6.

____ / 6
Total

DAY 132

NAME: ____________________

DIRECTIONS Solve each problem.

SCORE

1. ☺ 😐
2. ☺ 😐
3. ☺ 😐
4. ☺ 😐
5. ☺ 😐
6. ☺ 😐

___ / 6 Total

1. Write the missing number.

17 ______ 19 20

2. Add.

2 + 1 = ______

1 + 2 = ______

3. Circle what will come next.

 **?** ___

4. Circle the tallest animal.

5. Circle the solid that looks like the object.

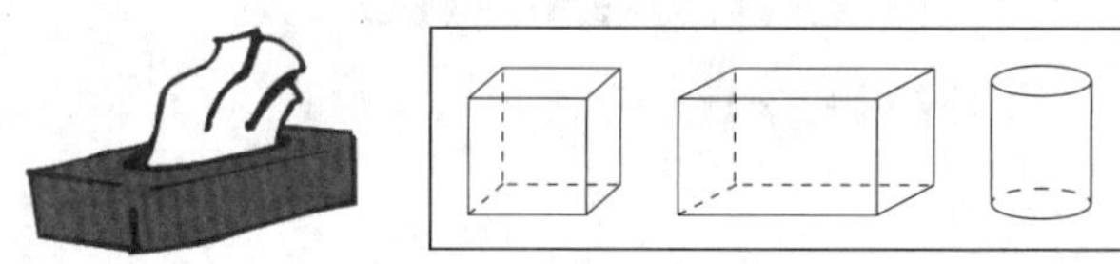

6. Peter ate 2 cookies on Monday, 1 cookie on Tuesday, and 2 cookies on Wednesday. How many cookies did Peter eat in all?

____

Monday	Tuesday	Wednesday

NAME: ____________________

DIRECTIONS Solve each problem.

SCORE

1. Draw a set of 6 squares. Draw a set of fewer than 6 triangles.

6	fewer than 6

2. Add.

1 + 4 = ______

1 + 3 = ______

1 + 2 = ______

3. Circle what will come next in this pattern.

 ? ____

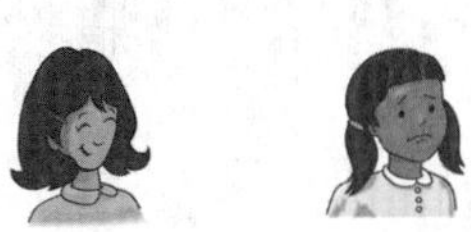

4. Circle about how many keys are on a computer keyboard.

6 60

5. Draw a boy on the bed.

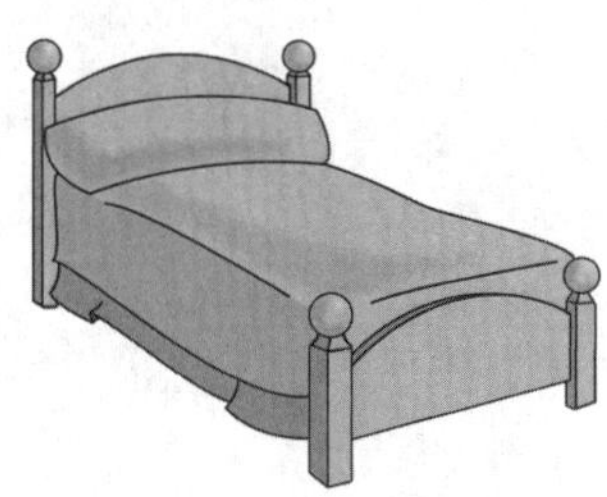

6. What time will it be in 1 hour?

______ o'clock

1. ☺ 😐
2. ☺ 😐
3. ☺ 😐
4. ☺ 😐
5. ☺ 😐
6. ☺ 😐

____ / 6 Total

NAME: ____________________

DIRECTIONS Solve each problem.

SCORE

1.

2.

3.

4.

5.

6.

___ / 6 Total

1. Put these numbers in order.

9 7 8

_____ _____ _____

2. Draw a picture to show 1 + 1 = 2.

3. Circle the part that repeats.

4. How tall is the boot?

_____ cubes

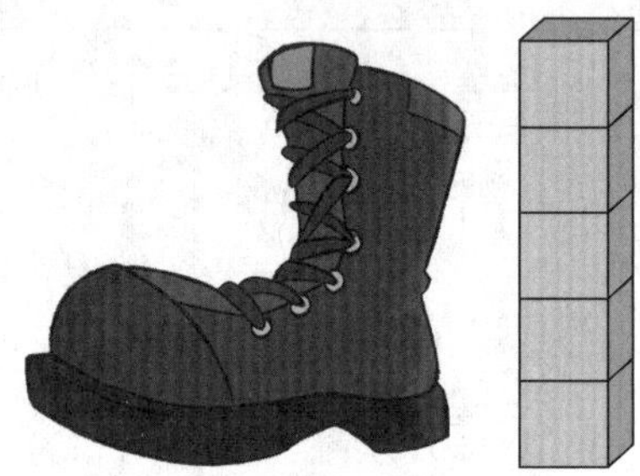

5. Draw a circle with a triangle in the middle.

6. Megan starts on the number 5. She counts backward 1. What number is she on now?

____

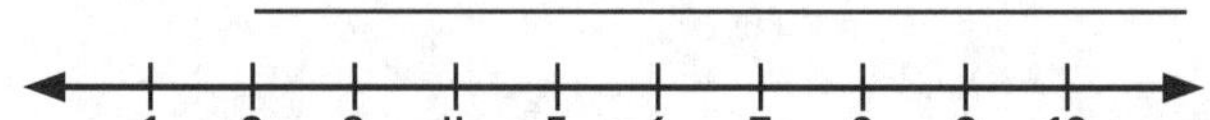

NAME: ______________________________

DIRECTIONS Solve each problem.

1. Count the ice cream cones. What is 1 more?

____

2. Draw a picture to show 4 – 3 = 1.

3. Make the same pattern using letters.

___ ___ ___ ___ ___ ___

4. Circle the best time to play with a friend.

2:00 A.M. 2:00 P.M.

5. Does the solid have any flat surfaces? Circle the answer.

yes no

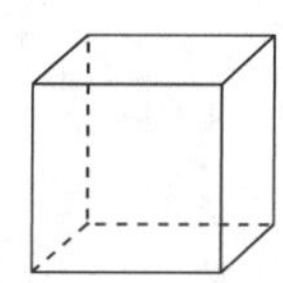

6. There are 6 triangles. One is red. One is green. The rest of them are blue. How many triangles are blue?

____

SCORE

1. ☺ 😐

2. ☺ 😐

3. ☺ 😐

4. ☺ 😐

5. ☺ 😐

6. ☺ 😐

____ / 6 Total

DAY
136

NAME: ______________________________

DIRECTIONS Solve each problem.

SCORE

1. ☺ 😐
2. ☺ 😐
3. ☺ 😐
4. ☺ 😐
5. ☺ 😐
6. ☺ 😐

____ / 6
Total

1. Circle the smaller number.

7 6 9

2.

$$\begin{array}{r} 3 \\ +\ 3 \\ \hline \end{array}$$

3. Create an AB pattern using these shapes.

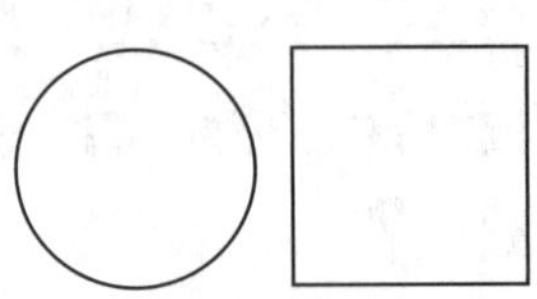

A B A B A B

4. What tool is best to measure how much a bucket can hold?

5. The pillow is ______ the boy's head.

on under out

6. What is the missing sign?

1 ☐ 1 = 2

NAME: ____________________________

DIRECTIONS Solve each problem.

SCORE

1. Count the mice. Draw a set of circles that is less than the mice.

2.

$$\begin{array}{r} 2 \\ -\ 0 \\ \hline \end{array}$$

3. Write what will come next.

10 20 30 40 ______

4. Circle the object that weighs the least.

5. How many sides does a triangle have?

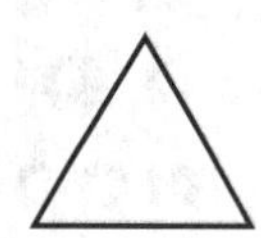

____

6. Marty picked 5 oranges. He ate 2 of them. How many oranges does he still have?

____

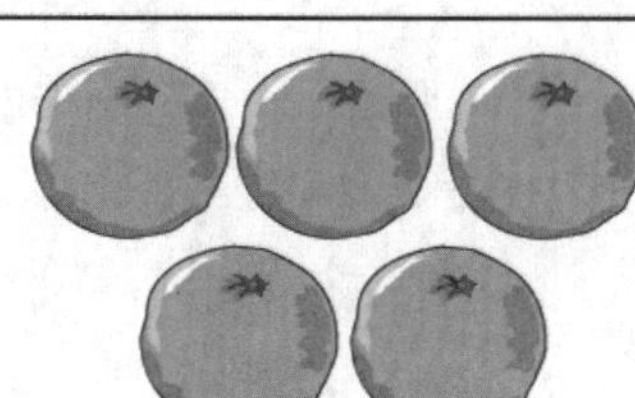

1. ☺ 😐

2. ☺ 😐

3. ☺ 😐

4. ☺ 😐

5. ☺ 😐

6. ☺ 😐

____ / 6
Total

DAY 138

NAME: ____________________

DIRECTIONS Solve each problem.

SCORE

1. ☺ 😐
2. ☺ 😐
3. ☺ 😐
4. ☺ 😐
5. ☺ 😐
6. ☺ 😐

____ / 6 Total

1. Draw 3 triangles in each circle. How many triangles are in all?

____

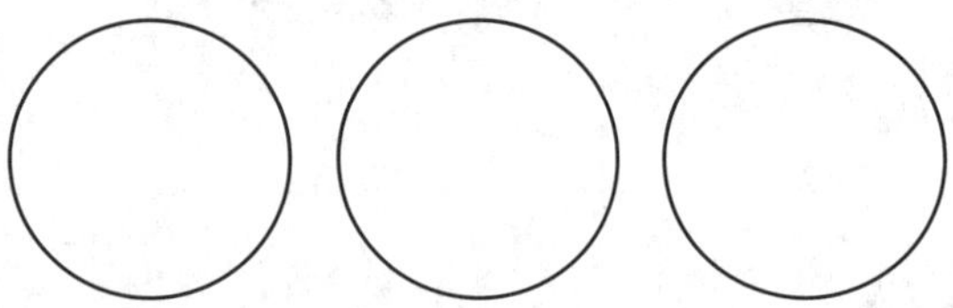

2. Draw a picture using apples to show 3 + 2 = 5.

3. Circle the part that repeats.

4. What day of the week is December 4th?

____

December						
Sun	Mon	Tues	Wed	Thurs	Fri	Sat
			1	2	3	4
5	6	7	8	9	10	11
12	13	14	15	16	17	18
19	20	21	22	23	24	25
26	27	28	29	30	31	

5. Will the solid stack? Circle the answer.

yes no

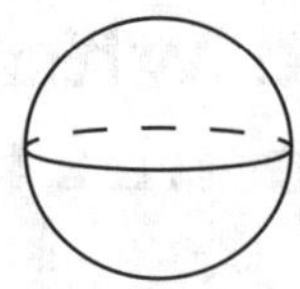

6. Write the word for each number.

3 ____________________

4 ____________________

5 ____________________

NAME: ____________________

DIRECTIONS Solve each problem.

1. Circle the ladybug with fewer than 9 spots.

2. 4 − 1 = ______

3. Draw a pattern using these fruits.

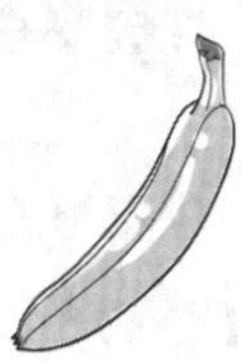

4. Circle about how long it would take to watch a movie.

1 minute

2 hours

5 hours

5. Circle the picture that shows the girl in the middle.

6. Draw a picture to match.

There are 3 fish swimming. Then 2 more fish come.

SCORE

1. ☺ 😐

2. ☺ 😐

3. ☺ 😐

4. ☺ 😐

5. ☺ 😐

6. ☺ 😐

____ / 6

Total

NAME: ____________________

DIRECTIONS Solve each problem.

SCORE

1. ☺ 😐
2. ☺ 😐
3. ☺ 😐
4. ☺ 😐
5. ☺ 😐
6. ☺ 😐

____ / 6
Total

1. Count how many.

____

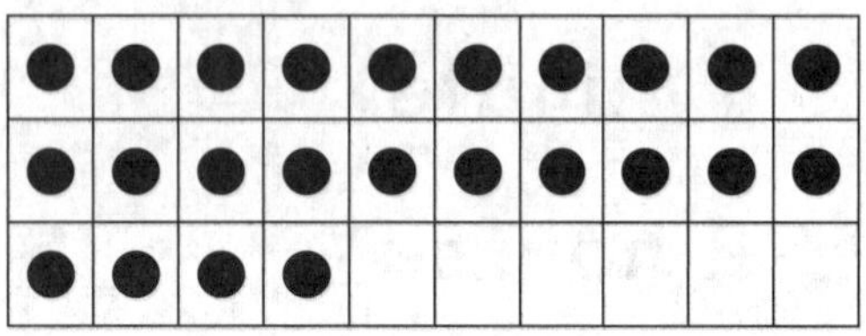

2.

$$\begin{array}{r} 3 \\ +\ 3 \\ \hline \end{array}$$

3. Write what will come next.

5 6 7 8 ______

4. Draw a container that holds more than a bucket.

5. Draw a line of symmetry.

6. I have 4 sides.

I have 4 corners.

I have 2 longer sides.

I have 2 shorter sides.

What shape am I?

____

DAY

141

NAME: ______________________

DIRECTIONS Solve each problem.

1. Circle an equal number of squares.

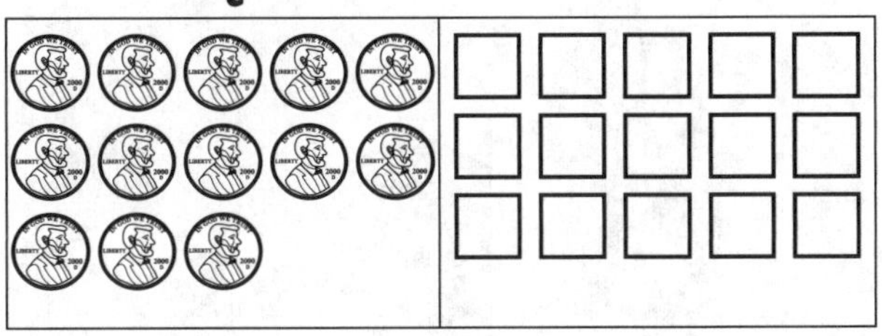

2. Draw a picture using suns to show 5 – 1 = 4.

3. Make the same pattern using letters.

___ ___ ___ ___ ___ ___

4. What time is it?

____ : ____

5. Circle the name of the shapes.

triangles squares

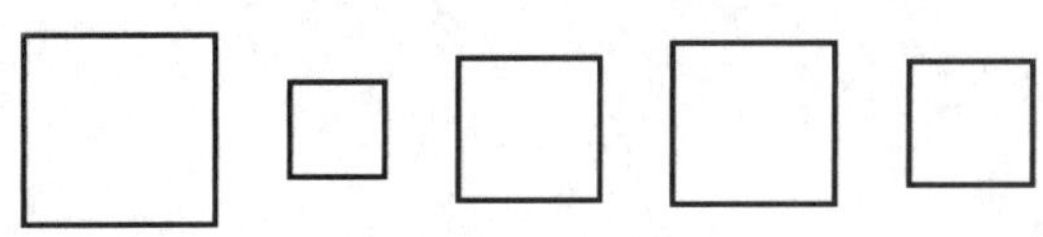

6. How many groups of 2 are there?

____

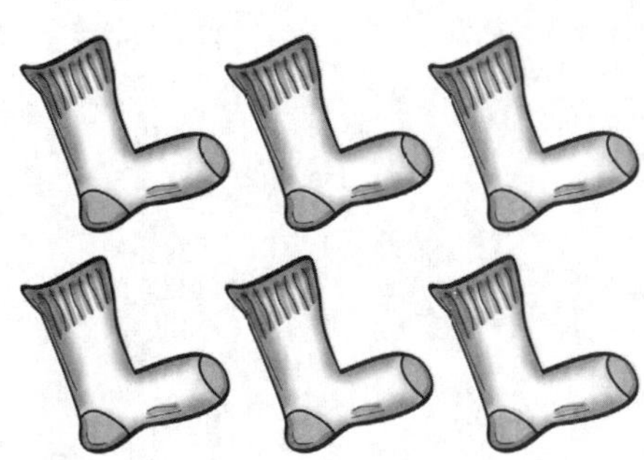

SCORE

1. ☺ 😐

2. ☺ 😐

3. ☺ 😐

4. ☺ 😐

5. ☺ 😐

6. ☺ 😐

___ / 6

Total

DAY 142

NAME: ____________________

DIRECTIONS Solve each problem.

SCORE

1. ☺ 😐
2. ☺ 😐
3. ☺ 😐
4. ☺ 😐
5. ☺ 😐
6. ☺ 😐

____ / 6 Total

1. Write the missing number.

22 23 ______ 25

2. 2 + 1 = ______

3. Draw a pattern using these figures.

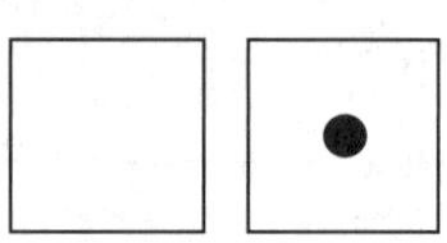

4. Circle the shortest stack of blocks.

5. Circle the solid that looks like the object.

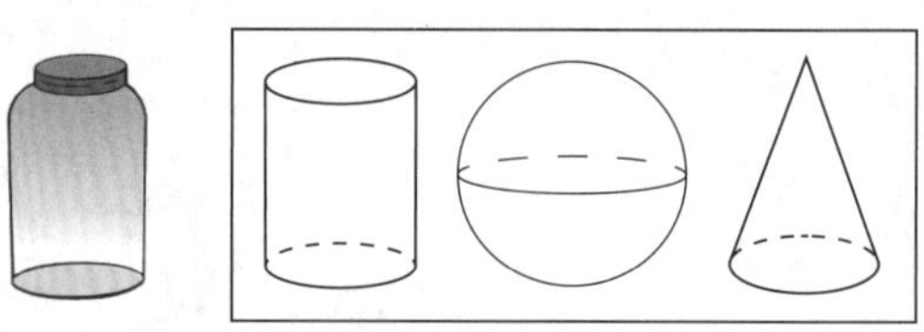

6. Owen saw 2 airplanes land at the airport. Then he saw one more land. How many airplanes did Owen see land?

____

NAME: ____________________

DIRECTIONS Solve each problem.

1. Draw a set of 8 circles. Draw a set of more than 8 squares.

8	more than 8

2. 5 – 5 = ______

3. Write what number will come next.

60 70 80 90 ______

4. Circle about how many buttons you can hold in your hand.

3 30

5. Draw noodles in the bowl.

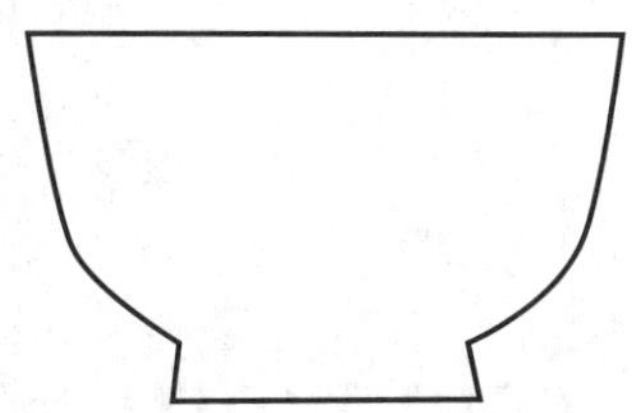

6. I am the number that is 1 more than 3.

What number am I?

____

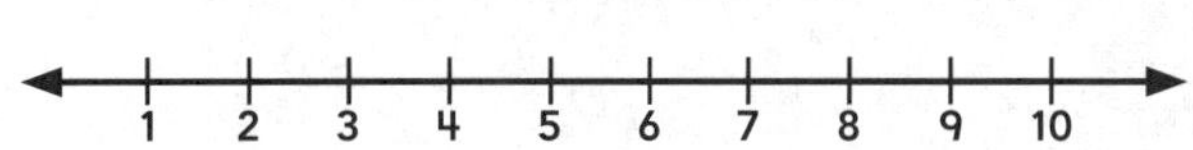

SCORE

1. ☺ 😐

2. ☺ 😐

3. ☺ 😐

4. ☺ 😐

5. ☺ 😐

6. ☺ 😐

___ / 6

Total

DAY 144

NAME: ______________________

DIRECTIONS Solve each problem.

SCORE

1. ☺ 😐

2. ☺ 😐

3. ☺ 😐

4. ☺ 😐

5. ☺ 😐

6. ☺ 😐

___ / 6

Total

1. Put these numbers in order from largest to smallest.

9 11 15

_______ _______ _______

2. Draw a picture using happy faces to show 5 + 0 = 5.

3. Circle what will come next.

? ___

4. How long is the toothbrush?

_______ cubes

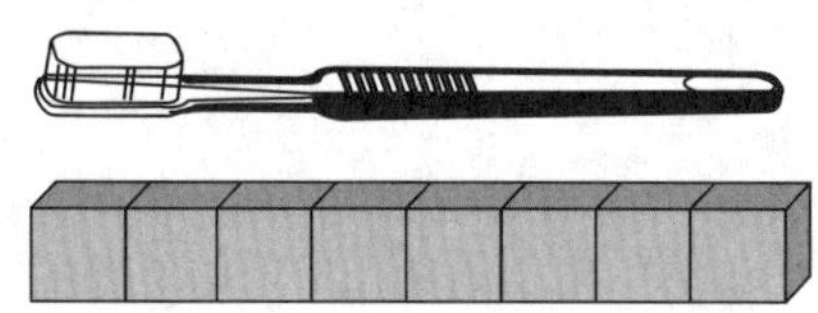

5. Draw a square around a triangle.

6. One ant is 1 cube long. How long are 3 ants?

_____________cubes

NAME: ____________________

DIRECTIONS Solve each problem.

1. Count the sea horses. What is 1 more?

____

2.

$$\begin{array}{r} 5 \\ -\ 3 \\ \hline \end{array}$$

3. Draw a pattern using these shapes.

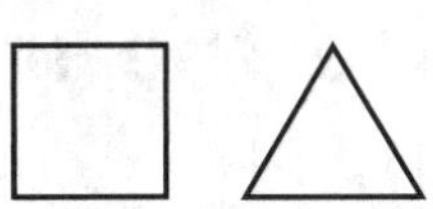

4. Circle the best time to eat breakfast.

7:00 A.M.   7:00 P.M.

5. How many sides does an octagon have?

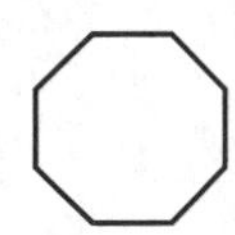

____

6. Sonya starts on the number 5. She counts forward 3. What number is she on now?

____

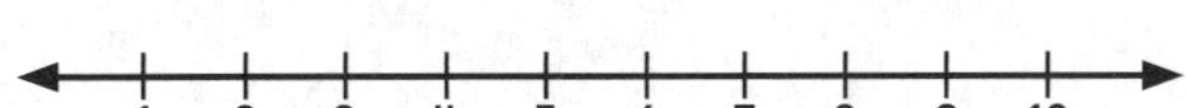

SCORE

1. ☺ 😐
2. ☺ 😐
3. ☺ 😐
4. ☺ 😐
5. ☺ 😐
6. ☺ 😐

____ / 6 Total

DAY
146

NAME: ____________________

DIRECTIONS Solve each problem.

SCORE

1. ☺ 😐
2. ☺ 😐
3. ☺ 😐
4. ☺ 😐
5. ☺ 😐
6. ☺ 😐

____ / 6
Total

1. Circle the larger number.

11   9

2. 4 + 1 = ______

3. Write what number will come next.

12 13 14 15 ______

4. Circle the tool you can use to tell when school starts.

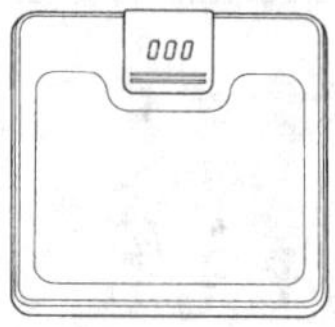

5. Is the dog on the right or the left? Circle the answer.

right   left

6. Write the missing sign.

2 ☐ 1 = 1

NAME: ______________________________

DIRECTIONS Solve each problem.

1. Count the balloons. Draw a set of circles that is more than the balloons.

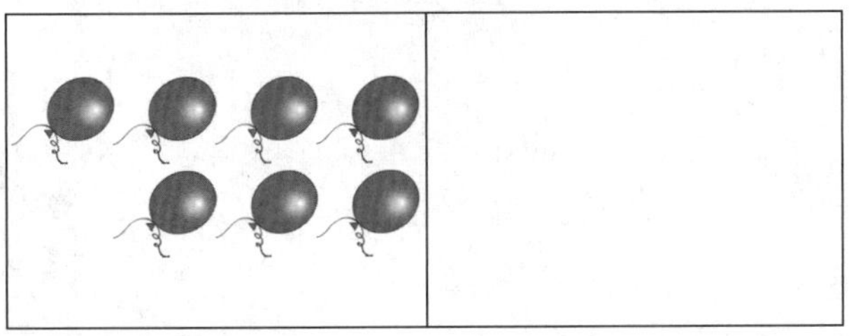

2. 3 – 3 = ______

3. Draw what will come next.

 ? ____

4. Draw or write something that weighs more than a crayon.

5. How many corners does a hexagon have?

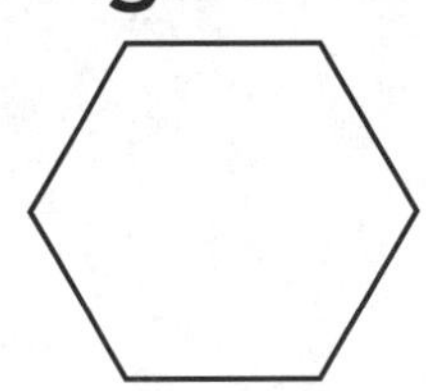

____

6. Kiko had 3 jackets. She lost one. How many jackets does she still have?

____

SCORE

1. ☺ 😐

2. ☺ 😐

3. ☺ 😐

4. ☺ 😐

5. ☺ 😐

6. ☺ 😐

____ / 6

Total

DAY
148

NAME: ____________________________

DIRECTIONS Solve each problem.

SCORE

1. ☺ 😐

2. ☺ 😐

3. ☺ 😐

4. ☺ 😐

5. ☺ 😐

6. ☺ 😐

____ / 6
Total

1. Draw 2 legs on each bird. How many legs on 2 birds?

____

2.

$$\begin{array}{r} 1 \\ +\ 3 \\ \hline \end{array}$$

3. Draw a pattern using these shapes.

4. Circle what day comes after Monday.

Tuesday   Friday

5. Will the solid slide? Circle the answer.

yes   no

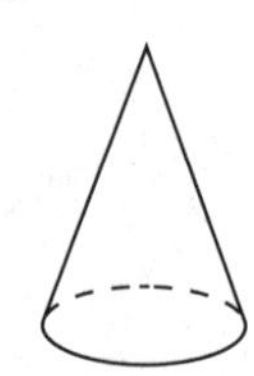

6. Write the number for each word.

one ____________

two ____________

three ____________

NAME: ____________________

DIRECTIONS Solve each problem.

1. Circle the machine with more than 11 pieces of gum.

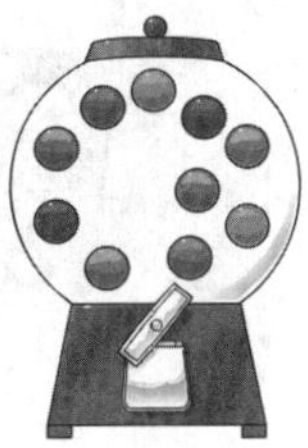

2.

$$\begin{array}{r} 4 \\ -\ 0 \\ \hline \end{array}$$

3. Write what number will come next.

9 8 7 6 ☐

4. Circle about how long it takes to count to 100.

10 seconds

1 minute

1 hour

5. Circle where the glue is.

below the paper

above the paper

6. Maggie has two bags. She has 4 pieces of candy. Circle the bags she has.

SCORE

1. ☺ 😐

2. ☺ 😐

3. ☺ 😐

4. ☺ 😐

5. ☺ 😐

6. ☺ 😐

___ / 6
Total

DAY 150

NAME: ____________________

DIRECTIONS Solve each problem.

SCORE

1. ☺ 😐
2. ☺ 😐
3. ☺ 😐
4. ☺ 😐
5. ☺ 😐
6. ☺ 😐

____ / 6
Total

1. Count how many.

____

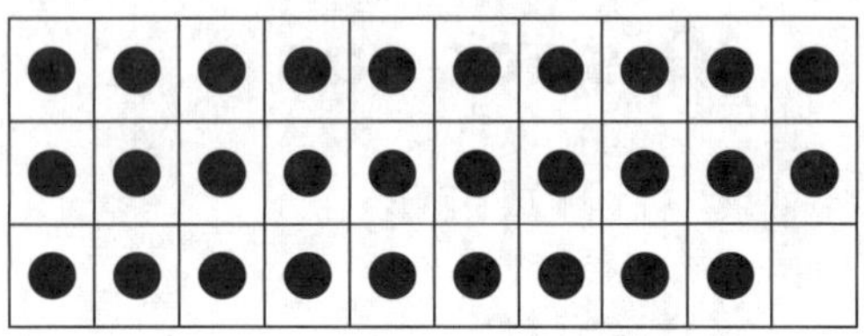

2. 1 + 2 = ______

3. Circle the part that repeats.

4. Circle the container that holds the least.

5. Draw a line of symmetry.

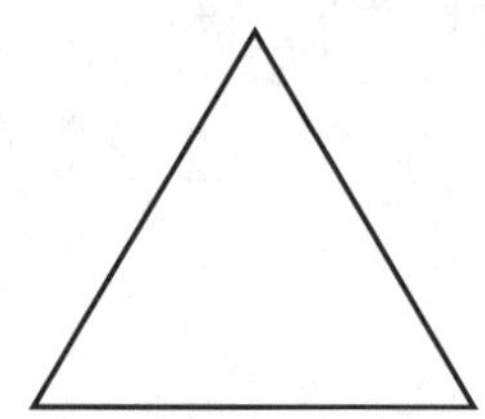

6. Circle the solids with flat faces.

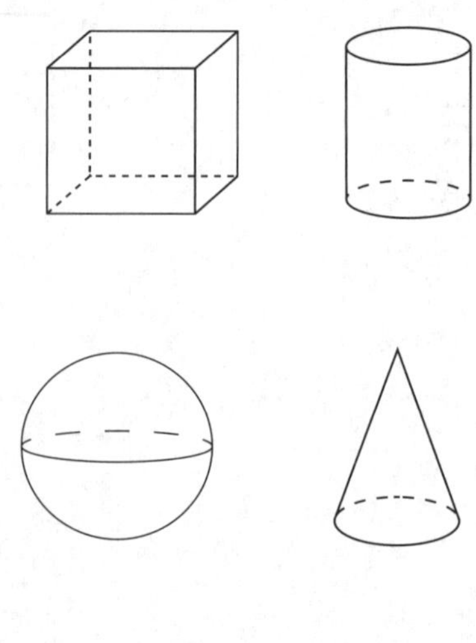

NAME: ____________________

DIRECTIONS Solve each problem.

1. Color an equal number of triangles.

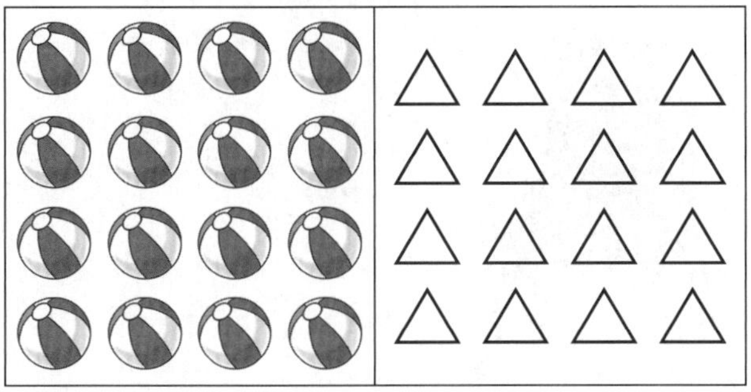

2. 1 – 1 = ______

3. Make a pattern using these shapes.

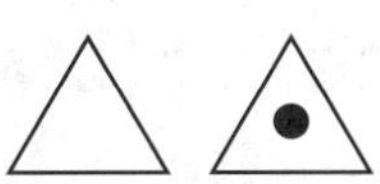

4. What time is it?

______ o'clock

5. Circle the name of the shapes.

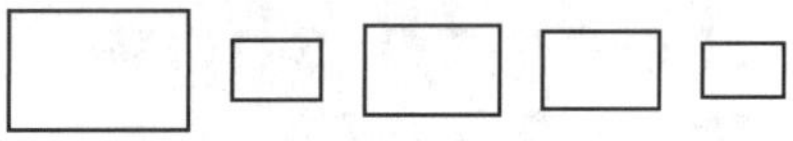

squares

rectangles

hexagons

6. How many numbers are on the faces of two clocks?

____

SCORE

1. ☺ 😐

2. ☺ 😐

3. ☺ 😐

4. ☺ 😐

5. ☺ 😐

6. ☺ 😐

____ / 6 Total

NAME: ____________________

DIRECTIONS Solve each problem.

SCORE

1. ☺ 😐
2. ☺ 😐
3. ☺ 😐
4. ☺ 😐
5. ☺ 😐
6. ☺ 😐

____ / 6
Total

1. Write the missing number.

25 26 ______ 28

2. Draw a picture of trees to show
2 + 3 = 5.

3. Write what number will come next.

30 40 50 60 ______

4. Draw something that is shorter than a chair.

5. Circle the solid that looks like the object.

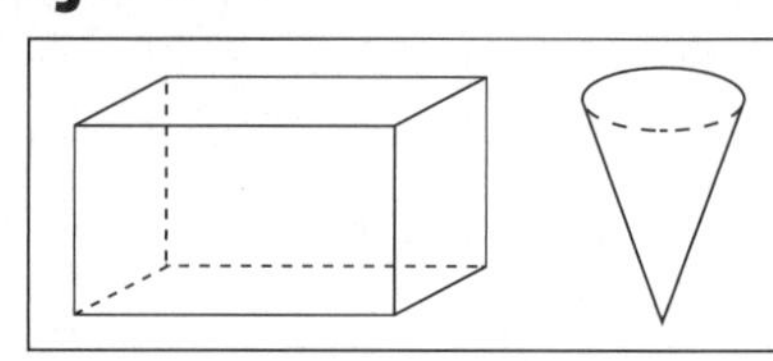

6. Lilo made 4 pots out of clay. Then she made one more. How many pots did she make?

____

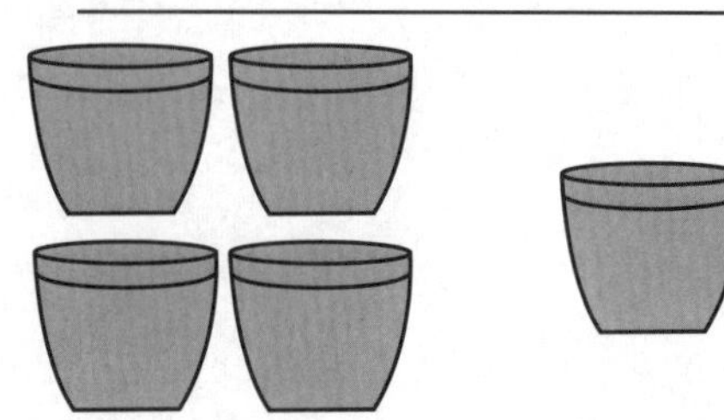

NAME: ____________________

DIRECTIONS Solve each problem.

1. Draw a set of 9 triangles. Draw an equal set of dots.

9	equal to 9

2.

$$\begin{array}{r} 3 \\ -\ 1 \\ \hline \end{array}$$

3. Make the same pattern using letters.

___ ___ ___ ___ ___ ___

4. Circle how many elephants could fit in your classroom.

4 40

5. Draw an apple in the bag.

6. Circle the numbers that have both straight lines and curved lines.

0 1 2 3 4

5 6 7 8 9

SCORE

1. ☺ 😐

2. ☺ 😐

3. ☺ 😐

4. ☺ 😐

5. ☺ 😐

6. ☺ 😐

___ / 6 Total

DAY 154

NAME: ____________________

DIRECTIONS Solve each problem.

SCORE

1. ☺ ☹
2. ☺ ☹
3. ☺ ☹
4. ☺ ☹
5. ☺ ☹
6. ☺ ☹

____ / 6 Total

1. Put these numbers in order from smallest to largest.

12 16 14

______ ______ ______

2. 1 + 4 = ______

3. Draw a pattern with your own pictures.

4. How tall is the robot?

______ cubes

5. Draw a pentagon next to a triangle.

6. Britney starts on the number 9. She counts backward 3. What number is she on now?

____

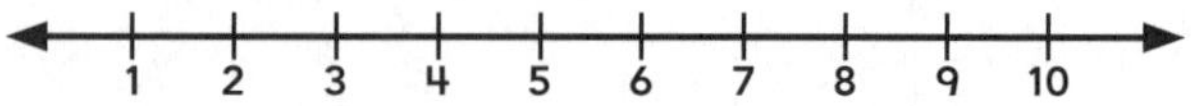

NAME: ______________________

DIRECTIONS Solve each problem.

1. Count the donuts. What is 1 more?

____

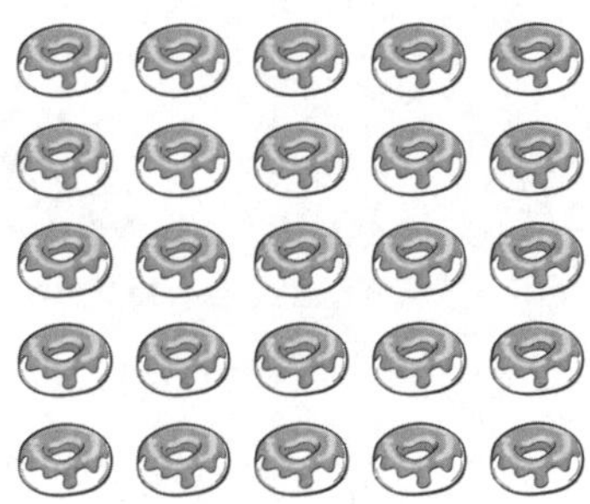

2. 5 – 4 = ______

3. Write what number will come next.

15 16 17 18 ______

4. Circle the best time to go to bed.

8:00 A.M. 8:00 P.M.

5. Does the solid have any curved surfaces? Circle the answer.

yes no

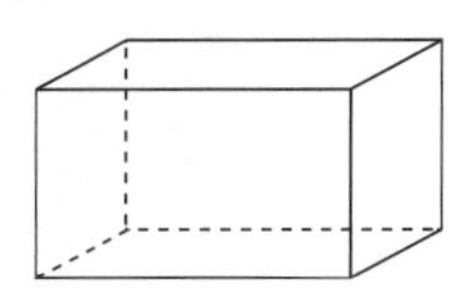

6. Draw 5 squares. Color 2 of them blue. Color the rest green. How many are green?

____

SCORE

1. ☺ 😐

2. ☺ 😐

3. ☺ 😐

4. ☺ 😐

5. ☺ 😐

6. ☺ 😐

____ / 6

Total

NAME: ____________________

DIRECTIONS Solve each problem.

SCORE

1.

2.

3.

4.

5.

6.

___ / 6

Total

1. Circle the smaller number.

8 12

2.

$$\begin{array}{r} 1 \\ +\ 3 \\ \hline \end{array}$$

3. Circle what will come next.

 ?

4. Circle the best tool to measure how tall a door is.

5. The circle is ______ the square.

below on above

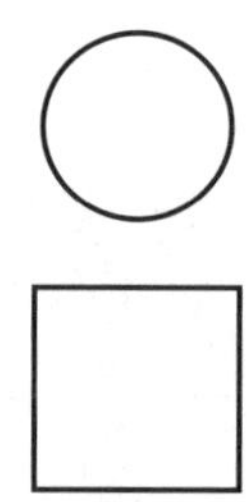

6. Write the missing sign.

3 ☐ 1 = 4

NAME: ____________________

DAY 157

DIRECTIONS Solve each problem.

1. Count the bananas. Draw a set of circles that is less than the bananas.

2. Draw a picture of kites to show 1 + 4 = 5.

3. Make a pattern using these shapes.

4. Circle the object that weighs the least.

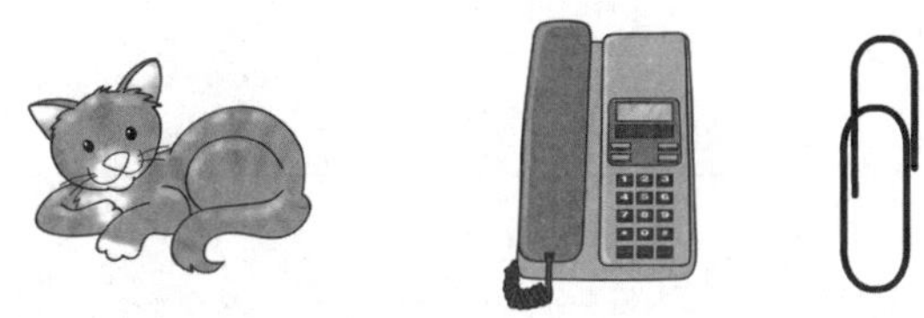

5. How many sides does a square have?

____

6. Trina had 4 jacks. She lost all of them. How many jacks does she have left?

____

SCORE

1. ☺ 😐

2. ☺ 😐

3. ☺ 😐

4. ☺ 😐

5. ☺ 😐

6. ☺ 😐

____ / 6 Total

DAY
158

NAME: ______________________

DIRECTIONS Solve each problem.

SCORE

1. ☺ 😐
2. ☺ 😐
3. ☺ 😐
4. ☺ 😐
5. ☺ 😐
6. ☺ 😐

____ / 6
Total

1. Draw 4 legs on each cat. How many legs are on 3 cats?

____

2.

$$\begin{array}{r} 4 \\ -\ 2 \\ \hline \end{array}$$

3. Write what will come next.

12 11 10 9 8 ______

4. What is the date of the second Sunday in May?

____

May						
Sun	Mon	Tues	Wed	Thurs	Fri	Sat
	1	2	3	4	5	6
7	8	9	10	11	12	13
14	15	16	17	18	19	20
21	22	23	24	25	26	27
28	29	30	31			

5. Name the solid.

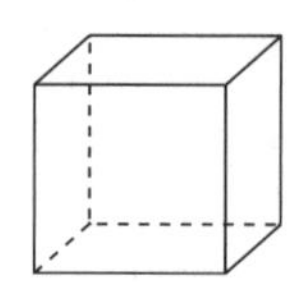

____

6. Write the names for the numbers.

5 ______________________

6 ______________________

7 ______________________

NAME: ______________________________

DIRECTIONS Solve each problem.

1. Circle the box with fewer dots.

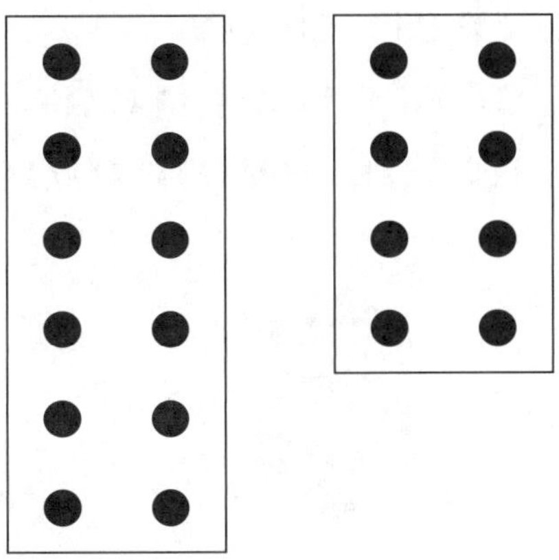

2. 2 – 2 = ______

3. Circle what will come next.

 ?

4. Circle about how long it takes to take a bath.

15 seconds

15 minutes

15 hours

5. Circle the picture that shows a boy on the balance beam.

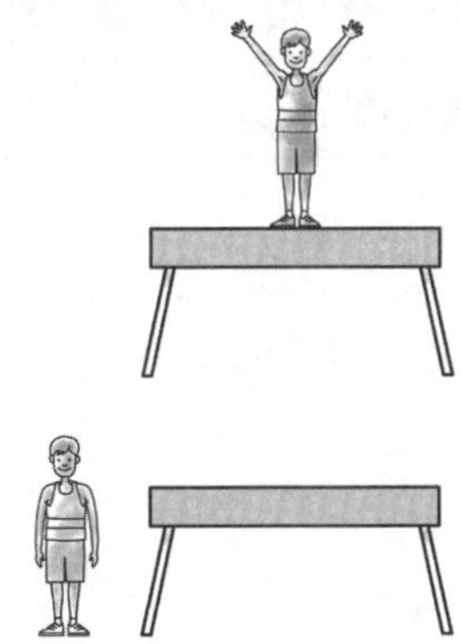

6. There are 6 apples and 3 baskets. How many apples go in each basket so it is fair?

____

SCORE

1.

2.

3.

4.

5.

6.

____ / 6

Total

DAY
160

NAME: ______________________

DIRECTIONS Solve each problem.

SCORE

1. ☺ 😐
2. ☺ 😐
3. ☺ 😐
4. ☺ 😐
5. ☺ 😐
6. ☺ 😐

____ / 6
Total

1. Count how many.

____

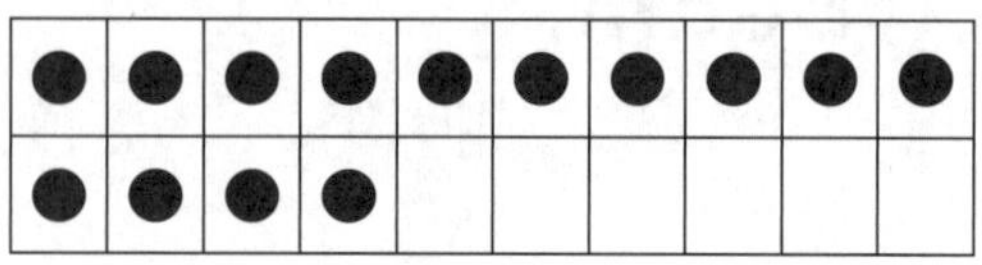

2.

$$\begin{array}{r} 1 \\ +\ 3 \\ \hline \end{array}$$

3. Draw a pattern using these shapes.

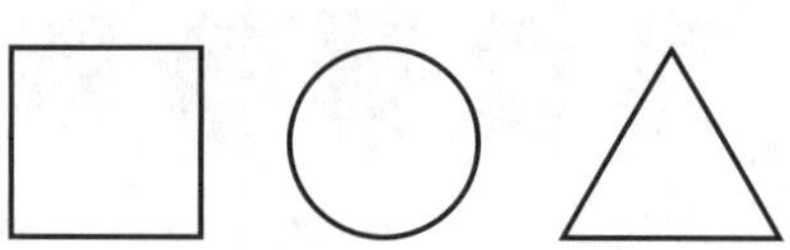

4. Circle the container that holds the most. Then draw a container that holds even more.

5. Draw a line of symmetry.

6. Do more people like basketball or soccer? Write the answer.

____

basketball	𝍸 |
soccer	𝍸 |||

DAY **161**

NAME: ____________________

DIRECTIONS Solve each problem.

1. Color an equal number of circles.

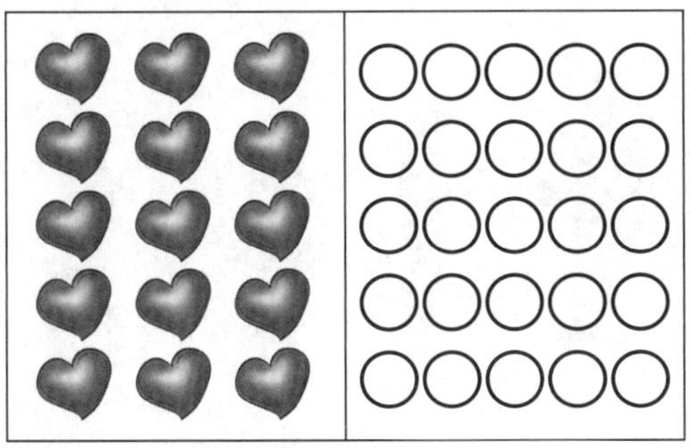

2.
$$\begin{array}{r} 3 \\ -\ 2 \\ \hline \end{array}$$

3. Write what will come next.

2 4 6 8 ______

4. What time is it?

_____ : _____

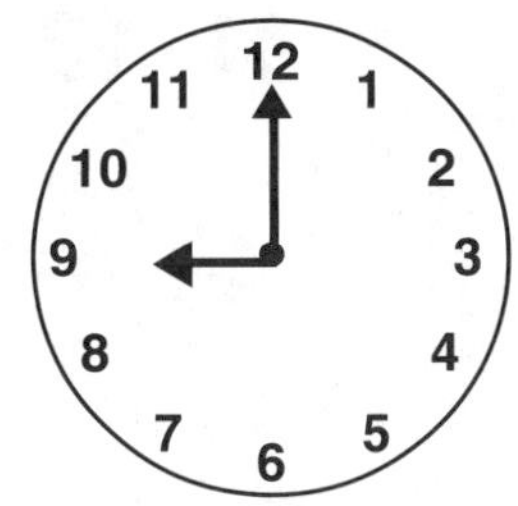

5. Circle the name of the shapes.

squares

rectangles

hexagons

6. How many groups of 3 can you make?

____

SCORE

1. ☺ 😐

2. ☺ 😐

3. ☺ 😐

4. ☺ 😐

5. ☺ 😐

6. ☺ 😐

____ / 6

Total

DAY
162

NAME: ______________________

DIRECTIONS Solve each problem.

SCORE

1. ☺ 😐
2. ☺ 😐
3. ☺ 😐
4. ☺ 😐
5. ☺ 😐
6. ☺ 😐

____ / 6
Total

1. Write the missing number.

______ 11 12 13

2. 4 + 1 = ______

3. Draw a pattern using these shapes.

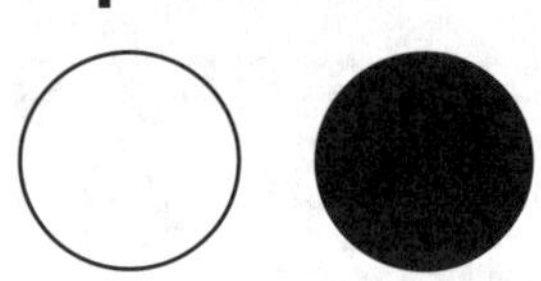

4. Circle the tallest person.

5. Draw a bug on the leaf.

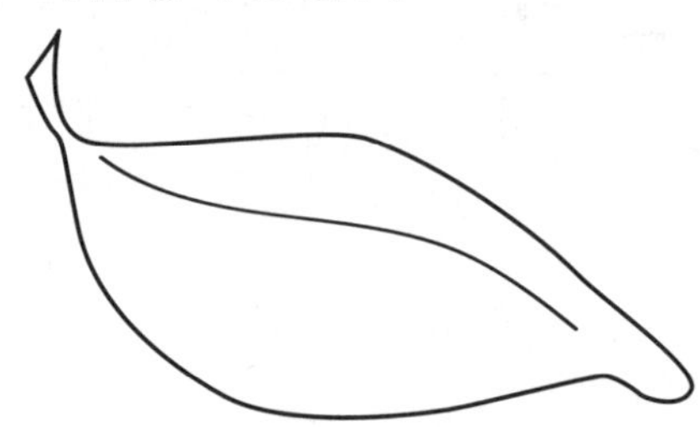

6. Rex has 3 dollars. Grandma gave him 1 more. How much money does Rex have now?

____

NAME: ______________________

DIRECTIONS Solve each problem.

1. Draw a set of 10 squares. Draw a set of fewer triangles.

10	Fewer than 10

2. 2 – 1 = ______

3. Circle the part that repeats.

4. Circle about how many people can fit in a car.

6 60

5. Circle the solid that looks like the object.

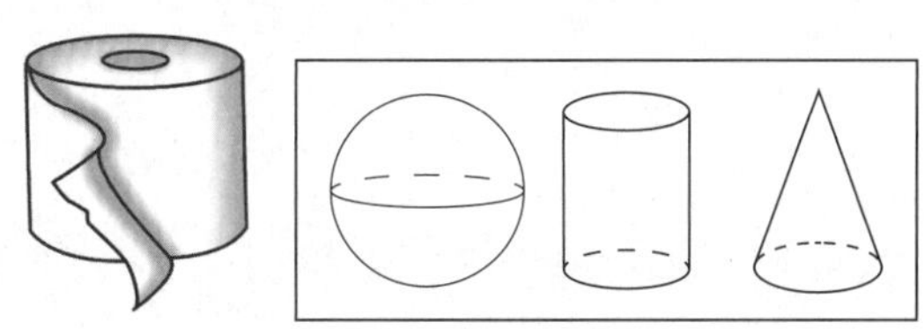

6. I am the number that is one less than 6. What number am I?

____

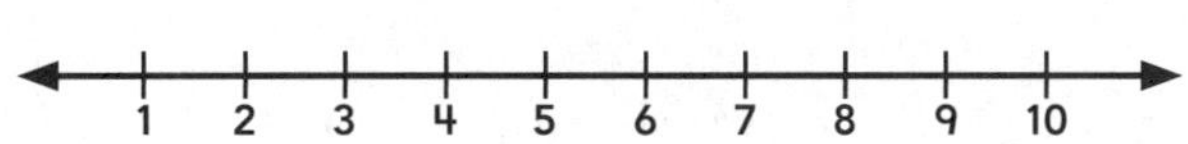

SCORE

1. ☺ 😐

2. ☺ 😐

3. ☺ 😐

4. ☺ 😐

5. ☺ 😐

6. ☺ 😐

____ / 6

Total

DAY
164

NAME: ______________________

DIRECTIONS Solve each problem.

SCORE

1. ☺ 😐
2. ☺ 😐
3. ☺ 😐
4. ☺ 😐
5. ☺ 😐
6. ☺ 😐

____ / 6
Total

1. Put these numbers in order.

4   12   9   15   5

______ ______ ______

______ ______

2.

$$\begin{array}{r} 2 \\ +\ 2 \\ \hline \end{array}$$

3. Write what will come next.

21 22 23 24 25 ____

4. How long is the stick?

______ paperclips

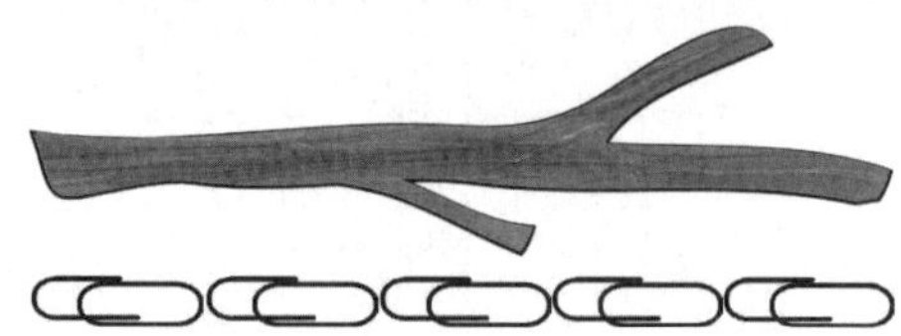

5. Draw a circle above a rectangle.

6. What time will it be 1 hour from now?

______ o'clock

NAME: ____________________

DIRECTIONS Solve each problem.

1. Count the roses. What is 1 more?

____

2. Draw a picture to show 4 – 4 = 0.

3. Make the same pattern using letters.

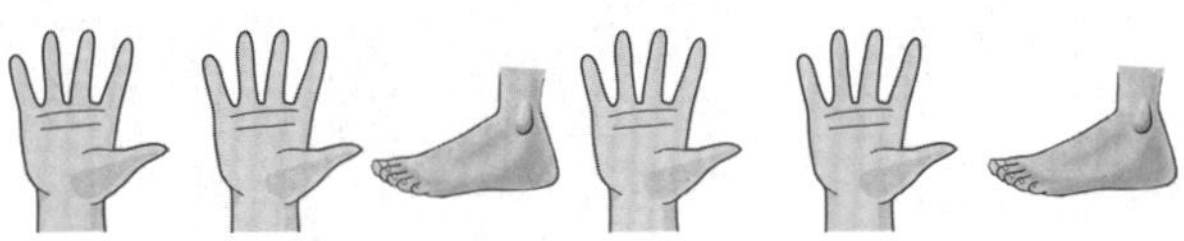

___ ___ ___ ___ ___ ___

4. Circle the best time to go to recess.

10:00 A.M. 10:00 P.M.

5. How many straight sides does an oval have?

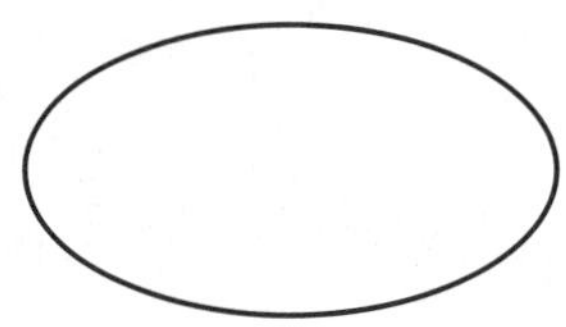

____

6. Kaylee starts on the number 8. She counts forward 2. What number is she on now?

____

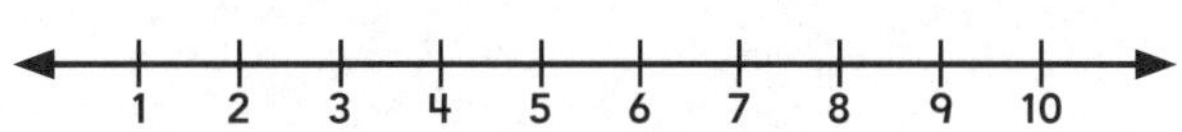

SCORE

1. ☺ 😐

2. ☺ 😐

3. ☺ 😐

4. ☺ 😐

5. ☺ 😐

6. ☺ 😐

___ / 6
Total

NAME: ____________________

DIRECTIONS Solve each problem.

SCORE

1. ☺ 😐
2. ☺ 😐
3. ☺ 😐
4. ☺ 😐
5. ☺ 😐
6. ☺ 😐

____ / 6
Total

1. Circle the larger number.

6 16

2. 3 + 1 = ______

3. Draw a pattern using these shapes.

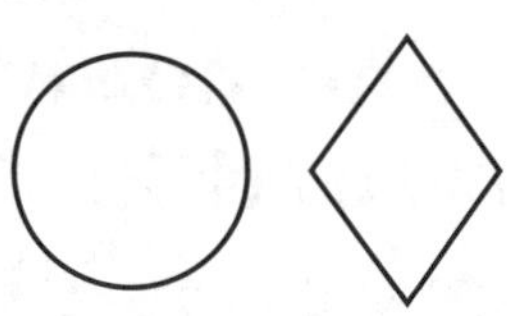

4. Circle the tool that is best to measure how much a dog weighs.

 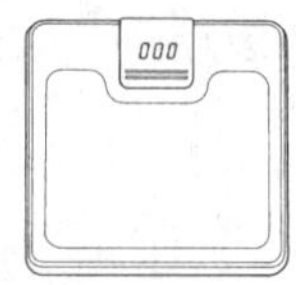

5. The clouds are ______ the sun.

above below in

6. Write the missing sign.

3 □ 1 = 2

DAY 167

NAME: ______________________

DIRECTIONS Solve each problem.

1. Count the jacks. Draw a set of circles that is more than the jacks.

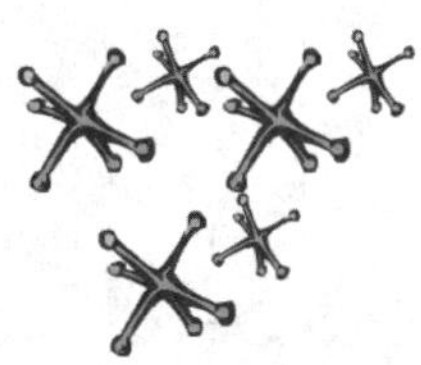

2. 5 – 2 = ______

3. Write what will come next.

8 9 10 11 12 ______

4. Draw or write something that weighs more than a dog.

5. How many corners does a rectangle have?

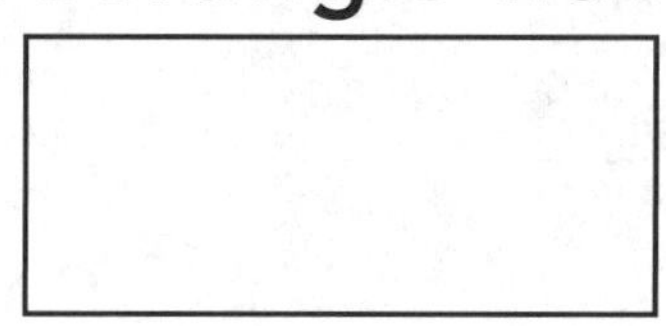

______ corners

6. A pizza was cut into 6 pieces. Michelle ate 2 of the pieces. How many pieces are left?

____

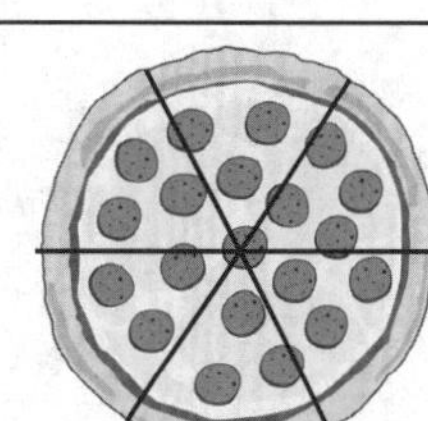

SCORE

1. ☺ 😐

2. ☺ 😐

3. ☺ 😐

4. ☺ 😐

5. ☺ 😐

6. ☺ 😐

____ / 6 Total

DAY
168

NAME: ______________________________

DIRECTIONS Solve each problem.

SCORE

1. ☺ ☹
2. ☺ ☹
3. ☺ ☹
4. ☺ ☹
5. ☺ ☹
6. ☺ ☹

____ / 6
Total

1. Draw 3 legs on each stool. How many legs are on 2 stools?

____

2.

$$\begin{array}{r} 2 \\ +\ 3 \\ \hline \end{array}$$

3. Circle what will come next.

? ____

4. Circle the day that comes before Tuesday.

Sunday Monday

5. Name the solid.

____

6. Write the numbers for the names.

three ____________

six ____________

nine ____________

NAME: ____________________

DIRECTIONS Solve each problem.

1. Circle the group that has more than 13 dots.

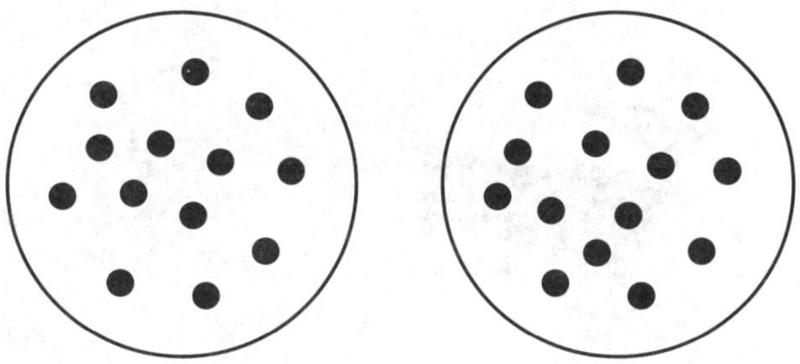

2.

$$\begin{array}{r} 1 \\ -\ 0 \\ \hline \end{array}$$

3. Draw a pattern using these shapes.

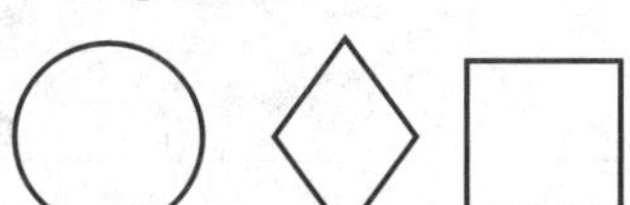

4. Circle how long it would take you to write a letter to your grandma.

10 minutes

10 hours

5. Circle where the bird is.

above the tree

below the tree

6. Wendy eats a yogurt every day. How many yogurts will she eat in one week?

____

SCORE

1. ☺ 😐

2. ☺ 😐

3. ☺ 😐

4. ☺ 😐

5. ☺ 😐

6. ☺ 😐

____ / 6 Total

NAME: ____________________

DIRECTIONS Solve each problem.

SCORE

1. ☺ 😐
2. ☺ 😐
3. ☺ 😐
4. ☺ 😐
5. ☺ 😐
6. ☺ 😐

____ / 6 Total

1. Count how many.

____

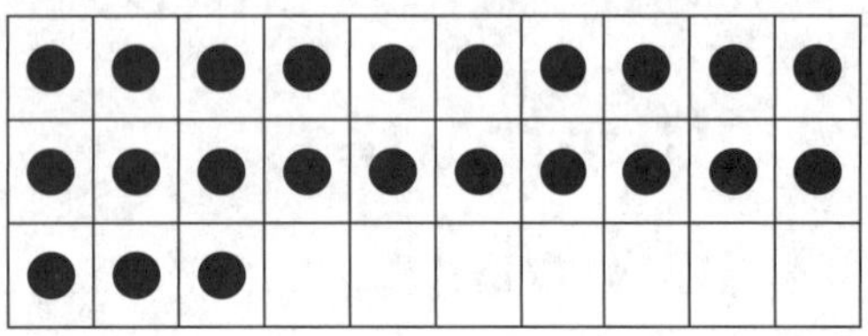

2. Solve.

3 + 1 = ______

4 − 1 = ______

3. Write what number will come next.

5 10 15 20 ______

4. Circle the container that holds the most.

5. Draw a line of symmetry.

6. One grasshopper is 2 cubes long. How long are 2 grasshoppers?

______________ cubes

NAME: ____________________

DIRECTIONS Solve each problem.

1. Color an equal number of squares.

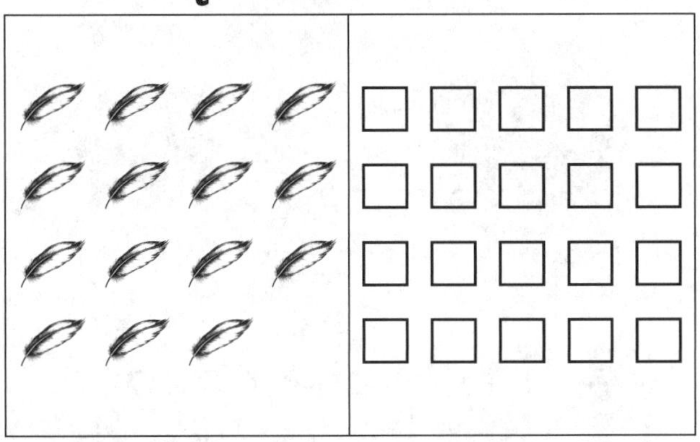

2. Solve.

1 + 1 = ______

2 – 1 = ______

3. Draw what will come next.

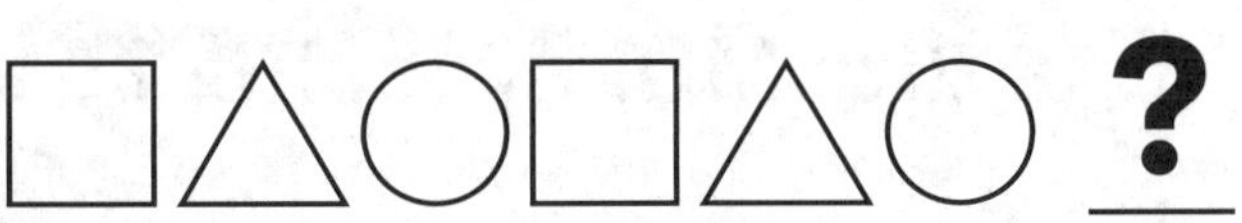

4. What time is it?

_____ o'clock

5. Circle the name of the shape.

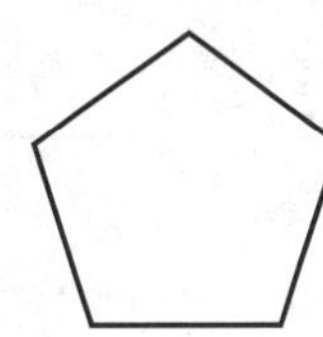

rectangle

pentagon

6. How many pairs of mittens are there? _____

SCORE

1. ☺ 😐

2. ☺ 😐

3. ☺ 😐

4. ☺ 😐

5. ☺ 😐

6. ☺ 😐

___ / 6

Total

DAY 172

NAME: ____________________

DIRECTIONS Solve each problem.

SCORE

1.

2.

3.

4.

5.

6.

___ / 6

Total

1. Write the missing number.

_____ 18 19 20

2. Solve.

4 + 0 = _____

4 – 0 = _____

3. Draw a pattern using these shapes.

4. Circle the shortest animal.

5. Circle the solid that looks like the object.

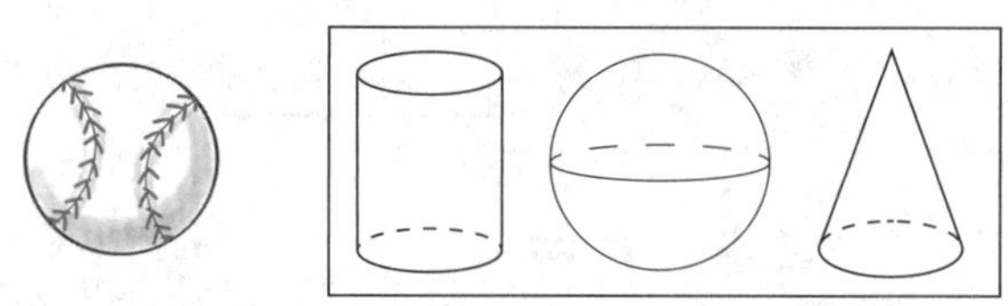

6. Marcy drinks 3 glasses of water. Later, she drinks 2 more glasses of water. How many glasses of water did Marcy drink?

____

NAME: ____________________

DIRECTIONS Solve each problem.

1. Draw a set of 10 squares. Draw an equal set of circles.

10	equal to 10

2. Solve.

2 + 3 = ______

5 – 3 = ______

3. Write what will come next.

30 40 50 60 70 ____

4. Circle how many bagels you could eat for breakfast.

2 20

5. Draw a flower in the vase.

6. Garren read 4 books in April. He read the rest in May. How many books did he read in May?

____

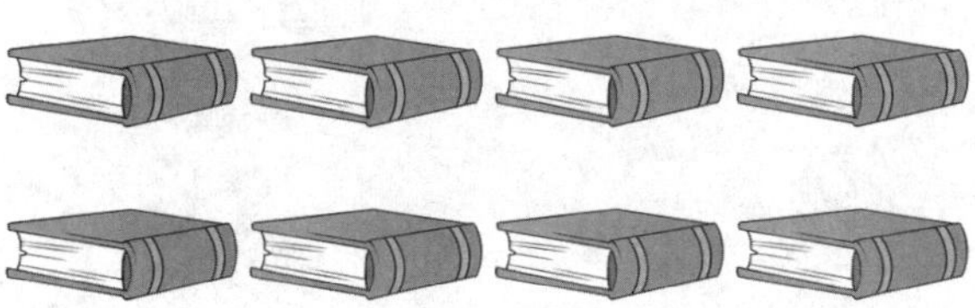

SCORE

1.

2.

3.

4.

5.

6.

___ / 6

Total

DAY
174

NAME: ______________________

DIRECTIONS Solve each problem.

SCORE

1. ☺ 😐
2. ☺ 😐
3. ☺ 😐
4. ☺ 😐
5. ☺ 😐
6. ☺ 😐

___ / 6
Total

1. Put these numbers in order.

24 13 19 17 6

______ ______ ______

______ ______

2. Solve.

1 + 4 = ______

5 – 4 = ______

3. Circle the part that repeats.

4. How tall is the purse?

______ cubes

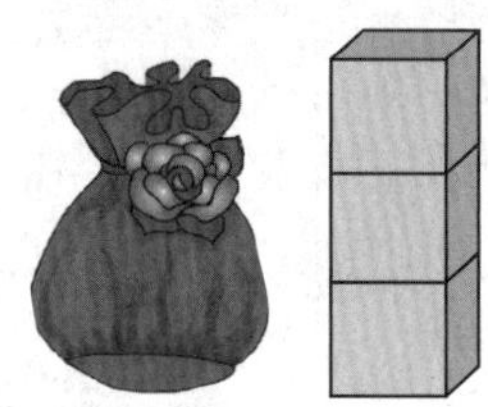

5. Draw a hexagon below a square.

6. Follow the directions.

Draw a circle first.

Draw a triangle second.

Draw a square third.

NAME: ______________________

DIRECTIONS Solve each problem.

1. Count the caps. What is 1 more?

____

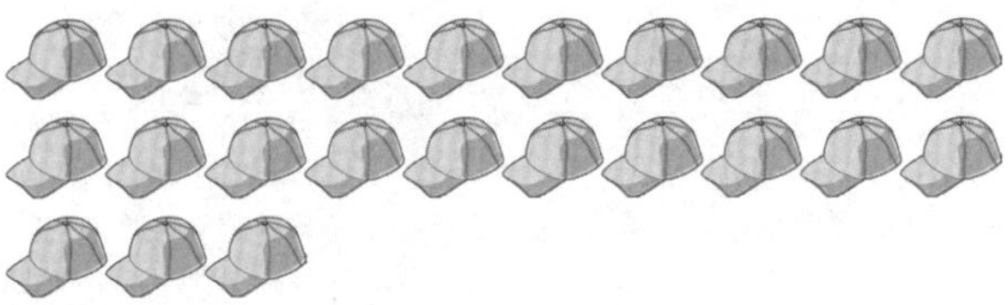

2. Solve.

2 + 2 = ______

4 – 2 = ______

3. Draw a pattern using these shapes.

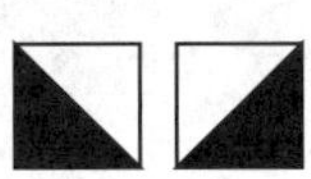

4. Circle the best time to go to a park.

3:00 A.M.   3:00 P.M.

5. Does the solid have any flat surfaces? Circle the answer.

yes   no

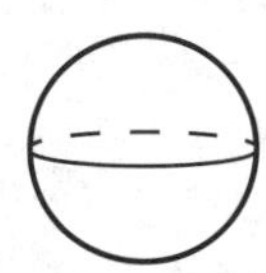

6. How many more flowers are there than vases?

____

SCORE

1. ☺ 😐

2. ☺ 😐

3. ☺ 😐

4. ☺ 😐

5. ☺ 😐

6. ☺ 😐

___ / 6 Total

DAY
176

NAME: ____________________

DIRECTIONS Solve each problem.

SCORE

1. ☺ 😐

2. ☺ 😐

3. ☺ 😐

4. ☺ 😐

5. ☺ 😐

6. ☺ 😐

___ / 6
Total

1. Circle the smaller number.

12   17

2. Solve.

3 + 0 = ______

3 – 0 = ______

3. Write what will come next.

16 15 14 13 12 ______

4. Circle the tool that is used to show what time you eat.

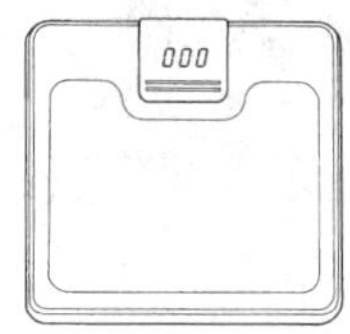

5. The dog is ______ the desk. Circle the answer.

under   on   above

6. Write the missing sign.

2 ☐ 2 = 4

NAME: ______________________________

DIRECTIONS Solve each problem.

SCORE

1. Count the objects. Draw a set of circles that is less than the cookies.

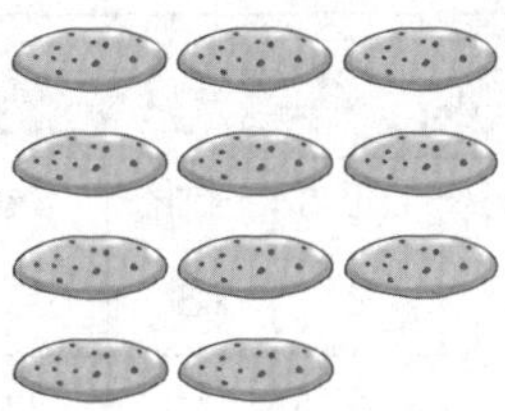

2. Solve.

   $4 + 1 =$ ______

   $5 - 1 =$ ______

3. Make the same pattern using letters.

___ ___ ___ ___ ___ ___

4. Draw or write something that weighs less than a boy.

5. How many sides does a triangle have? Write the answer.

   ______ sides

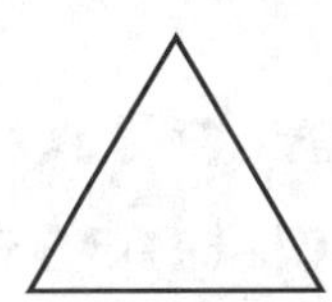

6. Ray has 4 games. He has played them all except one. How many games has he played?

   ____

1.
2.
3.
4.
5.
6.

___ / 6
Total

DAY 178

NAME: ____________________

DIRECTIONS Solve each problem.

SCORE

1. ☺ 😐

2. ☺ 😐

3. ☺ 😐

4. ☺ 😐

5. ☺ 😐

6. ☺ 😐

____ / 6

Total

1. Draw 2 legs on each person. How many legs on 3 people? ______

2. Solve.

1 + 3 = ______

4 – 3 = ______

3. Draw a pattern using these shapes.

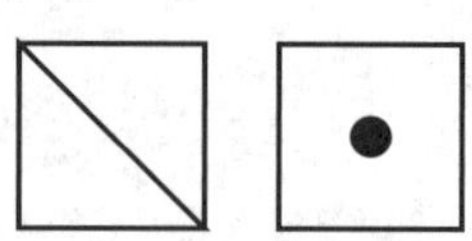

4. How many Wednesdays are in December?

____

December						
Sun	Mon	Tues	Wed	Thurs	Fri	Sat
			1	2	3	4
5	6	7	8	9	10	11
12	13	14	15	16	17	18
19	20	21	22	23	24	25
26	27	28	29	30	31	

5. Name the solid.

____

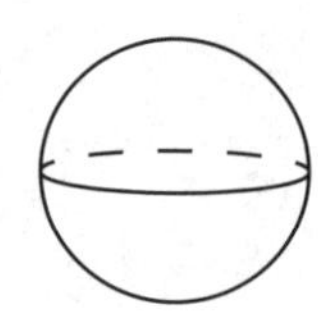

6. Write the names for the numbers.

8 ____________________

9 ____________________

10 ____________________

NAME: ____________________

DIRECTIONS Solve each problem.

1. Circle the group with less than 14 dots.

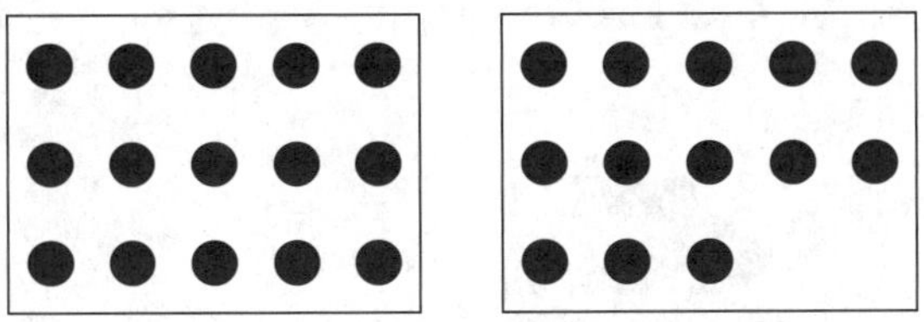

2. Solve.

2 + 1 = ______

3 – 1 = ______

3. Write what will come next.

6 8 10 12 14 ______

4. Circle about how long it takes to make dinner.

30 minutes

30 hours

5. Circle the picture that shows the book below the chair.

6. Draw a pattern. Use a square and a heart.

SCORE

1. ☺ 😐

2. ☺ 😐

3. ☺ 😐

4. ☺ 😐

5. ☺ 😐

6. ☺ 😐

____ / 6 Total

DAY 180

NAME: ______________________

DIRECTIONS Solve each problem.

SCORE

1. ☺ ☹
2. ☺ ☹
3. ☺ ☹
4. ☺ ☹
5. ☺ ☹
6. ☺ ☹

____ / 6 Total

1. Count how many.

____

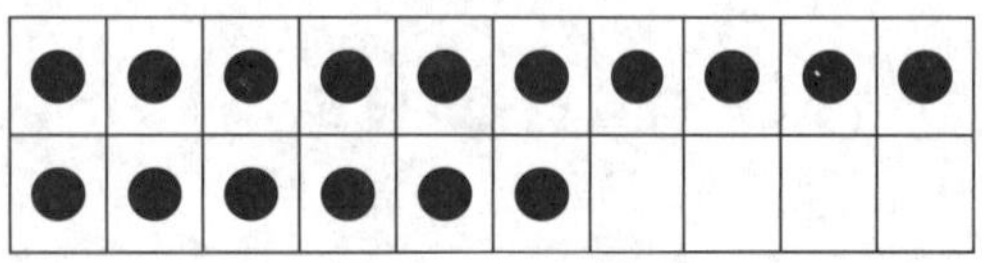

2. Solve.

$3 + 2 =$ ______

$5 - 2 =$ ______

3. Circle what will come next.

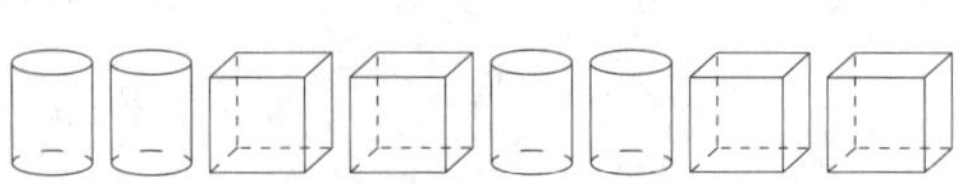

?
___

4. Draw a container that holds more than the milk carton.

5. Draw a line of symmetry.

6. If you spin the spinner below, are you more likely to land on white or black? Write the answer.

____

ANSWER KEY

Day 1
1. 3 blocks should be colored.
2. 3
3. a circle
4. 2
5. 3 circles should be colored.
6. 8

Day 2
1. 2 circles should be colored.
2. 4
3. bear
4. mouse
5. cone
6. 4

Day 3
1. 1 more circle should be drawn.
2. 5
3. blue
4. 30
5. 1 fishbowl should be drawn.
6. 3

Day 4
1. The fishbowl with 5 fish should be circled.
2. 3
3. boy patting head (right image)
4. 4
5. A triangle should be drawn.
6. 3 large paperclips should be circled.

Day 5
1. 6
2. 4
3. banana
4. 7:00 in the morning
5. 3
6. 5 petals should be drawn.

Day 6
1. yes
2. 3
3. a square with a dot in it
4. clock
5. top
6. 1 more banana should be drawn.

Day 7
1. 3 circles should be drawn.
2. 5
3. a circle
4. bottle of glue
5. closed
6. 2

Day 8
1. 4 legs should be drawn.
2. 3
3. ladybug
4. Tuesday
5. yes
6. apple

Day 9
1. The hive with 3 bees should be circled.
2. 5
3. green
4. 1 minute
5. on the plate
6. 4 eggs should be drawn.

Day 10
1. 4 apples should be colored.
2. 5
3. big car (right image)
4. bucket
5. yes
6. 1 dot should be added.

Day 11
1. 2 seals should be circled.
2. 5
3. 
4. 4
5. 2 squares should be colored.
6. 8

Day 12
1. 5
2. 3
3. 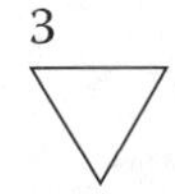
4. shorter boy
5. sphere (center image)
6. 3

Day 13
1. 4 more pencils should be drawn.
2. 4
3. cat
4. 10
5. A road should be drawn.
6. 1, 4, 7

Day 14
1. The machine with 3 pieces of gum should be circled.
2. 5
3. girl touching toes (right image)
4. 5
5. A circle should be drawn.
6. 1 triangle should be crossed out.

7. **Day 15**
1. 8
2. 6
3. yellow
4. in the afternoon
5. yes
6. 8

Day 16
1. no
2. 4
3. dolphin (right image)
4. scale
5. right
6. bird

Day 17
1. 5 circles should be drawn.
2. 3
3. ice cream bar (right image)
4. donut
5. open
6. 1

Day 18
1. 2 legs should be drawn.
2. 5
3. 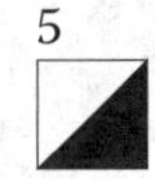
4. May
5. yes
6. The largest middle triangle should be circled.

Day 19
1. The log with 5 frogs should be circled.
2. 4
3. star
4. 1 minute
5. The dog inside the doghouse should be circled.
6. forward

ANSWER KEY *(cont.)*

Day 20

1. 5 pumpkins should be colored.
2. 5
3. ant (right image)
4. jar
5. yes
6. 1 sun and 3 clouds should be drawn.

Day 21

1. 4 cars should be colored.
2. 3
3. blue
4. 6:00
5. 3 triangles should be colored.
6. 6

Day 22

1. 3 more dots should be drawn.
2. 5
3. boy patting head (left image)
4. Something taller than a door should be drawn.
5. sphere (right image)
6. 5

Day 23

1. 5 more dots should be drawn.
2. 6
3. sad girl (left image)
4. 1
5. An apple should be drawn in the bowl.
6. 6

Day 24

1. The cup with 10 pencils should be circled.
2. 4
3. ▯ (left image)
4. 6
5. A square should be drawn.
6. 4 small buttons should be circled.

Day 25

1. 5
2. 4
3. car
4. 12:00 in the afternoon
5. 4
6. A shape with more than 3 sides should be drawn.

Day 26

1. The group with 5 fish should be circled.
2. 5
3. yellow
4. ruler
5. under the desk
6. 2 more apples should be drawn.

Day 27

1. 7 circles should be drawn.
2. 4
3. 2
4. book
5. closed
6. 0

Day 28

1. 6 legs should be drawn.
2. 5
3. girl hopping (left image)
4. Sunday
5. yes
6. pencil

Day 29

1. The giraffe should be circled.
2. 3
3. B
4. 1 minute
5. on the web
6. 4

Day 30

1. 3 suns should be circled.
2. 4
3. triangle with one dot inside
4. cup
5. no
6. 1 square should be crossed out.

Day 31

1. 7 bells should be colored.
2. 5
3. a circle
4. 1
5. 3 rectangles should be colored.
6. 10

Day 32

1. 7
2. 4
3. fish
4. crayon
5. cube
6. 4

Day 33

1. 3 more snakes should be drawn.
2. 6
3. green
4. 20
5. A bee should be drawn outside of the hive.
6. 1 red circle and 3 blue circles should be drawn; 3

Day 34

1. The box with 4 flowers should be circled.
2. 3
3. boy jumping (right image)
4. 4
5. A rectangle should be drawn.
6. 8; 6

Day 35

1. 10
2. 5
3. small carrot (left image)
4. 8:00 in the evening
5. no
6. 0

Day 36

1. no
2. 4
3. △
4. calendar
5. in the nest
6. The triangle should be crossed out.

ANSWER KEY *(cont.)*

Day 37
1. 9 circles should be drawn.
2. 4 + 1 = 5
3. star
4. chair
5. open
6. 0

Day 38
1. 3 circles should be drawn.
2. 5 + 1 = 6
3. P
4. 30
5. yes
6. color

Day 39
1. The box with 5 paint colors should be circled.
2. 3
3. black
4. 1 hour
5. The robot in the box should be circled.
6. 2 plates with 1 cracker on each plate should be drawn; yes

Day 40
1. 5 crayons should be colored.
2. 2 + 2 = 4
3. pig
4. bathtub
5. yes
6. Tim

Day 41
1. 9 pretzels should be colored.
2. 4
3. large turtle (left image)
4. 8
5. 3 triangles should be circled.
6. 12

Day 42
1. 10
2. 1
3. dot
4. The taller tower should be circled.
5. cylinder (left image)
6. 4

Day 43
1. 1 more cherry should be drawn.
2. 2 + 2 = 4
3. square (right image)
4. 10
5. A butterfly should be drawn below the net.
6. 9

Day 44
1. The right image should be crossed out.
2. 1
3. E
4. 4 paperclips
5. An oval should be drawn.
6. 1 group of 10; 2 left over

Day 45
1. 15
2. 2 + 2 = 4
3. yellow
4. in the morning
5. 3
6. 2 large leaves should be circled.

Day 46
1. yes
2. 1
3. square (left image)
4. measuring cup
5. on the bed
6. 4 more clouds should be drawn.

Day 47
1. 8 circles should be drawn.
2. 3 + 3 = 6
3. A
4. The older, heavier person should be circled.
5. closed
6. 1

Day 48
1. 1 kite string should be drawn.
2. 2
3. red
4. Friday
5. yes
6. The middle child (girl) should be circled.

Day 49
1. The ladybug on the right should be circled.
2. 1 + 2 = 3
3. girl clapping hands (right image)
4. 1 minute
5. by the pot
6. the circle

Day 50
1. 9
2. 4 + 1 = 5
3. sun (left image)
4. basket
5. yes
6. 3 more triangles should be drawn.

Day 51
1. All 10 stars should be colored.
2. 2
3. square (right image)
4. 9
5. 2 squares and 1 rectangle should be colored.
6. 6

Day 52
1. 12
2. 2 + 2 = 4
3. 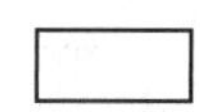
4. Something shorter than a woman should be drawn.
5. cone (right image)
6. 5

Day 53
1. 6 more moons should be drawn.
2. 1
3. candy (right image)
4. 8
5. 1 bird should be drawn in the tree.
6. 3

Day 54
1. The group of 5 worms on the right should be circled.
2. 0
3. red
4. 6
5. A heart should be drawn.
6. backward

ANSWER KEY *(cont.)*

Day 55
1. 17
2. 2 + 2 = 4
3. rabbit
4. 5:00 in the evening
5. yes
6. 3

Day 56
1. no
2. 3 – 1 = 2
3. 
4. calendar
5. on
6. The square should be crossed out.

Day 57
1. 6 circles should be drawn.
2. 6
3. The balloon and kite should be circled together.
4. piece of paper
5. open
6. 1

Day 58
1. 2 legs should be drawn.
2. 2 + 1 = 3
3. large pencil (right image)
4. Wednesday
5. yes
6. John should be circled.

Day 59
1. The machine on the left should be circled.
2. 3
3. boy hopping (left image)
4. 1 minute
5. right image
6. 3 apples and 3 bananas should be drawn; yes

Day 60
1. 9
2. 3 + 2 = 5
3. orange
4. bathtub
5. no
6. The smallest square should be circled.

Day 61
1. All 13 balls should be colored.
2. 1 + 2 = 3
3. Two boats and one plane should be circled.
4. 10
5. The triangle should be circled.
6. 0 or none

Day 62
1. 14
2. 5 – 5 = 0
3. shorts
4. bookcase
5. sphere (right image)
6. 3

Day 63
1. 3 more cookies should be drawn.
2. 6
3. 
4. 10
5. A present should be drawn in the wagon.
6. Any 4-sided shape should be drawn.

Day 64
1. The set with more bananas should be circled.
2. 1
3. hand
4. 5 cubes
5. A hexagon should be drawn.
6. 6

Day 65
1. 20
2. 3
3. A shoe and two boots should be circled.
4. 3:00 in the afternoon
5. 4
6. 2 groups of 10; 1 left over

Day 66
1. yes
2. 1
3. green
4. scale
5. A plate should be drawn under the cookie
6. 7

Day 67
1. 9 circles should be drawn.
2. 4
3. paintbrush
4. basket of fruit
5. closed
6. 0

Day 68
1. 4 legs should be drawn.
2. 3 – 0 = 3
3. 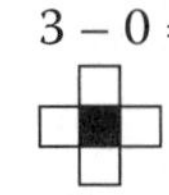
4. Thursday
5. no
6. The middle dog should be circled.

Day 69
1. The box with 8 dots should be circled.
2. 7
3. 
4. 1 hour
5. on the rug
6. triangle

Day 70
1. 11
2. 1
3. cake
4. bowl
5. yes
6. 1 banana should be drawn.

Day 71
1. 14 bees, all but 1, should be circled.
2. 7
3. red
4. 5
5. 2 triangles should be colored.
6. 15

ANSWER KEY *(cont.)*

Day 72
1. 15
2. 5 – 3 = 2
3. large square (left image)
4. bed
5. cube
6. 6

Day 73
1. 8 more Xs should be drawn.
2. 4 + 1 = 5
3. Pat, snap, snap should be circled.
4. 30
5. A star should be drawn to the left of the sun.
6. 0, 3, 6, 8, 9

Day 74
1. 1, 2, 3, 4, 5
2. 7
3. square
4. 5
5. A circle should be drawn inside a square.
6. 6

Day 75
1. 8
2. 3
3. triangle with 1 dot (left image)
4. 2:00 in the afternoon
5. yes
6. 12

Day 76
1. no
2. 1
3. A rectangle should be drawn.
4. clock
5. in
6. The circle should be crossed out.

Day 77
1. 14 circles should be drawn.
2. 4
3. A
4. crayon
5. open
6. 2

Day 78
1. 10 squares should be drawn.
2. 4
3. red
4. Saturday
5. yes
6. 1 one; 2 two; 3 three; 4 four

Day 79
1. The group on the right with 12 dots should be circled.
2. 1
3. boy hopping (right image)
4. second
5. The box with the pencil in it should be circled.
6. no

Day 80
1. 13
2. 3 + 1 = 4
3. A banana should be drawn.
4. bowl
5. no
6. a circle

Day 81
1. All 16 fish should be circled.
2. 1
3. 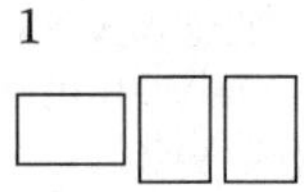
4. 3:00
5. 2 squares and 1 rectangle should be colored.
6. 8

Day 82
1. 18
2. 3
3. rhombus (left image)
4. Something taller than a book should be drawn.
5. rectangular prism (left image)
6. 6

Day 83
1. 9 more triangles should be drawn.
2. 1
3. fish (left image)
4. 10
5. A ball should be drawn outside the box.
6. 6

Day 84
1. 5, 6, 7, 8, 9
2. 2
3. red
4. 1 cube
5. A triangle should be drawn next to an oval.
6. forward

Day 85
1. 8
2. 2
3. girl skipping (left image)
4. 5:00 in the afternoon
5. 5
6. 2 groups of 10; 0 left over

Day 86
1. yes
2. 5
3. sun (left image)
4. measuring cup
5. bottom
6. A shape with fewer than 6 sides should be drawn.

Day 87
1. 12 circles should be drawn.
2. 3 – 1 = 2
3. The set of 2 squares should be circled.
4. phone
5. 0
6. 5

Day 88
1. 3 legs should be drawn.
2. 5
3. pentagon (right image)
4. Thursday
5. yes
6. 6 six; 7 seven; 8 eight; 9 nine; 10 ten

Day 89
1. The group of 14 squares on the left should be circled.
2. 2
3. A
4. 1 minute
5. on the road
6. 7

ANSWER KEY *(cont.)*

Day 90
1. 14
2. 4
3. black
4. The milk carton should be circled.
5. yes
6. 2 worms should be crossed out.

Day 91
1. 8 squares should be circled.
2. 3
3. A, B, A, B
4. 11
5. 3 circles should be colored.
6. 10

Day 92
1. 20
2. 5
3. A, B, C
4. elephant
5. cylinder (left image)
6. 3

Day 93
1. 4 more pumpkins should be drawn.
2. 2
3. worm
4. 3
5. A ball should be drawn in the mitt.
6. The middle cat should be circled.

Day 94
1. 15
2. 1 + 3 = 4
3. Dog, cat, fish should be circled.
4. 5
5. A circle with a diamond inside should be drawn.
6. Karla

Day 95
1. 21
2. 0
3. A, B, C
4. 6:00 in the evening
5. yes
6. 2 squares should be drawn; 1 square should be colored orange.

Day 96
1. 7
2. 3
3. The car should be circled.
4. The calendar should be circled.
5. left
6. 9:00

Day 97
1. 6 circles should be drawn.
2. 3
3. A circle should be drawn.
4. dog
5. 6
6. 1

Day 98
1. 7 circles should be drawn.
2. 6
3. A, A, B
4. Wednesday
5. no
6. 7

Day 99
1. The hive with 4 bees should be circled.
2. 3
3. candy (left image)
4. 1 second
5. The second group should be circled.
6. 4 apples should be drawn with 1 crossed out; 3

Day 100
1. 13
2. 4 + 1 = 5
3. small triangle (left image)
4. A container smaller than a bucket should be drawn.
5. no
6. square

Day 101
1. 6 squares should be drawn.
2. 3 – 2 = 1
3. One balloon and one plane should be circled.
4. 7:00
5. 2 squares. 1 rectangle, and 1 triangle should be colored.
6. 16

Day 102
1. 5
2. 1 – 0 = 1
3. A, A, B
4. The boy on the right should be circled.
5. cone (right image)
6. 4

Day 103
1. 2 triangles and 3 or more circles should be drawn.
2. 2 + 2 = 4
3. book
4. 100
5. Eggs should be drawn in the basket.
6. 2

Day 104
1. 18, 19, 20
2. 2; 3; 4
3. square (right image)
4. 4
5. A square with an oval in it should be drawn.
6. 1 first; 2 second; 3 third

Day 105
1. 22
2. 3 + 2 = 5
3. One mouse and one bird should be circled.
4. 12:00 P.M.
5. 4
6. 7

Day 106
1. 3
2. 4; 3; 2
3. A, B, B
4. scale
5. above
6. 2

Day 107
1. 13 circles should be drawn.
2. 3; 4; 5
3. sunflower (left image)
4. elephant
5. 4
6. 1

ANSWER KEY *(cont.)*

Day 108

1. 5 squares should be drawn.
2. 2 – 2 = 0
3. pants (left image)
4. Monday
5. yes
6. 9

Day 109

1. The log with 3 frogs should be circled.
2. 4; 5; 6
3. One present, one balloon, and one cake should be circled.
4. 15 minutes
5. at the top
6. cylinder (right image).

Day 110

1. 14
2. 4; 4
3. A, A, B
4. bathtub
5. yes
6. 4 apples should be crossed out.

Day 111

1. 9 triangles should be circled.
2. 3; 2; 1
3. cloud (left image)
4. 2
5. 2 pentagons should be circled.
6. 7

Day 112

1. 8
2. 2 + 2 = 4
3. A banana should be drawn.
4. building
5. sphere (center image)
6. 5

Day 113

1. 4 circles; 3 or fewer squares
2. 5; 5
3. One ice cream bar and two cookies should be circled.
4. 20
5. A toy should be drawn outside the tub.
6. 8

Day 114

1. 21, 22, 23
2. 2; 3; 4
3. crayon (right image)
4. 4
5. A rectangle should be drawn to the right of an oval.
6. The box with 2 apples should be circled.

Day 115

1. 25
2. 4 – 0 = 4
3. Answers will vary but may include A, B, C, A, B, C.
4. 8:00 A.M.
5. yes
6. 3

Day 116

1. 9
2. 2; 1; 0
3. girl touching toes (right image)
4. ruler
5. next to
6. 3 cookies should be drawn.

Day 117

1. 1 or 2 circles should be drawn.
2. 1 + 5 = 6
3. starfish (left image)
4. worm
5. 4
6. 2

Day 118

1. 12 eggs should be drawn.
2. 5; 5
3. Pat, clap, clap should be circled.
4. Monday
5. yes
6. 0, 1, 2

Day 119

1. grasshopper
2. 4; 3; 2
3. Answers will vary but may include A, B, B, A, B, B.
4. 15 minutes
5. The airplane above the clouds should be circled.
6. triangle

Day 120

1. 27
2. 3; 3
3. shirt (left image)
4. A container smaller than a milk carton should be drawn.
5. no
6. backward

Day 121

1. 12 circles should be colored.
2. 3 – 3 = 0
3. cookie
4. 4:00
5. circle
6. 2

Day 122

1. 14
2. 4; 3; 2
3. Two birds and two mice should be circled.
4. Something shorter than a can should be drawn.
5. cube (middle image)
6. 5

Day 123

1. 5 squares and 6 or more circles should be drawn.
2. 3; 3
3. Answers will vary but may include A, B, B, A, B, B.
4. 5
5. A person should be drawn in the tent.
6. 8

Day 124

1. 25, 26, 27, 28, 29
2. 1; 2; 3
3. flower
4. 5
5. A circle should be drawn to the left of a diamond.
6. 4

Day 125

1. 23
2. 1 + 2 = 3
3. large square (left image)
4. 12:00 P.M.
5. 6
6. 4

ANSWER KEY *(cont.)*

Day 126

1. 8
2. 6; 6
3. One circle and two lines should be circled.
4. calendar
5. on
6. triangle

Day 127

1. 4 or more circles should be drawn.
2. 4; 3; 2
3. Answers will vary but may include A, B, A, B, A, B.
4. house
5. 3
6. 1

Day 128

1. 4 legs should be drawn on each tiger; 8
2. 1; 1
3. 4-hole button (right image)
4. Tuesday
5. yes
6. 6, 7, 8, 9

Day 129

1. The plate with 8 strawberries should be circled.
2. 2 – 1 = 1
3. 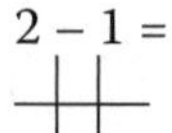
4. Answers will vary.
5. left of the apple
6. 8

Day 130

1. 30
2. 4; 4
3. One triangle and one circle should be circled.
4. The smallest container should be circled.
5. 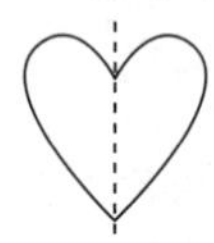
6. 2 crayons

Day 131

1. 13 triangles should be circled.
2. 1 + 3 = 4
3. Answers will vary but may include A, B, C, A, B, C.
4. 6
5. triangle
6. 8

Day 132

1. 18
2. 3; 3
3. cow
4. giraffe
5. rectangular prism (center image)
6. 5

Day 133

1. 6 squares and 5 or fewer triangles should be drawn.
2. 5; 4; 3
3. happy girl (left image)
4. 60
5. A boy should be drawn on the bed.
6. 6

Day 134

1. 7, 8, 9
2. Answers will vary.
3. One mouse and one cheese should be circled.
4. 5
5. A circle with a triangle in it should be drawn.
6. 4

Day 135

1. 29
2. Answers will vary.
3. Answers will vary but may include A, A, B, A, A, B.
4. 2:00 P.M.
5. yes
6. 4

Day 136

1. 6
2. 6
3. square, circle or circle, square, etc.
4. cup
5. under
6. +

Day 137

1. 4 or fewer circles should be drawn.
2. 2
3. 50
4. pen
5. 3 sides
6. 3

Day 138

1. 3 triangles per circle should be drawn; 9
2. 5 apples should be drawn.
3. One bird and two mice should be circled.
4. Saturday
5. no
6. three, four, five

Day 139

1. The ladybug on the left should be circled.
2. 3
3. Answers will vary.
4. 2 hours
5. boy, girl, boy (right image)
6. 5 fish should be drawn.

Day 140

1. 24
2. 6
3. 9
4. A container that holds more than a bucket should be drawn.
5. 
6. rectangle

ANSWER KEY *(cont.)*

Day 141

1. 13 squares should be circled.
2. 5 suns with one crossed out should be drawn.
3. Answers will vary but may include A, A, B, A, A, B.
4. 1:00
5. square
6. 3 groups of 2

Day 142

1. 24
2. 3
3. Answers will vary.
4. The shortest tower should be circled.
5. cylinder (left image)
6. 3

Day 143

1. 8 circles and 9 or more squares should be drawn.
2. 0
3. 100
4. 3
5. Noodles should be drawn in the bowl.
6. 4

Day 144

1. 15, 11, 9
2. 5 happy faces should be drawn.
3. turtle
4. 8
5. A square should be drawn around a triangle.
6. 3

Day 145

1. 28
2. 2
3. Answers will vary.
4. 7:00 A.M.
5. 8
6. 8

Day 146

1. 11
2. 5
3. 16
4. clock
5. right
6. –

Day 147

1. 8 or more circles should be drawn.
2. 0
3. An apple should be drawn.
4. Something that weighs more than a crayon should be drawn or written.
5. 6
6. 2

Day 148

1. 4
2. 4
3. Answers will vary.
4. Tuesday
5. yes
6. 1, 2, 3

Day 149

1. The machine on the right should be circled.
2. 4
3. 5
4. 1 minute
5. above the paper
6. The middle and last bags should be circled.

Day 150

1. 29
2. 3
3. One balloon, one car, and one boat should be circled.
4. The cup should be circled.
5. 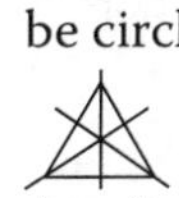
   Any line of symmetry may be drawn.
6. The cube (top left), cylinder (top right), and cone (bottom right) should be circled.

Day 151

1. All 16 triangles should be colored.
2. 0
3. Answers will vary.
4. 8
5. rectangles
6. 24

Day 152

1. 27
2. 5 trees should be drawn.
3. 70
4. An object shorter than a chair should be drawn.
5. rectangular prism (left image)
6. 5

Day 153

1. 9 triangles and 9 dots should be drawn.
2. 2
3. Answers will vary but may include A, B, B, A, B, B.
4. 4
5. An apple should be drawn in the bag.
6. 2, 5

Day 154

1. 12, 14, 16
2. 5
3. Answers will vary.
4. 5
5. A pentagon should be drawn next to a triangle.
6. 6

Day 155

1. 26
2. 1
3. 19
4. 8:00 P.M.
5. no
6. 2 blue squares and 3 green squares should be drawn; 3

ANSWER KEY *(cont.)*

Day 156
1. 8
2. 4
3. The bear should be circled.
4. ruler
5. above
6. +

Day 157
1. 8 or fewer circles should be drawn.
2. 5 kites should be drawn.
3. Answers will vary.
4. paperclip
5. 4
6. 0

Day 158
1. 12
2. 2
3. 7
4. May 14
5. cube
6. five, six, seven

Day 159
1. The box with 8 dots (right image) should be circled.
2. 0
3. A butterfly should be circled.
4. 15 minutes
5. boy on balance beam (top image)
6. 2

Day 160
1. 14
2. 4
3. Answers will vary.
4. The carton of milk should be circled and a larger container should be drawn.
5. Any line of symmetry may be drawn.

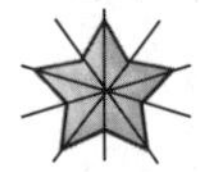

6. soccer

Day 161
1. 15 circles should be colored.
2. 1
3. 10
4. 9:00
5. hexagons
6. 3

Day 162
1. 10
2. 5
3. Answers will vary.
4. The man should be circled.
5. A bug should be drawn on the leaf.
6. $4.00

Day 163
1. 10 squares and 9 or fewer triangles should be drawn.
2. 1
3. One pencil, one crayon, and one pair of scissors should be circled.
4. 6
5. cylinder (center image)
6. 5

Day 164
1. 4, 5, 9, 12, 15
2. 4
3. 26
4. 5
5. A circle should be drawn above a rectangle.
6. 3

Day 165
1. 17
2. Answers will vary, but should show a set of 4 things. The things should be crossed out to show 0.
3. Answers will vary but may include A, A, B, A, A, B.
4. 10:00 A.M.
5. 0
6. 10

Day 166
1. 16
2. 4
3. Answers will vary.
4. scale
5. below
6. – (minus sign)

Day 167
1. 7 or more circles should be drawn.
2. 3
3. 13
4. Something that weighs more than a dog should be drawn or written.
5. 4
6. 4

Day 168
1. 3 legs should be drawn on each stool; 6
2. 5
3. shorts (left image)
4. Monday
5. cone
6. 3, 6, 9

Day 169
1. The group on the right should be circled.
2. 1
3. Answers will vary.
4. 10 minutes
5. above the tree
6. 7

Day 170
1. 23
2. 4; 3
3. 25
4. bathtub
5. 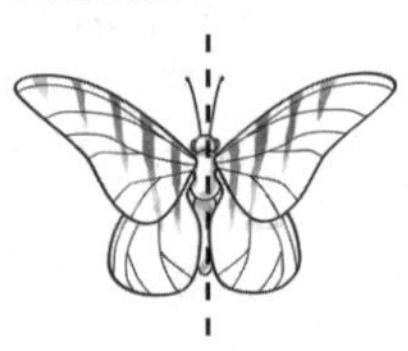
6. 4

Day 171
1. 15 squares should be colored.
2. 2; 1
3. A square should be drawn.
4. 3
5. pentagon
6. 5

ANSWER KEY *(cont.)*

Day 172

1. 17
2. 4; 4
3. Answers will vary.
4. mouse
5. sphere (center image)
6. 5

Day 173

1. 10 squares and 10 circles should be drawn.
2. 5; 2
3. 80
4. 2
5. A flower should be drawn in the vase.
6. 4

Day 174

1. 6, 13, 17, 19, 24
2. 5; 1
3. Head pat, head pat, toe touch should be circled.
4. 3
5. A hexagon should be drawn below a square.
6. The right order is circle, triangle, square.

Day 175

1. 24
2. 4; 2
3. Answers will vary.
4. 3:00 P.M.
5. no
6. 2

Day 176

1. 12
2. 3; 3
3. 11
4. clock
5. under
6. +

Day 177

1. 10 or fewer circles should be drawn.
2. 5; 4
3. Answers will vary but may include A, A, B, A, A, B.
4. Answers will vary.
5. 3
6. 3

Day 178

1. 2 legs should be drawn on each person; 6
2. 4; 1
3. Answers will vary.
4. 5
5. sphere
6. eight, nine, ten

Day 179

1. The group on the right should be circled.
2. 3; 2
3. 16
4. 30 minutes
5. chair with the book (center image)
6. AB pattern: square, heart OR heart, square

Day 180

1. 16
2. 5; 3
3. The cylinder should be circled.
4. A container that holds more than a milk carton should be drawn.
5. 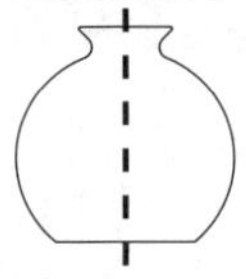
6. black

REFERENCES CITED

Kilpatrick, J., J. Swafford, and B. Findell, eds. 2001. *Adding it up: Helping children learn mathematics.* Washington, DC: National Academies Press.

Marzano, R. 2010. When practice makes perfect…sense. *Educational Leadership* 68 (3): 81–83.

McIntosh, M. E. 1997. Formative assessment in mathematics. *Clearing House* 71 (2): 92–96.

DIGITAL RESOURCES

Accessing the Digital Resources

The digital resources can be downloaded by following these steps:

1. Go to www.tcmpub.com/digital
2. Use the ISBN number to redeem the digital resources.
3. Respond to the question using the book.
4. Follow the prompts on the Content Cloud website to sign in or create a new account.
5. The content redeemed will now be on your My Content screen. Click on the product to look through the digital resources. All resources are available for download. Select files can be previewed, opened, and shared. For questions and assistance with your license key card, or to report a lost card, please contact Shell Education.

   mail: customerservice@tcmpub.com
   phone: 800-858-7339

CONTENTS OF THE DIGITAL RESOURCES

Teacher Resources

- Practice Page Item Analysis Chart
- Student Item Analysis Chart

Student Resources

- Practice Pages

NOTES

NOTES

NOTES

NOTES

NOTES